How To Find a Great Lab Breeder

1. Ask other Lab owners for recommendations.

2. Ask your veterinarian for recommendations.

3. Visit several breeders before choosing.

4. Don't buy from a breeder who pressures you.

5. Ask for a tour. Facilities should be clean, and the dogs should look happy and healthy.

6. Good breeders will let you see at least one of the parents of the puppy.

7. Good breeders will want to interview you, too, to make sure you will provide their pups with a good home.

8. Does the breeder seem like someone you can trust?

9. Good breeders are up-front about both the good qualities and the challenging aspects of Lab ownership.

10. Check out the way the dogs react to the breeder. Good breeders are loved by their Labs.

D0569926

How To Find a Goc Canine Behavic

1. Ask for recommendations from friends, neighbors and relatives who have friendly, well-behaved dogs.

2. Ask pet professionals, such as veterinarians, vet techs, groomers, boarding kennel managers, humane societies and rescue groups.

3. Call the Association of Pet Dog Trainers at 1-800-PET-DOGS and ask for the names of dog trainers and canine behavior consultants who use positive training methods such as lure-and-reward and clicker training.

4. Join one of the doggy e-mail lists listed in Appendix B.

5. A good dog trainer/canine behavior consultant will understand how dogs learn.

6. A good dog trainer/canine behavior consultant will also understand how to communicate with you about how to manage and train your Lab, in terms you understand.

7. A good dog trainer/canine behavior consultant will have extensive experience educating owners and their pets. Ask about experience, and ask for references. And check them!

8. A good dog trainer/canine behavior consultant will not advocate or use physical punishment (shock collars, leash jerks, hitting).

9. A good dog trainer/canine behavior consultant will be familiar with the work of pioneers in the field of positive dog training, such as Dr. Ian Dunbar and Karen Pryor.

10. A good dog trainer/canine behavior consultant will give you the feeling that training will be fun for you and your Labrador!

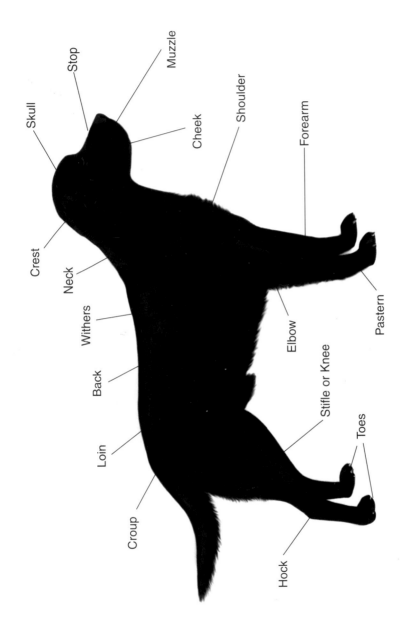

Skull
Stop
Muzzle
Cheek
Shoulder
Forearm
Crest
Neck
Withers
Back
Loin
Croup
Elbow
Stifle or Knee
Pastern
Toes
Hock

External Features of the Labrador Retriever

What They're Saying About The Complete Idiot's Guide to Labrador Retrievers

"This book is so well-written and user-friendly, I ended up glued to it for hours. Not only is the training and behavior information sound and plentiful, there is frank and empowering information on a myriad of other topics. I loved the tone and I have no suggestions other than 'Get it out there!' It will set the standard for breed books of the 21st century."

—**Jean Donaldson,** author of *THE CULTURE CLASH: A Revolutionary New Way of Understanding the Relationship Between Humans and Domestic Dogs,* and *DOGS ARE FROM NEPTUNE: Candid Answers to Urgent Questions About Aggression and Other Aspects of Dog Behavior*

"This book is a friendly, sensible, up-to-date, well-organized, positive book about getting a new puppy—ANY puppy, not just Labs! The authors show you in clear, fun-to-read detail how to organize your puppy's environment and manage its behavior with new-style positive reinforcement training. Do as they say, and your puppy will be a pleasure from day one, and will grow up to be a safe, calm, fun-loving yet well-behaved companion."

—**Karen Pryor,** author of *DON'T SHOOT THE DOG: The New Art of Teaching and Training,* and *A DOG & A DOLPHIN: An Introduction to Clicker Training*

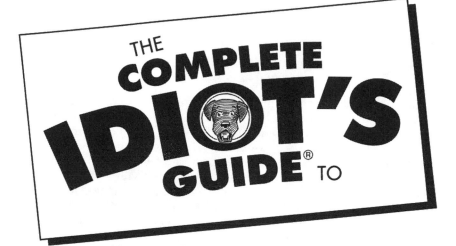

THE
COMPLETE
IDIOT'S
GUIDE® TO

Labrador
Retrievers

by Joel Walton and Eve Adamson

Howell Book House   Alpha Books
Divisions of Macmillan General Reference USA
A Pearson Education Macmillan Company
1633 Broadway, New York, NY 10019-6785

Macmillan General Reference books may be purchased for business or sales promotional use. For information please write: Special Markets Department, Macmillan Publishing USA, 1633 Broadway, New York, NY 10019-6785.

International Standard Book Number: 1-58245-030-7
Library of Congress Catalog Card Number available upon request

01   00   99   8   7   6   5   4   3   2   1

Interpretation of the printing code: The rightmost number of the first series of numbers is the year of the book's printing; the rightmost number of the second series of numbers is the number of the book's printing. For example, a printing code of 99-1 shows that the first printing occurred in 1999.

Printed in the United States of America

Alpha Development Team

Publisher
Kathy Nebenhaus

Editorial Director
Gary M. Krebs

Managing Editor
Bob Shuman

Marketing Brand Manager
Felice Primeau

Acquisitions Editor
Jessica Faust

Development Editors
Phil Kitchel and Amy Zavatto

Assistant Editor
Georgette Blau

Production Team

Acquisitions Editor
Dominique DeVito

Production Editor
Stephanie Mohler

Copy Editor
Heather Stith

Cover Designer
Mike Freeland

Photo Editor
Richard Fox

Cartoonist
Bryan Hendrix

Designers
Scott Cook and Amy Adams of DesignLab

Indexer
Johnna VanHoose Dinse

Layout/Proofreading
Laura Goetz and Sean Monkhouse

Contents at a Glance

Contents

Foreword

If you are already Labradorian, or are considering becoming so, buying this book is the very smartest thing you can do. It's brilliant! Excellent!! Awesome!!!

Utterly comprehensive, overflowing with oodles of useful up-to-date, cutting-edge training tidbits, Labradorian Lore and Lingo, it offers a marvelous in-depth insight into the hearts, minds and souls of Labradors. Written in an engaging, easy-to-read style that is a sheer delight to read, it will be hard for you to put this book down. It's so refreshing to read a book written from the dog's point of view. A book that emphasizes dogs' needs and feelings above everything else, and shows and teaches them to be good companions using gentle, dog-friendly methods. This is a book written from the heart, with the best interests of dogs as its focus.

The MRE System is definitely the way to go: Managing behavior, developing a grrreat Relationship and Educating your dog. Indeed, the chapter on managing puppy problems is worth the price of the book alone. If you are not familiar with these modern-day lure/reward training techniques, it is unlikely your dogs will ever achieve their full potential. I can vividly remember Joel at my very first Puppy Training Workshop. I have never seen anyone make such a speedy and complete transition from disbeliever to disciple. Joel's transition took the same amount of time as it took dear Cocoa's two little pups to learn to come, sit, lie down and rollover while playing off-leash with a pack of puppies. Just seconds! Since that day, Joel has devoted his time to spreading the electronic word to dog owners worldwide on The Web. It is a good day for dogs that Joel's message is now readily available in bookstores.

I do have just a single criticism. This book was written exclusively for Labrador folk, and it's simply not fair. All the sections are excellent and all the excellent information therein applies to all dogs. So let's hope Joel Walton and Eve Adamson soon return with *The Complete Idiot's Guide to Raising the Practically Perfect Puppy*, so that dog owners of all breeds may benefit from their infinite wisdom and their wonderful way with words.

—Ian Dunbar, PhD, MRCVS
(Lives with a Malamute and a Mutt in Berkeley, California, but was raised by a Labrador)
Founder, Association of Pet Dog Trainers; author of *Dog Behavior: An Owner's Guide to a Happy Healthy Pet* and the video, *Sirius Puppy Training*.

Introduction

The first time I (Joel) saw a *Complete Idiot's Guide,* it was on a computer subject and two thoughts went through my mind. "What a strange title for a book," and "Gosh, it looks like it covers the subject in a concise, easy-to-use format!" Despite my hesitancy over the title, I bought the book. I'm glad I did! I think you'll be glad you bought this book, too.

Over the last decade I have had the privilege of working with families and their pet dogs. I see families who are thinking about getting a Labrador Retriever, just starting to train their first puppy, experiencing their dog's adolescence, dealing with training and behavior problems and finally, dealing with the loss of a beloved pet. This book is intended to help you on this journey with your Labrador Retriever.

When I (Eve) decided to become a full-time writer three years ago (upon the birth of my first child), I was interested in many subjects and didn't know where I would find my niche. I had no idea dog writing, fun as it is, would supply me with an actual income! When I began writing *Complete Idiot's Guides,* I knew I had found another niche. Their easy, humorous tone and user-friendly approach is just the kind of writing I love. The opportunity to blend my knowledge of dogs with the *Complete Idiot's Guide* style seemed just right, and here is the result: a book that is fun to read and easy to use.

Not a coffee table book, an esoteric treatise or a book filled with complex dog terms and dog world lingo, this book is, instead, a book meant for your life and your Lab. This is a book to sink your teeth into, a book that can change the way you act with, react to, train, live with and love your Lab. We hope you enjoy reading it as much as Joel and I enjoyed writing it!

Extras

While you're reading the book, keep an eye out for these icons that highlight important warnings, helpful tips, interesting facts and useful definitions.

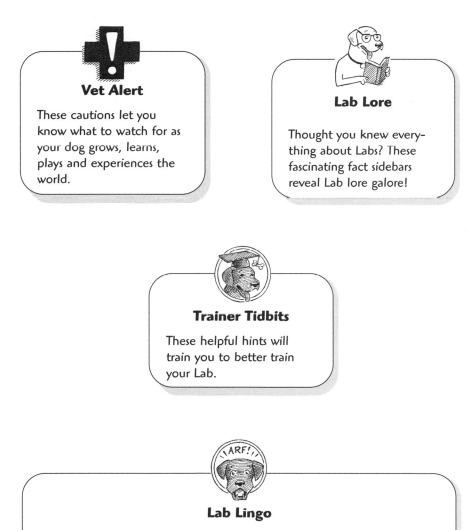

Vet Alert

These cautions let you know what to watch for as your dog grows, learns, plays and experiences the world.

Lab Lore

Thought you knew everything about Labs? These fascinating fact sidebars reveal Lab lore galore!

Trainer Tidbits

These helpful hints will train you to better train your Lab.

Lab Lingo

Dog terminology doesn't always make sense to the dog lover on the street. We'll clear things up for you with these helpful sidebars.

Acknowledgments

Many people and dogs helped to make this book a reality, so we would like to thank them all generally and a few special individuals particularly.

Thanks to Janet, my wife, the hardest working person I have ever known. Untold people and dogs are happy because of her efforts. And she has put up with me for over 33 years! I also thank Cocoa, who taught me that you cannot train all dogs by jerking them around; Ian Dunbar, who taught me how to train dogs without jerking them around; and Gus Viergutz, my father-in-law, who taught me that you have to be smarter than the dog. This book would not have been possible without Dominique DeVito's faith and Eve Adamson's skill.

—Joel Walton

Thanks to my kiddos, Angus and Emmett, who demonstrate on a daily basis how much training babies has in common with training dogs. To my parents, Richard and Penny Watson, whose grandparenting skills allowed me to finish this book—I could not possibly have done it without them! Thanks to Joel for his good nature and great knowledge and to Madelyn Larsen and Dominique DeVito for their support and patience. Thanks to Marylou Zarbock for always taking time out of an impossible schedule to answer my questions, and for always having an answer. Last of all, I send out my heartfelt thanks and love to the Chewdog, Whiskey, Bart, Valis, Ed and Zeke, all gone, but never, ever forgotten.

—Eve Adamson

About the Authors

Joel Walton, his wife, Janet, and their two boys, David and Jimmy, got their first Labrador Retriever, Bart, in September 1969. Bart crossed the Rainbow Bridge in 1981. The Waltons had their first Labrador litter in 1983. Although some Walton Family Labradors have excelled in obedience, drug detection, hunting and hunt tests and other doggy activities, the Waltons continue to focus on breeding the best possible family pets. Joel has been a member of the Labrador Retriever Club of the Potomac for many years and helped found Lab Rescue of LRCP, Inc., serving as its first secretary.

Karen Pryor opened Joel's mind to the science of positive dog training when she passed through the Washington, D.C., area giving her famous "Don't Shoot the Dog" seminars based on her classic book of the same title. In June of 1987, Joel and Janet took Cocoa and her two pups, Bear and Ginger, to Dr. Ian Dunbar's first-ever Puppy Training Workshop. Joel immediately adopted lure-and-reward training and stopped using the old-fashioned methods involving punishing dogs by giving them a leash correction with a choke collar when they made a mistake. Joel says it is much more fun to reward dogs when they get it right!

Walton Family Dog Training, LLC was founded in 1986. Joel trains families in the Washington, D.C., area to train their puppies and dogs. Joel provides classes for aspiring positive dog trainers and operates five Internet e-mail lists for pet dog trainers and pet dog owners. Joel and Janet continue to breed a few Labrador litters each year. Joel shares his bedroom with nine Labradors and one Rottweiler.

Eve Adamson is a freelance writer in Iowa City, Iowa, who specializes in pet and holistic health subjects. She is a frequent contributor to *Dog Fancy* and many other pet-related publications and a member of the Dog Writers' Association of America. She holds an MFA in creative writing from the University of Florida and has co-authored many books, including several other *Complete Idiot's Guides*.

Part 1

Finding and Acquiring Your Practically Perfect Labrador Retriever

So you think a Lab is the dog for you? In this first section, we'll help you make sure you are the right kind of companion for a Labrador Retriever. We'll also fill you in on what to expect from your Lab, and what not to expect. Not everything you've heard about Labs is true!

Next, we'll show you the breed standard and translate it into plain English even complete idiots can understand! We'll give you the low-down on whether a great pet needs to meet every aspect of the breed standard, and which parts of the standard are particularly important for pet owners.

For history buffs, we'll let you know how the Lab came to be the Lab it is today (no, it didn't originate in Labrador!). We'll talk about your Lab options (colors, types, ages), and we'll end up with some great tips on how to find a good breeder, as well as the individual Lab that is right for you.

Chapter 1

Is a Lab the Dog for You?

In This Chapter

➤ Analyze your Labrador Retriever expectations

➤ Would you be a good Lab companion? Test yourself

➤ Survey your personal resources: Do you have the time, energy, space and money to keep a Labrador Retriever?

You have a picture in your head. A picture of you with your practically perfect dog. You've always preferred big dogs, and the practically perfect dog in your head is sturdy, strong and energetic, yet gentle and completely in tune to your needs, your whims and your every move. Maybe you imagine the two of you jogging in the park, your dog in a perfect heel, watching out for your safety and enjoying your company. Maybe you imagine curling up on the sofa with your cozy, beautiful dog as a soft pillow and trustworthy confidante. Maybe you picture teaching your dog the ins and outs of obedience, agility, flyball and Frisbee or simply "Sit," "Stay" and "Fetch the Sunday paper, please."

Whatever your dream of the practically perfect dog, we're guessing that if you're flipping through the pages of this book, you have a Labrador Retriever in mind. After all, the Labrador Retriever is the most popular dog in the United States according to *American Kennel Club* registrations. Labs are beautiful, friendly, adaptable, easygoing, brave, loyal, dependable and intelligent. What could be better?

Lab Lingo

The **American Kennel Club (AKC)** is a nonprofit organization, established in 1884, devoted to the advancement of purebred dogs. The AKC maintains a record of all registered dogs; publishes ideal standards for each recognized breed; sponsors a variety of dog events including dog shows, obedience and field trials, agility and the Canine Good Citizen program; and publishes educational information.

Why Do You Want a Lab?

But popularity is no reason to choose a breed. You know that. You probably have other reasons why that practically perfect picture in your head looks an awful lot like a Labrador Retriever. Are your reasons good ones? Let's spend a little time examining your motives. Ask yourself the following questions and take some time to examine the following statements. Then circle all those that sound like what you've been thinking. Be honest!

1. I want a Lab because I used to have a Lab in the past, and I want another one just like her.

2. I want a Lab because my friend/neighbor/coworker/boss has one, and I want one just like her.

3. Everyone likes Labs, so if I get a Lab, everyone will like me!

4. I want a big dog for protection.

5. I want a good hunting dog.

6. Labs are easy. I won't have to spend time on training because they quickly pick up on what to do.

7. I think they're cute.

8. I feel a kinship with the breed and feel ready to spend the time and energy necessary to raise and train my dog so that she can become a companion and friend for life.

Do any of the above sound like you? Well, guess what? Only one of the items on the above list is a good reason to bring a Labrador Retriever into your life. You guessed it, number eight. What's wrong with the other reasons?

First of all, no matter how many Labs you've known and admired or even loved in the past, the Lab you bring home won't be the same. Dogs, like people, are individuals, and although breeds do have certain consistent characteristics, personalities can be as different as black and white (or black, yellow and chocolate). You probably wouldn't make the mistake of saying that, for example, everyone from Minnesota is nice and easygoing or everyone from Idaho loves to go jogging. Why should all Labrador Retrievers be the same? They shouldn't, and they aren't. It's unfair to expect any dog to conform to some idea you have of how some other dog once behaved. You have to get to know your own dog and love her for who she is.

Lab Lore

Labrador Retrievers come in three colors: black, yellow and chocolate. Apart from a permissible white chest spot, the American Kennel Club (AKC) breed standard allows solid colors only.

As far as a Lab's being your ticket to popularity, although many people like Labrador Retrievers, not everyone does. Besides, your dog won't influence people's opinion of you. If you are a good person and a good dog owner, people might think better of you because of it. But if you are generally irritable, impatient or unkind (or worse, an animal-hater), getting a dog won't fool anyone, especially if they sense that your dog fears or distrusts you.

Although some dogs are better protectors than others, getting any dog solely for protection is a bad reason to get a dog. Dogs are thinking, feeling, sentient beings that deserve more than a job as a security guard. They deserve to be members of the family, and they need your commitment of time, energy and love. Besides, Labs have less of a guard-dog instinct than some other breeds. However, if you want a Lab for all the right reasons and you also want some protection, get a dark-colored (black or chocolate) Lab. For some reason, dark-colored dogs seem to serve as a better deterrent than yellow

You'll own a Lab for all the right reasons if you examine why you want one before you get one and remember that all dogs are individuals, just like you.

dogs. People tend to ask, "Is she friendly?" when they meet a black or chocolate Lab, whereas people tend to assume yellow Labs are always friendly. Don't ask us why!

We can't deny that Labs are excellent retrievers for hunting purposes, but if they aren't also beloved family members, you won't be making the most of your Lab.

Labs are intelligent and ready to please, but no dog is easy to train. All dogs require time, energy and consistency if they are to become well trained, and Labs are no exception. If you don't train your Lab, chances are she will end up behaving in ways you don't appreciate. You may even end up feeling that you have to give up the dog. You don't want to contribute to the epidemic of abandoned dogs in this country, do you?

Sure, Labs are cute. Heck, we'd even say adorable. But that's no reason to buy a dog.

But you say you feel a kinship with the breed and are ready to spend the time and energy necessary to raise and train your Labrador Retriever so that she can become a companion and friend for life? Now we're talking!

Great Lab Expectations

Everyone has great expectations for a new pet, but too often, those expectations soon turn to disappointment. Why? Because bringing a new dog into the family isn't easy. It's work. Anyone who has brought a new baby home knows that babies don't come fed, burped, diapered and potty-trained; in fact, new babies don't come with very many skills at all. Don't expect much more from your new puppy. Even if you bring home an older dog that has mastered some basics, she may also have mastered some behaviors you aren't at all happy to tolerate.

Before you bring home a Labrador Retriever—or any dog—you have to think long and hard about what's involved. You have to be ready to make a serious commitment to the care, training and development of a relationship. Otherwise, you'll have a dog that's more trouble than fun, and the poor dog will probably end up either banished to the solitude of the backyard for life or at the local animal shelter, where she may then become someone else's problem or worse.

So don't buy a Lab on impulse. Labs are big, energetic and sometimes boisterous dogs (especially as puppies), and they don't take care of themselves. They need you. Don't let them need you unless you are ready to be needed.

Trainer Tidbits

You love dogs, but you have to work all day, and you can't come home for lunch. Hire a dog walker, pet sitter or doggy daycare center to fill in when you can't be there. More and more such services are popping up all over the country as people become increasingly aware of the importance of meeting their pets' needs. Check your phone book.

Lab Lore

More Labrador Retrievers are used as guide dogs for the sight-impaired than any other breed. Approximately 60 to 70 percent of the working guide dogs in the United States are Labrador Retrievers.

Are You Meant for a Lab? A Self-Test

By now, you may be pretty sure that you are ready for a dog. But is a Lab the dog for you? Sure, they're popular. Lots of people have them. But far fewer actually should have them, and are able to bring out the best in them. You could be one of those precious few, the God's-Gift-to-Labrador-Retrievers kind of human companion. Or maybe you at least have the potential. (Humans usually need some training, too!)

Questions

Take our test and see if you are meant for a Lab:

1. How would you describe your lifestyle?

   A. Weekend warrior

   B. Home body

   C. Desk jockey

   D. Party animal

   E. Couch potato

2. How would you describe your energy level?

   A. Volleyball league? Office softball? Running club? You're there!

   B. Pretty good, as long as the activity is pleasant and enjoyable, such as long walks around the neighborhood or in a park on a nice day.

   C. You exercise to stay healthy, but you don't enjoy it. You may wonder whether exercise would be more fun with a dog in tow.

   D. Football? Basketball? Hockey? What channel is it on? Better yet, what sports bar is showing the game?

   E. You read this book, and every book, about two pages at a time because you keep falling asleep.

3. How do you feel about getting periodically slapped with a huge, wagging tail or having your knees buckled by a rambunctious dog body barreling by?

A. Bring it on! Sounds like a dog that would be great at jogging or catching a Frisbee.

B. The more tail wagging and enthusiasm, the better. It means my dog is happy!

C. I guess I could put up with it for a few months, until my dog matures and can be trained.

D. *My* Lab would never do that.

E. Hmm, I'm not sure something like that wouldn't knock me right off my feet. Can I order a Lab that just sleeps most of the time?

4. How often is someone home at your house?

   A. You work but could come home for lunch, and your evenings and weekends are usually free or filled with some dog-friendly activity.

   B. You work at home and are there most of the day.

   C. You're away for about ten hours per weekday, and then when you get home, you have a quick dinner and collapse in front of the TV to unwind.

   D. You often go out after work with coworkers for drinks, a few rounds of pool or office gossip over nachos and pretzels. Weekends are the time for a social life.

   E. You work long hours and are at home so seldom that you wonder why you bother to pay for electricity! When you do get home, you usually go straight to bed.

5. Where do you live?

   A. Out in the country on several fenced acres—dog heaven!

   B. A house in town with a large fenced yard.

   C. An apartment or town house with a small, enclosed yard.

   D. An apartment or condo in the city with no yard.

   E. A place where they don't allow dogs, but you're thinking you could sneak one in.

6. What do you see happening in your life in the next ten years?

   A. You've got a good job, lots of friends and commitments. You're not going anywhere.

   B. You may move, get married or change jobs, but you couldn't see your life without a dog and wouldn't live somewhere that wasn't dog-friendly.

   C. You hope to meet someone, maybe get married, maybe have kids and certainly advance in your career. If a dog doesn't fit in later, you'll cross that bridge when you come to it.

   D. Your job is your life. Wherever it takes you, you're willing to go.

   E. You don't like to make a habit of thinking beyond tomorrow. You're a go-with-the-flow sort of person.

7. How is your financial situation?

   A. No problems. You make plenty to support yourself and your family. If your dog needs medical care, you're willing to do whatever it takes.

   B. You spend pretty much what you make, but you save a little, and in emergencies, you always find a way to meet the bills.

   C. Pretty tight, but dogs aren't expensive, are they?

   D. You certainly wouldn't spend more than $40 or $50 dollars at a veterinarian. After all, it's just a dog.

   E. You think you'll be able to convince the phone company to turn the phone back on sometime in the next month. Meanwhile, no phone means the creditors can't keep bugging you!

8. How do you spend your leisure time?

   A. You're as active as possible: hiking, camping, biking, swimming, jogging or just being outside in the fresh air.

   B. You like to go to new places and try new things: relaxing on a beach, exploring a new town, going on car trips and so on.

C. You get things done around the house or simply catch up on your sleep or the soaps. You pretty much prefer to stick close to home.

D. When you're not at work, you like to go out and party with your friends.

E. Leisure time? What leisure time?

9. How do you imagine a dog fitting into your life?

    A. Companion and pal on your many adventures.

    B. Confidante, best friend and family member, always with you whether you're taking a walk or taking a nap.

    C. A pet to keep you company, make you feel safe, and generally add to the atmosphere of your home.

    D. Home security system or backyard guard.

    E. A dog is a dog. They hang out in the backyard and eat dog food. What more is there to say?

10. What is the most important thing to know before getting a dog?

    A. What their physical and emotional needs will be.

    B. The characteristics and tendencies of the particular breed.

    C. What to feed them and what medical care they'll need.

    D. What kind of dog will take the least effort.

    E. Where to get a free one.

Answers

What kind of a potential Labrador Retriever companion are you? Tally up your answers and check your profile.

If you had mostly As and/or Bs, congratulations. You would probably make a great Labrador Retriever companion. You have a good energy level and can provide your dog with the activity she requires. You also value dogs as family members, are willing to find out what their

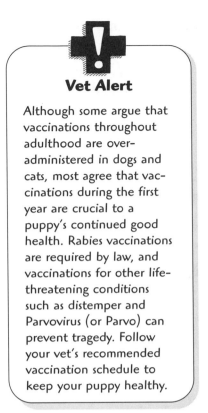

Vet Alert

Although some argue that vaccinations throughout adulthood are over-administered in dogs and cats, most agree that vaccinations during the first year are crucial to a puppy's continued good health. Rabies vaccinations are required by law, and vaccinations for other life-threatening conditions such as distemper and Parvovirus (or Parvo) can prevent tragedy. Follow your vet's recommended vaccination schedule to keep your puppy healthy.

needs are and are then willing to meet those needs. Whether you are an athlete extraordinaire or the stay-at-home type, you understand that dogs aren't impulse purchases but long-term commitments, and you're ready to take the plunge. Of course, that doesn't mean you know it all, so don't chuck this book aside just yet. There's always more to learn about our canine companions, so keep reading.

If you had mostly Cs, you have potential, but you have some misconceptions about Labrador Retrievers and/or pet ownership. You may not be quite active enough or home often enough to be the ideal dog owner. You also haven't given a whole lot of thought to the commitment involved. Maybe you grew up with a dog but weren't responsible for her care and maintenance. You see a dog as a pet that would be nice to have around, but shouldn't be too much trouble. You like dogs, however, and if you are willing to make some changes in your life, a dog could become a valuable and beloved family member. Perhaps adopting an older dog that doesn't require the rigorous attention and training of a puppy would be best for you, but you still need to do some research about Labs and be sure you are ready for an active, exuberant dog that requires your love and constant attention.

If you had mostly Ds and Es, you should probably think twice about bringing home a Labrador Retriever. We're not saying you absolutely shouldn't have one, but your lifestyle isn't ideal for a dog, and your ideas about dog ownership could use some revamping. Of course, that's what this book is for.

We'll be filling you in on everything involved in Labrador Retriever ownership, so please read this entire book *before* bringing home a dog. Then do some serious thinking about whether you're ready for the commitment. Dogs aren't temporary amusements to be discarded when they become inconvenient. They require time, money, energy and responsibility. After reading this book, if you have doubts, do yourself (and your potential pet) a favor and hold off. If, on the other hand, you feel like you've learned a lot and are ready to do what it takes, we'll be glad to have helped.

Lab Lingo

Parvovirus, commonly known as **Parvo,** targets bone marrow, the gastrointestinal lining, lymph nodes or the heart. Symptoms of the enteric form include loss of appetite, vomiting, diarrhea, fever and depressed behavior. The myocardial form usually occurs in young puppies, may cause sudden death and may also result in chronic congestive heart failure. Parvovirus is transmitted through contaminated feces. It's extremely contagious and is one of the biggest killers of puppies.

Got the Time?

You may feel ready to take on the responsibility of a dog, but you may not realize how much time a Lab, or any social animal, requires. Your Lab will need daily training sessions, lots of purposeful socialization as a puppy and time to simply hang around with you. You and your Lab need to form a relationship, and any successful relationship takes time. If you aren't home very often or have too much on your plate when you are home, enjoy a friend's Labrador Retriever now and then. Don't take on your own until you can pencil in lots of time for your new family member. You wouldn't have a child if you didn't have the time to raise it well, would you? Give your Lab the same courtesy.

Lab Lore

Labrador Retrievers didn't originate in Labrador, as their name would imply, but in Newfoundland.

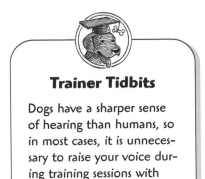

Trainer Tidbits

Dogs have a sharper sense of hearing than humans, so in most cases, it is unnecessary to raise your voice during training sessions with your Labrador Retriever.

Got the Energy?

Labs, unlike some other dogs, require as much energy as time. If you are a certified couch potato, your Lab *might* adjust, but inactive dogs (like inactive people) are less healthy, and Labs that aren't provided outlets for their energy might become destructive. Labs aren't small dogs and can't get sufficient activity running back and forth across the living room like a Chihuahua. (If your Lab did get its exercise this way, you'd probably soon be in need of some new furniture!)

Well-trained Labs that get sufficient exercise shouldn't be hyperactive and can certainly adapt to different levels of activity, but your Lab will need to be walked at least once a day, taken for occasional swims and given the opportunity to do lots of retrieving, the thing she loves best. If you aren't up to the physical challenge, consider a less-active or smaller dog or perhaps a cat.

Vet Alert

Although active, Labrador Retrievers can easily become overweight. Overfeeding and table scraps can quickly lead to obesity, which is the most common nutritional health problem in dogs, according to many vets. Try using halved baby carrots or small broccoli florets as treats rather than dog biscuits, which are often too caloric to be used daily.

Got the Space?

If you don't have the living space for a large dog, don't bring home a Labrador Retriever. The ideal situation is a single-family detached house with a fenced yard and dog-friendly neighbors or a country home with lots of fenced land. Other situations can work, too, especially if you walk your Lab religiously and train her well. However, if your living space doesn't allow dogs or if your apartment walls are paper thin, if you live in a tiny apartment with no yard and can't walk your dog every day, or if you like your home immaculate and value your collection of ceramic figurines or glassware or antique china above all else, please consider another type of dog. Labs need lots of exercise, puppies can sometimes be loud in the middle of the night and those Lab tails can be downright destructive if your house isn't Lab-proofed.

Got the Money?

Purchasing a Labrador Retriever through a breeder can cost anywhere from $300 to $1,000 (more if you want a quality show or field trial dog). Maybe you think that if you get a dog at an animal shelter or through a rescue group, it will be cheap or even free. But the cost of acquiring a dog is insignificant compared to the cost of keeping a dog healthy and well behaved throughout its life.

The cost of health maintenance, including vaccinations, heartworm preventive, parasite control and regular checkups, plus the cost of good food, a quality kennel or other enclosure, a supply of chew toys, obedience classes, trainers and/or behaviorists and any emergency medical costs or treatment for serious health problems or accidents can add up to quite a sum. Can you say college fund? If you can barely afford groceries or medical bills for yourself and your own family, don't bring a dog into your home until you're on a firmer financial footing.

Trainer Tidbits

Never underestimate the importance of identification tags. Even a well-trained dog may get separated from its humans, and puppies that haven't been fully trained may wander away and be unable to find the way home. Identification tags can mean your dog is quickly returned to you. Your dog's absence can land her in the animal shelter, where you may not find her in time.

The Least You Need to Know

➤ The Labrador Retriever is a popular and wonderful breed, but not right for everyone.

➤ Before purchasing any dog, make sure your lifestyle, priorities and level of commitment match the dog's requirements.

➤ If you aren't willing to make your Labrador Retriever a member of the family by providing her with plenty of exercise, training, socialization, companionship, proper health care and affection, you shouldn't bring a Lab into your home.

➤ Labs take significant time, energy, space and financial resources to be happy, healthy and rewarding pets.

Chapter 2

What Is a Labrador Retriever?

In This Chapter

➤ Labs versus other retrievers

➤ How does the AKC describe the perfect Lab?

➤ How does England (and Europe) describe a perfect Lab?

➤ How should you describe your perfect Lab?

You can probably recognize a Lab, or even a Lab mix, when you see one on the street. You know that friendly face, that sturdy build and those floppy ears. But beyond your first impression, you may not know what exactly makes a Labrador Retriever a Labrador Retriever. Are they from Labrador? (No.) Are they good at bringing stuff back to you? (Yes.) But there's much, much more.

Of course, standards for the Labrador Retriever vary depending on what country you are in and even what your priorities are. A great hunting dog, for example, may not necessarily win any prizes for conformation in the show ring. However, the *Labrador Retriever Club, Inc. (LRC)* emphasizes that fanciers and judges should remember the Lab was brought to the United States to retrieve waterfowl or game for hunters and that the field Lab and the show ring Lab should have the same characteristics and should be judged accordingly.

Lab Lingo

The **Labrador Retriever Club, Inc. (LRC)** is an AKC–sanctioned national breed club. The LRC's current breed standard (a description of the ideal Labrador Retriever) was approved by the AKC in 1994. The LRC issues working certificates for Labrador Retrievers, sponsors Labrador Retriever events and educates the public about Labrador Retrievers, including maintaining a directory of breeders.

What Makes the Lab Unique?

You probably know that Labrador Retrievers aren't the only retrieving dogs. Golden Retrievers, Chesapeake Bay Retrievers, Curly-Coated Retrievers and Flat-Coated Retrievers are other AKC-approved retriever breeds. What distinguishes the Lab from these other retrievers?

Many retrievers have Newfoundland dogs and spaniels in their backgrounds, and all were bred to aid hunters in retrieving game. Labrador Retrievers, however, are unique in that they were first discovered in Newfoundland, a chillier and icier climate than that of the British Isles, where most other retrievers were probably developed (except for the Chesapeake Bay Retriever, an American original). Labs have a shorter coat than some other retrievers; this coat prevents ice from clinging to it when the dog exits the water.

All retrievers should be friendly, intuitive and willing helpers that learn quickly and are eager to please, but the Labrador Retriever isn't the most popular dog in the United States by accident. Particularly agreeable, trainable, outgoing and ready to go to any lengths to please his owner, the Lab is a definite charmer and, in many ways, the ideal medium-to-large dog (if properly trained, of course).

The Breed Standard

Both the American Kennel Club and the Kennel Club of England have developed breed standards for the Labrador Retriever. *A breed standard* is a complete and thorough description of the ideal Labrador

Retriever. Of course, no dog meets the ideal in every way, but breed standards provide a standard so that breeds can be continually improved in looks, health, temperament and skill.

Lab Lingo

A **breed standard** is a description of the ideal specimen of a particular breed. No dog is expected to completely match the standard, but breeders use this standard to help define and improve a breed. Dog show judges use breed standards to give them something by which to judge show dogs.

Breed standards are also chock-full of dog-world jargon, so in this book, we'll give you the best of both worlds. In the following sections, you'll find the official standard and a translation tailor made for anyone who doesn't feel they need to know about briskets, withers and pasterns to get a great pet. (In case you would like to know more about briskets, withers and pasterns, however, keep an eye out for the Lab Lingo sidebars, check out the section on the anatomy of the Labrador Retriever in Chapter 11 or refer to the illustration of the Lab's external features in the front of this book.)

The AKC Standard

Although Labrador Retrievers have been retrieving and otherwise aiding their human companions for centuries, the first Lab wasn't registered with the American Kennel Club until 1917. The official breed standard, presented in the following sections, was last updated by the Labrador Retriever Club of America and approved by the AKC on February 12, 1994, and became official on March 31, 1994.

General Appearance

The Labrador Retriever is a strongly built, medium-sized, short-coupled dog possessing a sound, athletic, well-balanced conformation that enables it to function as a retrieving gun dog; the substance and soundness to hunt waterfowl or upland game for long hours under difficult conditions; the character and quality to win in the show ring; and the temperament to be a family companion. Physical features and mental characteristics should denote a dog bred to perform as an efficient Retriever of game with a stable temperament suitable for a variety of pursuits beyond the hunting environment. The most distinguishing characteristics of the Labrador Retriever are its short, dense, weather resistant coat; an "otter" tail; a clean-cut head with broad back skull and moderate stop; powerful jaws; and its "kind" friendly eyes, expressing character, intelligence and good temperament. Above all, a Labrador Retriever must be well balanced, enabling it to move in the show ring or work in the field with little or no effort. The typical Labrador possesses style and quality without over refinement, and substance without lumber or cloddiness. The Labrador is bred primarily as a working gun dog; structure and soundness are of great importance.

Lab Lingo

A short-coupled dog is relatively short in length from the shoulder blades to the hips, as opposed to longer-bodied dogs such as German Shepherds.

The Complete Idiot's Guide Translation

The Labrador Retriever is a strong and athletic-looking, medium-sized dog with a short, dense coat; a clean-cut look; a broad skull; and warm, friendly eyes. The Lab's size and balanced body make him ideal for retrieving, as well as a wide variety of other activities. He should be hardy, healthy and sturdy enough to hunt for long hours under difficult conditions; and should have the character, personality and looks to do well in dog shows and the right temperament to be a great family companion.

Size, Proportion and Substance

Size   The height at the withers for a dog is 22½ to 24½ inches; for a bitch is 21½ to 23½ inches. Any variance greater than ½ inch above or below these heights is a disqualification. Approximate weight of dogs and bitches in working condition: dogs 65 to 80 pounds; bitches 55 to 70 pounds. The minimum height ranges set forth in the paragraph above shall not apply to dogs or bitches under twelve months of age.

Proportion Short-coupled; length from the point of the shoulder to the point of the rump is equal to or slightly longer than the distance from the withers to the ground. Distance from the elbow to the ground should be equal to one half of the height at the withers. The brisket should extend to the elbows, but not perceptibly deeper. The body must be of sufficient length to permit a straight, free and efficient stride; but the dog should never appear low and long or tall and leggy in outline.

Substance Substance and bone proportionate to the overall dog. Light, "weedy" individuals are definitely incorrect; equally objectionable are cloddy lumbering specimens. Labrador Retrievers shall be shown in working condition well-muscled and without excess fat.

Trainer Tidbits

To keep your Lab in good physical condition, allow him to get at least thirty minutes of exercise every day. To combat boredom (your Lab's or yours), alternate long walks, romps in the park, field trips to dog-friendly recreational areas, beaches or hiking trails and, of course, lots of retrieving activities.

Lab Lingo

The **withers** is the top of the shoulder blades, and is used to measure the height of dogs. The **brisket** may refer to the chest area, or to the entire front half of the torso (the thorax).

The Complete Idiot's Guide Translation

When measured from the ground to the top of the shoulder blade, the ideal Labrador Retriever should be between 22½ to 24½ inches for males and 21½ to 23½ inches for females. After they are 1 year old, males in good shape should weigh between 65 and 80 pounds, and females should weigh between 55 and 70 pounds. Any Lab over ½ inch above or below the standard would be disqualified from the show ring. Proportionally, a Lab should be relatively short from shoulder to hips, but just long and tall enough to make walking and running easy and efficient. Labs in good shape have lots of muscle and no excess fat.

Lab Lingo

When a dog looks **weedy,** he looks light-boned or has an insufficient amount of bone for his size. A **cloddy** dog, on the other hand, is low and thickset and looks relatively heavy.

Head

Skull   The skull should be wide; well developed but without exaggeration. The skull and foreface should be on parallel planes and of approximately equal length. There should be a moderate stop—the brow slightly pronounced so that the skull is not absolutely in a straight line with the nose. The brow ridges aid in defining the stop. The head should be clean-cut and free from fleshy cheeks; the bony structure of the skull chiseled beneath the eye with no prominence in the cheek. The skull may show some median line; the occipital bone is not conspicuous in mature dogs. Lips should not be squared off or pendulous, but fall away in a curve toward the throat. A wedge-shape head, or a head long and narrow in muzzle and back skull is incorrect as are massive, cheeky heads. The jaws are powerful and free from snippiness, the muzzle neither long and narrow nor short and stubby.

Lab Lingo

A dog's **foreface** is his muzzle area.

Nose   The nose should be wide and the nostrils well developed. The nose should be black on black on yellow dogs, and brown on chocolates. Nose color fading to a lighter shade is not a fault. A thoroughly pink nose or one lacking in any pigment is a disqualification.

Ch. Campbellcroft's P.B. Max, CD, JH won Best of Breed at the Labrador Retriever National Specialty in 1994. The CD and JH after his name mean he's earned obedience and hunting titles (which you'll read more about later in this book). (photo by Callea Photography)

Teeth   The teeth should be strong and regular with a scissors bite; the lower teeth just behind, but touching the inner side of the upper incisors. A level bite is acceptable, but not desirable. Undershot, over-shot, or misaligned teeth are serious faults. Full dentition is preferred. Missing molars or pre-molars are serious faults.

Lab Lingo

Scissors bite refers to a bite in which the outside of the lower six front teeth (**incisors**) touches the inner side of the top six front teeth (also incisors). A **level bite** occurs when the upper and lower incisors meet exactly, rather than overlapping one way or the other.

Ears   The ears should hang moderately close to the head, set rather far back and somewhat low on the skull; slightly above eye level. Ears should not be large and heavy, but in proportion with the skull and reach to the inside of the eye when pulled forward.

Eyes   Kind, friendly eyes imparting good temperament, intelligence and alertness are a hallmark of the breed. They should be of medium size, set well apart and neither protruding nor deep set. Eye color should be brown in black and yellow Labradors, and brown or hazel in choco-lates. Black, or yellow eyes give a harsh expression and are undesirable.

Small eyes, set close together or round prominent eyes are not typical of the breed. Eye rims are black in black and yellow Labradors; and brown in chocolates. Eye rims without pigmentation is a disqualification.

The Complete Idiot's Guide Translation

Skull

A Labrador Retriever's skull should be wide, but not so wide as to look exaggerated. The top of the skull should be parallel to the top of the muzzle, and both parts should be about the same length. The head should look clean-cut with strong jaws, but without fleshy cheeks or lips. The nose should be wide and black on black and yellow Labs; it should be brown on chocolate Labs. The teeth should be strong and even, with the bottom teeth just behind the top teeth when the mouth is closed.

Ears/Eyes

Ears should hang next to the head, relatively far back and low and should reach to the inside of the eye when pulled forward. The eyes should show good temperament, intelligence and alertness because these traits are so representative of the Labrador Retriever. Eyes should be brown with black rims in black and yellow Labs and should be brown or hazel with brown rims in chocolates.

Neck, Topline and Body

Neck   The neck should be of proper length to allow the dog to retrieve game easily. It should be muscular and free from throatiness. The neck should rise strongly from the shoulders with a moderate arch. A short, thick neck or a "ewe" neck is incorrect.

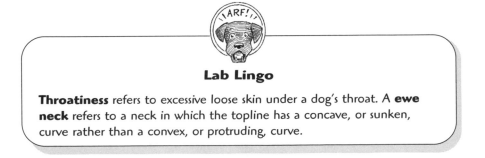

Lab Lingo

Throatiness refers to excessive loose skin under a dog's throat. A **ewe neck** refers to a neck in which the topline has a concave, or sunken, curve rather than a convex, or protruding, curve.

Topline   The back is strong and the topline is level from the withers to the croup when standing or moving. However, the loin should show evidence of flexibility for athletic endeavor.

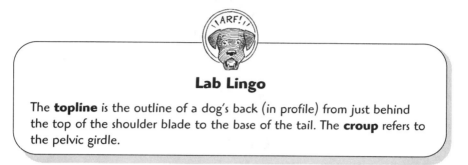

Lab Lingo

The **topline** is the outline of a dog's back (in profile) from just behind the top of the shoulder blade to the base of the tail. The **croup** refers to the pelvic girdle.

Body   The Labrador should be short-coupled, with good spring of ribs tapering to a moderately wide chest. The Labrador should not be narrow chested; giving the appearance of hollowness between the front legs, nor should it have a wide spreading, bulldog-like front. Correct chest conformation will result in tapering between the front legs that allows unrestricted forelimb movement. Chest breadth that is either too wide or too narrow for efficient movement and stamina is incorrect. Slab-sided individuals are not typical of the breed; equally objectionable are rotund or barrel chested specimens. The underline is almost straight, with little or no tuck-up in mature animals. Loins should be short, wide and strong; extending to well developed, powerful hindquarters. When viewed from the side, the Labrador Retriever shows a well-developed, but not exaggerated forechest.

Lab Lingo

The **underline** is the outline of the dog's underside (in profile) from the front of the chest to the base of the abdomen.

Tail   The tail is a distinguishing feature of the breed. It should be very thick at the base, gradually tapering toward the tip, of medium length and extending no longer than to the hock. The tail should be free from feathering and clothed thickly all around with the Labrador's short, dense coat, thus having that peculiar rounded appearance that has been described as the "otter" tail. The tail should follow the topline in repose or when in motion. It may be carried gaily, but should not curl over the back. Extremely short tails or long thin tails are serious faults. The tail completes the balance of the Labrador by giving it a flowing line from the top of the head to the tip of the tail. Docking or otherwise altering the length or natural carriage of the tail is a disqualification.

Lab Lingo

The **hock** is the hind-leg joint corresponding to the ankle joint on a human. **Docking** refers to the procedure of shortening a dog's tail by cutting it. In America, many breeds have their tails docked, although in many European countries the procedure will disqualify a dog from the show ring and is frowned upon as unethical.

The Complete Idiot's Guide Translation

The neck should be strong without loose skin and long enough to make retrieval easy. The back should be straight and level between the shoulder blade and the hips, and the body should have a nicely tapered rib cage (not too flat or too barrel-chested). The Lab tail should be very thick at the base and then taper off. The Lab tail should also be covered in thick, short fur all the way around (called an "otter tail") rather than long, feathery fur as on a Golden Retriever. The tail shouldn't curve over the back like a Husky tail and should continue the flow of a line from the top of the head to the tail tip.

Forequarters

Forequarters should be muscular, well coordinated and balanced with the hindquarters.

Shoulders The shoulders are well laid-back, long and sloping, forming an angle with the upper arm of approximately 90 degrees that permits the dog to move his forelegs in an easy manner with strong forward reach. Ideally, the length of the shoulder blade should equal the length of the upper arm. Straight shoulder blades, short upper arms or heavily muscled or loaded shoulders, all restricting free movement, are incorrect.

Lab Lingo

Forequarters are the front part of the dog, from shoulder blades to paws. **Hindquarters** are the back part of the dog, from hips to paws.

Front Legs   When viewed from the front, the legs should be straight with good strong bone. Too much bone is as undesirable as too little bone, and short legged, heavy boned individuals are not typical of the breed. Viewed from the side, the elbows should be directly under the withers, and the front legs should be perpendicular to the ground and well under the body. The elbows should be close to the ribs without looseness. Tied-in elbows or being "out at the elbows" interfere with free movement and are serious faults. Pasterns should be strong and short and should slope slightly from the perpendicular line of the leg. Feet are strong and compact, with well-arched toes and well-developed pads. Dewclaws may be removed. Splayed feet, hare feet, knuckling over, or feet turning in or out are serious faults.

Lab Lingo

Pasterns are the forelegs between the "ankle" and the joint where the toes begin. **Dewclaws** are "toes" on the inside of a dog's leg, separated from the other "toes" and comparable to a thumb, except that they aren't used. They are commonly removed because they serve no function.

The Complete Idiot's Guide Translation

The front part of the dog should be muscular (but not so much as to restrict movement) and balanced with the back part so that shoulders and hips are in proportion, as are front and back legs. Front legs should be straight with strong bones, and when viewed from the side, the dog's elbows should be directly beneath the top point of the shoulder blade. Feet should be strong and compact with arched toes and well-developed paws.

Hindquarters

The Labrador's hindquarters are broad, muscular and well-developed from the hip to the hock with well-turned stifles and strong short hocks. Viewed from the rear, the hind legs are straight and parallel. Viewed from the side, the angulation of the rear legs is in balance with the front. The hind legs are strongly boned, muscled with moderate angulation at the stifle, and powerful, clearly defined thighs. The stifle is strong and there is no slippage of the patella while in motion or when standing. The hock joints are strong, well let down and do not slip or hyperextend while in motion or when standing. Angulation of both stifle and hock joint is such as to achieve the optimal balance of drive and traction. When standing the rear toes are only slightly behind the point of the rump. Over angulation produces a sloping topline not typical of the breed. Feet are strong and compact, with well-arched toes and well-developed pads. Cow-hocks, spread hocks, sickle hocks and over-angulation are serious structural defects and are to be faulted.

Lab Lingo

The **hock** is the "heel" joint, the **stifle** is the "knee" joint, the **patella** is the knee cap and the **pasterns** are the knuckle joints. **Cow-hocks** refer to turned-in ankles and turned-out toes; **spread hocks** refer to hocks that point outward; **sickle hocks** refer to hocks that can't be straightened.

The Complete Idiot's Guide Translation

The dog's back half, the pelvis, hips, legs and paws, should be muscular and balanced. From the side, the angle of the rear legs should match the angle of the front legs. Hind legs should have strong bones and defined thighs with steady knees. When standing still, the dog's rear toes should stand just behind the top of the rump. Feet should be strong and compact, with arched toes and well-developed pads.

Coat

The coat is a distinctive feature of the Labrador Retriever. It should be short, straight and very dense, giving a fairly hard feeling to the hand. The Labrador should have a soft, weather-resistant undercoat that provides protection from water, cold and all types of ground cover. A slight wave down the back is permissible. Woolly coats, soft silky coats and sparse slick coats are not typical of the breed, and should be severely penalized.

The Complete Idiot's Guide Translation

Labs have a double coat, which means the coat has two layers: a thick, dense, hard, weather-resistant top layer and a soft, downy undercoat for insulation. Labs with woolly, soft or sparse coats are considered less desirable because they won't be as resistant to inclement weather conditions.

Color

The Labrador Retriever coat colors are black, yellow and chocolate. Any other color or a combination of colors is a disqualification. A small white spot on the chest is permissible, but not desirable. White hairs from aging or scarring are not to be misinterpreted as brindling.

Black   Blacks are all black. A black with brindle markings or a black with tan markings is a disqualification.

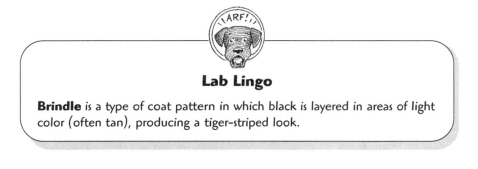

Lab Lingo

Brindle is a type of coat pattern in which black is layered in areas of light color (often tan), producing a tiger-striped look.

Yellow   Yellows may range in color from fox-red to light cream, with variations in shading on the ears, back and underparts of the dog.

Chocolate   Chocolates can vary in shade from light to dark chocolate. Chocolate with brindle or tan markings is a disqualification.

The Complete Idiot's Guide Translation

Labs come in black, yellow (from fox red to light cream) and chocolate (light to dark). Other color variations would disqualify a dog from the show ring.

29

Movement

Movement of the Labrador Retriever should be free and effortless. When watching a dog move toward oneself, there should be no sign of elbows out. Rather, the elbows should be held neatly to the body with the legs not too close together. Moving straight forward without pacing or weaving, the legs should form straight lines, with all parts moving in the same plane. Upon viewing the dog from the rear, one should have the impression that the hind legs move as nearly as possible in a parallel line with the front legs. The hocks should do their full share of the work, flexing well, giving the appearance of power and strength. When viewed from the side, the shoulders should move freely and effortlessly, and the foreleg should reach forward close to the ground with extension. A short, choppy movement or high knee action indicates a straight shoulder; paddling indicates long, weak pasterns; and a short, stilted rear gait indicates a straight rear assembly; all are serious faults. Movement faults interfering with performance including weaving; side-winding; crossing over; high knee action; paddling; and short, choppy movement, should be severely penalized.

The Complete Idiot's Guide Translation

When a Lab moves, he should look free, balanced and effortless. Elbows shouldn't turn out, the body should move straight without weaving, the legs should remain straight and all parts of the dog should move in concert.

Lab Lore

In England, Labrador Retrievers must earn working certificates to qualify as show champions.

Temperament

True Labrador Retriever temperament is as much a hallmark of the breed as the "otter" tail. The ideal disposition is one of a kindly, outgoing, tractable nature; eager to please and non-aggressive towards man or animal. The Labrador has much that appeals to people; his gentle ways, intelligence and adaptability make him an ideal dog. Aggressiveness towards humans or other animals, or any evidence of shyness in an adult should be severely penalized.

The Complete Idiot's Guide Translation

Temperament can make or break a Lab. The ideal Lab is kindly, outgoing, obedient, nonaggressive, gentle, intelligent, adaptable and, above all, eager to please.

The Labrador Retriever's gentle nature, as evident in this dog's expression, is one of the breed's most endearing qualities. (photo by Ann and Randy McCall)

Disqualifications

If you want to show your dog in dog shows, pay attention to the following disqualifications from the AKC standard. If not, don't give them a second thought. If your dog has any of these characteristics, he will be disqualified from show competition:

1. Any deviation from the height prescribed in the Standard.

2. A thoroughly pink nose or one lacking in any pigment.

3. Eye rims without pigment.

4. Docking or otherwise altering the length or natural carriage of the tail.

5. Any other color or a combination of colors other than black, yellow or chocolate as described in the Standard.

The English Standard

The standard for the Labrador Retriever in England is much the same as the AKC standard, but it's shorter and a little less in need of a translation, so we're going to print it as is. The standard is set by an organization called the FCI, which is made up of kennel clubs from most major countries in the world except the United States (Russia is the newest member). The FCI is similar to the AKC standard, but it's less detailed and has a few other differences. (For instance, the FCI does not disqualify dogs if they do not fall within the ideal size guidelines as the AKC does.) All member clubs use FCI breed standards:

General Appearance   Strongly built, short coupled, very active; broad in skull; broad and deep through chest and ribs; broad and strong over loins and hindquarters.

Characteristics   Good tempered, very agile. Excellent nose, soft; keen lover of water. Adaptable, devoted companion.

Temperament   Intelligent, keen and biddable, with a strong will to please. Kindly nature, with no trace of aggression or undue shyness.

Head and Skull   Skull broad with defined stop; clean cut without fleshy cheeks. Jaws of medium length, powerful not snipey. Nose wide, nostrils well-developed.

Eyes   Medium size, expressing intelligence and good temper; brown or hazel.

Ears   Not large or heavy, hanging close to head and set rather far back.

Mouth   Jaws and teeth strong with a perfect, regular and complete scissor bite, i.e. upper teeth closely overlapping lower teeth and set square to the jaws.

Neck   Clean, strong, powerful, set into well-placed shoulders.

Forequarters   Shoulders long and sloping. Forelegs well-boned and straight from elbow to ground when viewed from either front or side.

Body   Chest of good width and depth, with well sprung barrel ribs. Level topline. Loins wide, short coupled and strong.

Hindquarters   Well developed, not sloping to tail; well turned stifle. Hocks let down, cowhocks highly undesirable.

Feet   Round, compact; well-arched toes and well-developed pads.

Tail   Distinctive feature, very thick towards base, gradually tapering towards tip, medium length, free from feathering, but clothed thickly all round with short, thick, dense coat, thus giving "rounded" appearance described as "Otter" tail. May be carried gaily, but should not curl over back.

Gait/Movement   Free, covering adequate ground; straight and true in front and rear.

Coat   Distinctive feature, short dense without wave or feathering, giving fairly hard feel to the touch; weather resistant undercoat.

Colour   Wholly black, yellow or liver/chocolate. Yellows range from light cream to red fox. Small white spot on chest permissible.

Size   Ideal height at withers; dogs 56–57 cms (22–22½ ins); bitches 54–56 cms (21½ ins).

Faults   Any departure from the foregoing points should be considered a fault and the seriousness with which the fault should be regarded should be in exact proportion to its degree. NOTE: Male animals should have two apparently normal testicles fully descended into the scrotum.

Approved by the General Assembly on the 23rd and 24th June 1987 in Jerusalem.

Must Your Dog Fit the Standard?

Must your dog exactly match the AKC or English standard for a Labrador Retriever? Of course not. No Lab will exactly fit every aspect of the standard because no dog is perfect. But your dog might be perfect for you.

If you want a show dog, pay closer attention to the published standard because it is used to judge show dogs. But if you want a pet, you'll be more interested in certain aspects of the standard, such as temperament. If you live in a cold climate, you'll want a Lab with a good coat in addition to a good temperament. If you would like a hunting companion, you'll want a Lab that excels in retrieving and has lots of endurance and strength.

It can be interesting, and even helpful, to know what the perfect Lab is like, but your Lab need only meet your personal standard for perfection. And lots of that perfection will come from the way you raise, train and treat your dog. They don't come pre-perfected!

How to Register Your Lab with the American Kennel Club

If you buy a purebred Labrador Retriever from a breeder and your Lab is eligible for registration with the AKC, you'll want to register him, especially if you want to participate in dog shows or other AKC dog events that require registration.

When you buy your Lab, you should receive an AKC application form that has already been filled out correctly by the breeder or previous owner. When you complete the form, submit it to the AKC along with the specified fee. When the AKC processes your application, you will receive a registration certificate. Keep it in a safe place!

If the breeder or previous owner doesn't have the proper paperwork, but the dog you are purchasing is represented as eligible for registration, the breeder must give you records that provide all the necessary identifying information and the breeder's signature. This information includes the breed, sex, color, date of birth, registered names of the dog's sire (father) and dam (mother) and the name of the breeder. If the seller can't provide this information, don't buy the dog.

If you need help filling out the proper information, ask the breeder for help, or contact the American Kennel Club (see Appendix B for contact information).

The Least You Need to Know

➤ Labs have similarities to other retrievers but are unique in their country of origin and in their particularly agreeable temperaments.

➤ The American Kennel Club has a published standard to describe the perfect Labrador Retriever as a measure for show judges and breeders.

➤ England and other European countries have a separate but similar breed standard.

➤ Your Lab needn't meet any published breed standard, but he should fit into your unique situation.

Chapter 3

The Labrador Retriever Through the Ages

In This Chapter

➤ The history of the Lab in the United States

➤ The history of the Lab in England

➤ Ancient Lab history, such as it is

➤ The many ways Labs help us today

A book on Labrador Retrievers wouldn't be complete without a mini history lesson on their origin. Where did they come from? What forces and influences made them the dogs we know and love today? Just looking at a Lab will give you some clues about the traits humans have been encouraging in them for centuries. Their relatively small size (compared to the prodigious Newfoundland dog), distinct muscle tone, hardiness, no-fuss double coat, strong jaws and agreeable disposition are all evidence of their original purpose, which was (and still is) to best help humans survive and thrive.

As with many breeds, the distant history of the Labrador Retriever is a bit murky. So just for fun, let's look at the history of the Labrador Retriever in reverse. That way, we'll start on firmer footing, with the part of the Lab's history we do know because it is well documented.

Lab Lore

The American Kennel Club has ranked the Labrador Retriever as the most popular dog every year since 1991.

The Labrador Retriever in the United States

In 1997, the Labrador Retriever ranked number one in popularity with the American Kennel Club in number of purebred dogs registered, which is quite an impressive rise from a humble American beginning at the start of the twentieth century. Back in 1917, the first Labrador Retriever was registered with the American Kennel Club, and ten years later, only twenty-three retrievers of all types were registered (including Labradors, Goldens, Flat-coated, Curly-coated and Chesapeake).

In 1920s America, sportsmen developed a fascination with a Scottish sport called pass shooting. Desiring the authentic experience, many Americans imported both guns and dogs from the British Isles. The Labrador Retriever quickly caught on as a skilled hunting companion. By the 1930s, these shoots had become *field trials*, and in 1931, the Labrador Retriever Club was incorporated under the laws of the State of New York.

Lab Lingo

Field trials are special tests for certain breeds, including retrievers, spaniels, Beagles, Basset Hounds and Dachshunds. Each of these breeds was originally bred for a specific purpose, such as retrieving game, and field trials for each breed are meant to test an individual dog's ability to perform the function for which she was bred. Dogs can earn the title of Field Champion and Amateur Field Champion.

Today, the Labrador Retriever is right at home on American soil. Perfectly suited for hunting and/or fishing expeditions in the frigid north, the steamy south or the arid west, Labs are as versatile and proficient at their many tasks as they ever were—maybe more so. These days, you'll find Labs doing far more than hunting and fishing. They work as service dogs of all types, from leading the blind to locating explosives to rescuing hikers from avalanches. But we'll go into that in more detail later in this chapter.

The Lab in England

Most retrievers claim the British Isles as their original home, and who knows? The ancestors of the Labrador Retriever may have been brought from Britain to Newfoundland. We have no proof of this, but we do have proof of the Labrador Retrievers' illustrious history in Great Britain after they were imported from Newfoundland.

Many sources report that the dog known as the St. John's dog was brought to England on ships returning from Newfoundland in the early nineteenth century. The second Earl of Malmesbury (among others) is said to have taken these dogs from Newfoundland for use on his estate at Hurn in Dorset, where wild fowl often fell into the water after being shot. The English aristocracy proceeded to develop the St. John's dog into what is now known as the Labrador Retriever.

One of the first to refer to the dog as a Labrador was the third Earl of Malmesbury, who wrote in a letter to the sixth Duke of Buccleah, "We always call mine Labrador dogs, and I have kept the breed as pure as I could from the first I had—the real breed may be known by their having a close coat which turns water off like oil and, above all, a tail like an otter."

Not all breeders were as scrupulous as the third Earl of Malmesbury in keeping the breed pure, however. The Labrador dog was frequently crossed with other types of retrievers. Most descendants, usually resembling the original Labrador, were called Labradors.

England's Kennel Club first recognized the Labrador Retriever as a unique and separate breed in 1903. In 1905, they were classified as a variety of retriever.

Ancient History of the Labrador Retriever

Let's look back even further, into the misty depths of history, to the place where the appearance of a dog suspiciously similar to our

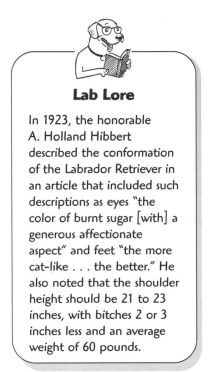

Lab Lore

In 1923, the honorable A. Holland Hibbert described the conformation of the Labrador Retriever in an article that included such descriptions as eyes "the color of burnt sugar [with] a generous affectionate aspect" and feet "the more cat-like . . . the better." He also noted that the shoulder height should be 21 to 23 inches, with bitches 2 or 3 inches less and an average weight of 60 pounds.

beloved Labrador Retriever was first recorded. Most books on Labrador Retrievers note that the Lab originated in Newfoundland, not Labrador. That's a little like saying a dog originated in Florida, not Georgia. In 1949, Newfoundland and Labrador together became Canada's easternmost province, and both areas were known collectively as Newfoundland until 1965, at which time the province name was changed to Newfoundland and Labrador. (Just look at one of their car license plates.)

Newfoundland proper is an island off the coast of Labrador; Labrador is part of the Canadian mainland. Yet both areas share similar geography, wildlife and climate. Both share many rivers, lakes and a rugged, irregular coastline. Until the twentieth century, both relied almost solely on fishing as an export.

The probable ancestor of the Labrador Retriever was apparently first observed on the island of Newfoundland rather than the mainland. In any case, the climate was cold, life was harsh and working hours for man, woman and dog alike were long and unforgiving.

However, before the Dorset Eskimos first settled in Newfoundland and began to fish, the area wasn't inhabited by any kind of dog—or at least, no evidence suggests it was. Chances are, the ancestors of both the Labrador Retriever and the Newfoundland dog were brought from elsewhere, probably from Europe by settlers and quite possibly from the British Isles.

The settlers of Newfoundland, mostly fishermen, needed dogs for hunting (you can eat only fish so many days in a row!) and for helping on the fishing boats. It took awhile before the smaller, short-coated, utilitarian dog so eager to please and so adept at retrieving was given a name that stuck. Called the Lesser Newfoundland (reflecting a previous belief that the Labrador Retriever was a descendant of the Newfoundland dog), the St. John's Water Dog (St. John's is the largest city in Newfoundland) or just plain retriever, these dogs were excellent hunters and could also fit in small fishing boats. (In fact, one of Joel's favorite Labs used to love to retrieve fish from rivers and ponds—evidence of her ancestry, perhaps?)

In 1662, the "small water dog" was described in the journal of W. E. Cormack, a St. John's native trekking across Newfoundland. Englishmen exploring the area took note of the breed's many abilities and soon began to revamp their hunting parties by replacing their pointers and setters with retrievers. By the nineteenth century, the dog found her way to England and graced the hunting parties of the English gentry. By the twentieth century, Labrador Retrievers had made their mark in the United States. For a more detailed history, check out some of the books on the list of resources in Appendix B.

Lab Lore

The province called Newfoundland and Labrador is the seventh-largest province in Canada. It measures 156,649 square miles, including 13,139 square miles of inland water. The island of Newfoundland makes up 43,359 square miles of this space and is separated from mainland Labrador by the Strait of Belle Isle. Newfoundland measures about 325 miles from north to south and about 300 miles from east to west. Most of Newfoundland and Labrador is rocky and unsuitable for farming, with lots of coastline, making fish one of the province's few exports.

The Lab at Work

One of the hallmarks of the Labrador Retriever is her eagerness to please. But Labs do much more than please their human companions. More Labrador Retrievers serve as guide dogs than any other breed (between 60 and 70 percent of working guide dogs). Labs also serve as assistance dogs for the deaf and the physically disabled. Labs make wonderful therapy dogs, brightening the days of hospitalized children and nursing-home residents alike. Lost in the mountains? Many Labs are adept at search and rescue, including specializations such as avalanche dogs. Labs are also great at sniffing out explosives and illegal drugs. What would we do without them?

Trainer Tidbits

Training your Labrador Retriever as a therapy dog, a search and rescue dog or in any other helping activity is good for your dog. Dogs like to have a job to do, and when the activity is performed with their human companions at their sides, Labs are in dog heaven. When considering a hobby, think of something that will involve your dog. Your relationship will be the better for it.

A History of Help

After this brief look at Labrador Retrievers from the distant past to the present moment, one thing becomes clear: Labrador Retrievers know how to help us. From increasing our ancestors' chances of survival by aiding them in the hunt to easing the loneliness and fear of a hospitalized child to rescuing a stranded mountain climber to providing love and companionship as a family pet, Labs know what we need. Labs love to help us and serve us, and they do it with consummate skill. The least we can do is learn all we can about how to make their lives long, happy and fulfilling. So keep on reading!

The Least You Need to Know

➤ The Labrador Retriever is the most popular breed in the United States.

➤ The Labrador Retriever was brought to England and further refined in the nineteenth century.

➤ The ancestors of the Labrador Retriever were first noted in Newfoundland in the sixteenth century.

➤ Labs are more than pets. They also make great guide dogs, hearing dogs, assistance dogs, therapy dogs, search and rescue dogs and explosive detection dogs.

➤ Labs have a history of helping humankind. We owe our pets healthy, happy and fulfilling lives.

Chapter 4

A Lab of Many Colors (and Types and Ages)

In This Chapter

➤ What type of Lab should you get?

➤ Does color matter?

➤ What about gender?

➤ Should you adopt a puppy or an older Lab?

Even if you are sure by this point that a Labrador Retriever is the perfect dog for you, you have a few more decisions to make before you rush out to find one. Not all Labs are the same. You should consider what type of Lab you want, what color, whether you prefer a male or a female and perhaps most important, what age of dog to bring into your home. In this chapter, we'll help you to determine the details of your practically perfect Lab, before we expound upon where to find him in the next chapter.

Which Type of Lab Fits Your Life?

There are two general types of Labs: the English type and the Field type. The English types are active pups that tend to settle down with good, positive training and can make great family companions. The Field types have lots of field titles in their *pedigree* and are usually much more active than most families want in a pet dog. Remember,

41

field trial champions are like Olympic athletes. Too high an activity level in a family pet is not desirable unless you plan to put the dog to work doing an extremely active task such as training for field trials.

Lab Lingo

A **pedigree** is the written record of a dog's ancestry and must go back at least three generations. A **show champion pedigree** means a dog is descended from dogs that have earned champion titles in dog shows.

First of all, you'll want to consider what type of Lab will fit into your life. Check all the qualities in the following list that appeal to you or are important to you in a dog:

- ☐ I want a dog with a *show champion pedigree* for showing and breeding.

- ☐ I want a dog with a show champion pedigree so I can brag about it!

- ☐ I want a dog that won't be more active than I can manage.

- ☐ I want a dog that I can train to become a well-behaved companion.

- ☐ I want a heavy-duty hunting dog.

- ☐ I want a dog to compete in *field trials*.

- ☐ I want a dog that I can train to be a good companion, but with whom I can also compete in the higher levels of AKC *obedience trials*.

If you checked any of the first four items, you'll probably want an English Lab. If you checked any of the last three items, look at Field Labs.

The English Lab

Although the term *English Lab* doesn't designate an actual sub-breed of Labrador Retriever, it does have meaning to dog people. It refers to a Lab with show dogs in his pedigree. If a dog has earned championship status in the show ring for conformation (being the closest specimen to the breed standard or ideal), he gets a *CH.* before his name. Lots of CH.s in the pedigree show that a dog had a lot of ancestors that were also judged to be closest to the ideal of the breed.

If showing and/or breeding Labs are your passion, you'll probably want to consider an English Lab. Consider joining your local or regional Labrador Retriever Club (check with the national Labrador Retriever Club, Inc., for a list of local and regional AKC-affiliated clubs or find an independent club). After doing your research, get on a waiting list for that special puppy that will have the potential to earn his Show Championship. If you want to breed your Labrador, you will want to get to know one or more excellent breeders and learn as much as you can from them. In every case, make sure your dog comes from a breeder who tests for the common problems that Labs have (more on that in the next chapter). Then get ready to learn a lot about handling a show dog, or consider hiring a *professional handler.*

Of course, a good family pet needn't have a championship title and needn't even be particularly close to the breed standard in appearance (though he should match the breed standard in personality and temperament). If you are looking for a Lab to join your family, a dog with obedience titles will probably be at least as important as a dog with conformation titles. If you just like the idea of having a dog with a champion pedigree, that's certainly okay (it's your money), but just be sure that isn't the only reason you want a dog. Dogs shouldn't be status symbols. They are living beings that need care and love.

The Field Lab

The Field Lab (not an official sub-breed, but a description of what purpose the dog was primarily bred to serve) is a great choice for someone who wants to participate actively with his or her dog in field trials and who has money and time to spare. Successful field trial dogs take a lot of training, and you'll need to learn the ropes, too. Attend some field trial events to see what it's all about. If you love the idea, look for a breeder who has demonstrated success at producing dogs that have done well in field trials. Then, once again, start researching, learning and practicing.

Lab Lingo

A **professional handler** is someone you hire to handle your dog in the show ring. Handlers are trained to bring out the best in a dog in the ring and can sometimes make the difference between winning and not even placing. Doing your own handling requires some education. Go to dog shows and research the subject to find out more.

The Titled Lab

Entering your Lab, whether an English or a Field Lab, in obedience trials is a great way to bond with your dog while training him to be ultimately well behaved, useful and fun. Most dogs can earn their CD (see the following list) with a little work. If the obedience bug bites you and you have a particularly high-energy dog, keep up the training and see how much the two of you can achieve. Active dogs need something to do, and training them for such events gives them a purpose as well as an outlet for their energy. Plus, they love to spend their days with you.

Labs can earn a variety of titles. Obedience titles have four levels of accomplishment:

➤ **Companion Dog (CD)** refers to a dog that has demonstrated the basics of heeling on and off a leash, standing for examination, coming when called and performing both a long sit and a long down.

➤ **Companion Dog Excellent (CDX)** refers to a dog that has earned a CD and can also drop on recall, retrieve on flat, retrieve over the high jump and perform a broad jump.

➤ **Utility Dog (UD)** refers to a dog that has earned his CDX and can also perform a signal exercise, two scent discrimination tests, a directed retrieve, directed jumping and group examination.

➤ **An Obedience Trial Champion (OTCH)** refers to a dog that has his UD title and has proceeded to win 100 points (according to AKC scoring regulations) in competition with other UD dogs. Many dogs with an OTCH are Field Labs.

Labrador Retrievers (either type) may also earn a Tracking Dog title (TD) by passing tests that demonstrate the dog's ability to follow a trail by scent. Passing more-advanced tracking tests will earn a Lab a Tracking Dog Excellent (TDX) title.

And of course, let's not forget that Labrador Retrievers are excellent hunting companions. Labs can participate in hunting tests that evaluate aspects of a dog's hunting ability. Labs can earn three levels of hunting titles: Junior Hunter (JH), Senior Hunter (SH) and Master Hunter (MH).

Vet Alert

If you're looking for a mellow, pleasant family dog to accompany you on leisurely walks around the block, don't go for the puppy with a pedigree rife with field and utility titles. If your dog is bred to be an ultra-achiever and you aren't willing to do the work it takes to channel that drive, you'll probably end up with a problem on your hands. Consider instead a dog in good health that has been bred to be an excellent pet.

The Rescued Lab

Even if you are interested in teaching your Lab obedience, you might want to consider a rescued Lab. You will not be able to show a rescued Lab in AKC Conformation because that is reserved for dogs that are not spayed/neutered and that can reproduce. However, rescued Labs are especially ideal as family pets. Many are former devoted family dogs that could no longer be kept for a number of reasons. Others may have certain behavioral problems that, if you are willing to put in the effort, can be worked out. Especially if you aren't particularly interested in showing your dog in conformation, a rescued Lab may be just the dog for you. See Chapter 5 for more information about adopting a rescued dog.

In selecting a puppy, remember that if you want a mellow companion like this gal, you should probably not get a Lab bred for field work, which requires a strong drive.

Details, Details, Details

Beyond the type of Lab you choose, you'll also have to make some more minor decisions. Color and gender are two issues people tend to overemphasize, as far as we are concerned. Better to focus on the individual puppy's or dog's personality and energy level. But if these issues are important to you (or even if they aren't), read on.

Pick a Color

Labrador Retrievers come in three colors: yellow (from light cream to fox red), chocolate and black. According to the breed standard, a small white spot on the chest is permissible. You may prefer a certain color, but don't believe anyone who tells you that any temperament or health differences are related to coat color. Let us repeat: *No temperament or health differences are related to coat color in the Labrador Retriever.*

No, black Labs aren't meaner. No, yellow Labs aren't nicer. No, none of those other things you've heard is true. Of course, that doesn't mean people won't think your black Lab is more protective or your yellow Lab is Friendliest Dog on Earth. They probably will. Considering that, if you are looking for a dog that will protect you and intimidate people, you might want to go for a dark-colored Lab. If you want a dog that won't intimidate people and you have properly socialized your dog to accept strangers patting him on the head, you might go for the lighter color. But that's up to you. As far as how your dog behaves, color doesn't make any difference at all. You'll be better off basing your decision on a dog's health, temperament, energy level and other factors (for more on how to choose the right puppy, see Chapter 6).

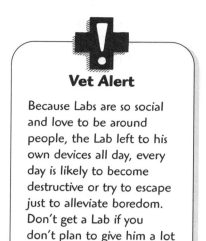

Vet Alert

Because Labs are so social and love to be around people, the Lab left to his own devices all day, every day is likely to become destructive or try to escape just to alleviate boredom. Don't get a Lab if you don't plan to give him a lot of attention.

Male or Female?

People have a lot of funny ideas about the differences between male and female dogs. Have you fallen prey to the misconceptions? Take this quiz to find out. Answer true or false to each statement:

1. Male dogs roam more than females.

2. Female dogs are more affectionate than male dogs.

3. Male dogs are harder to housetrain than female dogs.

4. Female dogs are better family dogs than male dogs.

5. Male dogs are more aggressive than female dogs.

6. Female dogs are more protective than male dogs.

If you answered any of these questions as true, you may have known a dog that happened to fit one of the stereotypes, but in just as many cases, the stereotypes aren't true. A female in heat is just as likely to roam as a male looking for a female in heat. Male dogs can be incredibly affectionate, easy to housetrain and unaggressive. Female dogs can be standoffish, difficult to housetrain and as aggressive as any male dog. Likewise, males may be extremely protective.

Dog behavior, in other words, is a product of many interrelated factors, including breeding, socialization (or lack of it), training, environment and health. Gender isn't one of those factors.

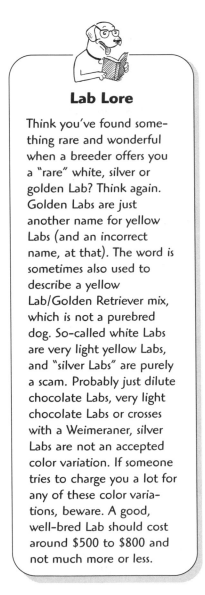

Lab Lore

Think you've found something rare and wonderful when a breeder offers you a "rare" white, silver or golden Lab? Think again. Golden Labs are just another name for yellow Labs (and an incorrect name, at that). The word is sometimes also used to describe a yellow Lab/Golden Retriever mix, which is not a purebred dog. So-called white Labs are very light yellow Labs, and "silver Labs" are purely a scam. Probably just dilute chocolate Labs, very light chocolate Labs or crosses with a Weimeraner, silver Labs are not an accepted color variation. If someone tries to charge you a lot for any of these color variations, beware. A good, well-bred Lab should cost around $500 to $800 and not much more or less.

Ages and Stages

Far more significant than color or gender is the age of the dog you choose to bring home. A world of difference exists between a young puppy and an adult dog, for example, or an adolescent dog and an aging dog. The age of your dog largely determines the amount of time you'll have to spend in training and socializing (although other factors, such as a dog's previous history, also contribute to the time commitment factor).

The Young Puppy

Housetraining, housetraining, housetraining! You'll think of little else when you first bring your tiny little Lab home with you. Sure, they're cute. Sure, you can cuddle them, teach them to walk on a leash and romp with them in the backyard. But you know what happens when you bring them back in? And again after every meal? And in the middle of the night?

Housetraining and lure-and-reward training will take up a lot of your time when you bring home a new puppy, and you may begin to believe that you can't handle the rigors of puppy care. But if you stay consistent and keep at it, your puppy will soon be trained, and you'll

What color Lab you choose is strictly a matter of personal preference. Whether black, chocolate or yellow, Labrador Retrievers share the same physical and temperamental characteristics. (photo by Lisa Weiss)

be on to obedience training, walks in the park and long evenings curled up on the sofa without a single accident.

The Older Puppy

Older puppies (3 to 6 months) tend to be a little easier to housetrain because they are physically more mature and more able to control their bodily functions. To make up for missing those early weeks or months, the most important thing to remember with older puppies is lots of training using positive reinforcement and lots of socialization.

The Adolescent Lab

Adopting an adolescent dog (6 months to 2 years) can be misleading. They look so grown-up, but inside, they still feel like puppies.

Vet Alert

Spaying (for female dogs) is far more complicated than castration (for male dogs). If you worry about subjecting your dog to major surgery or about accidentally ending up with an unwanted litter of puppies, consider a male. Of course, just because male dogs can't have puppies doesn't mean they can't make puppies, so help curb the epidemic of unwanted dogs and have your male castrated.

Vet Alert

In 1997, President Clinton introduced his new chocolate Labrador Retriever puppy to the world. Although Labs were popular before, less reputable breeders are sure to take advantage of the Lab's new status as presidential dog. Breeders breeding for pure profit and not for good family pets and the betterment of the breed are more likely to produce hyperactive and ill-tempered dogs, so do your homework!

Vet Alert

If an adult dog has been abused or otherwise mistreated, the previous owner very well may not reveal that fact, and the resulting behavioral problems may not be obvious at first. Don't let that scare you away from adopting an adult dog from a reputable source, however. They are much easier to bring into your home than a new puppy.

(Remember your teenage years? You know the feeling!) Adolescents are at an awkward stage. Not quite comfortable in their large bodies, they are often less than graceful. They are also energetic, even frisky. Of course, a frisky 75-pound dog that is clumsy to boot can be quite a challenge to handle. Adolescent dogs need to be consistently trained with positive reinforcement, and that takes patience. But you can do it! The payoff will be well worth the effort. And housetraining probably isn't something you'll have to worry about.

The Grown Lab

With an adult Lab (2 to 8 years), what you see is what you get. Genetic health problems that wouldn't be obvious in a puppy may be showing now, as would be the effects of how the dog was raised. If he wasn't properly socialized, for example, an adult Lab may be overly shy or nervous around strangers. If he was well trained, he will be friendly, obedient and compliant. Bringing home an adult dog can be a gamble, unless you spend sufficient time getting to know the dog. Even then, you may be in for a few surprises. But never fear! Most behavioral obstacles can be overcome with some good, consistent, positive-reinforcement-based training and lots of love.

The Aging Lab

The older Lab (over 8 years old) is a choice many people don't even consider. Why get to know and love a dog when you have only a few years left? Because older Labs can be the most wonderful Labs of all. Already trained, nicely mellowed by time and wise with experience, an older Lab can be a wonderful pet and can still learn your house rules, even if they were different from the rules by which he used to live.

Whatever your personal requirements for your Labrador Retriever, doing your homework along with some soul-searching about the kind of dog you need and then spending time evaluating your potential pet (see Chapter 5) will pay off in the long run. Then the fun of getting acquainted starts!

The Least You Need to Know

➤ The two general types of Labrador Retrievers are the English type and the Field type.

➤ The English type tends to make better family pets with good, positive training.

➤ The Field type tends to be much more active than most families can manage.

➤ When selecting a Labrador Retriever, be sure to choose a type that will best meet your particular needs.

➤ The best dog for you is more dependent on the dog's individual personality and energy level than on color or gender.

➤ Adopting a Lab of any age can mean particular challenges and particular joys.

Chapter 5

Where to Find Your Lab

In This Chapter

➤ Is a breeder the best place to find a Lab?

➤ How do you tell a good breeder from a not-so-good breeder?

➤ Do dogs come with guarantees?

➤ What about rescued Labs and Labs in animal shelters?

➤ What about your neighbor's litter, or that "free to good home" dog listed in the classified ads?

➤ Wouldn't it be easier to just go to a pet store?

By now, you probably have a pretty good idea about the type of Lab you would like. What's left to do but go out and buy one? Plenty! Finding that practically perfect Lab isn't as easy as looking up Labrador Retriever in the yellow pages. You have a lot of options and a lot of limitations, too, if you want to find the right dog for you.

The Breeder Option

Purchasing a dog from a reputable and responsible breeder is a good way to be assured your puppy will be healthy with good temperament and an appearance close to the breed standard. Finding your practically perfect puppy from a breeder is probably the safest route as far as knowing what you are getting.

53

Trainer Tidbits

The Internet can be a great place to make first contact with any number of breeders. Just type **http://www. k9web.com/breeders_ directory/** in your web browser for a list of Labrador Retriever breeders. If you can't find a breeder within driving distance, search on **Labrador Retriever breeders,** and you'll get a big list. Add your city or state to the search to find breeders in your area.

The trick is finding a good breeder. "Good" by some standards may not be good for you. Of course, now that you've read the first few chapters of this book, you have a much better idea of the qualities you prefer in a Lab. But how do you find the breeder who is breeding for those qualities?

Finding a Good Breeder

Time to do a little research! Different breeders have different priorities. Some breeders may strive to produce puppies that will excel in conformation or in field trials. You want to make sure these breeders are also very interested in puppies that will excel at being great family pets.

You can look for some clues that will help you separate the good from the less-than-good breeders. A good breeder will want to show you the dogs behind the puppies (the parents) and the puppies themselves, of course, but only after conveying lots of important information. Pay attention and take notes. Bring along the following breeder checklist and a pen. The checklist will help you with what to look for. You can tell a lot about the breeder by observing both the adult dogs and the place where the puppies are being raised.

Breeder Checklist

- [ ] Where are the puppies? If they are raised in the house with the family, that's a good sign. If they are raised in clean, well-maintained kennels, that could be okay as long as the puppies are being socialized properly. If the kennels are broken down and dirty (a few "piles" here and there aren't evidence of a dirty kennel—puppies shoot those out night and day) or if the dogs look like they rarely see a human being, that's a red flag.

☐ How do the puppies look? Are their coats clean or caked with dirt or feces around the rectum? Are they bright-eyed and energetic, or do they look sick or fatigued? Are their coats in good condition or are they missing patches of hair? Are their nails clipped or too long? Do they have fleas or ticks?

Trainer Tidbits

Ask the breeders you visit what their priorities are for their lines. If they are breeding for field champions, for example, their dogs may be too energetic and driven to be satisfied with a life as a family pet. The ideal breeder for someone looking for a family pet is one who breeds with good health and temperament as the top priorities.

☐ Does the breeder seem interested in how you are going to manage and raise the puppy, rather than just trying to put the puppy in your lap and have you take her home? Does he or she seem like someone you can or would trust, both in taking care of dogs and in business dealings? Does the breeder emphasize that he or she will be there to answer questions on the phone after you take the puppy home?

☐ How do the dogs act around the breeder? Are they jumping with joy to see their beloved caretaker, or do they shy away or act indifferently? The latter two are red flags.

☐ Is at least one of the parents available for you to see? If you can't see either parent, you have to wonder if you will really know what you are getting.

The Interview

Now that you've had a look around the premises, spend a little time asking some smart questions. Good breeders expect this "interview," and one of the best signs that you're talking to a good breeder is that you find yourself getting interviewed right back! Good breeders care just as much about placing their beloved charges into good homes as you care about bringing the right dog home with you.

What should you ask about, and what will the breeder ask you? We'll tell you! We'll also tell you what answers you'll want to hear, and what ones should raise red flags. First, let's cover what you should ask the breeder (and keep in mind that many good breeders will tell you the information before you ask, which makes your job a whole lot easier).

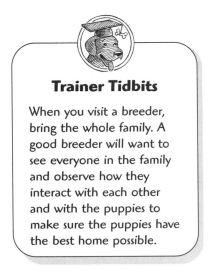

Trainer Tidbits

When you visit a breeder, bring the whole family. A good breeder will want to see everyone in the family and observe how they interact with each other and with the puppies to make sure the puppies have the best home possible.

1. What can you tell me about the breed, and about your particular Labs?

Good breeders really know their breed. They should be able to tell you what the standard characteristics are, both in conformation and in temperament, and should also know the specific qualities and tendencies of their particular lines, which will be more specific than the breed standard. For example, does the breeder breed for field champions? These dogs are probably super-energetic and may be more than an average pet owner wants to handle. Does the breeder breed for conformation and are there dog show champions in the pedigrees of the puppies? Does the breeder consider his or her "pet quality" dogs to be the dogs that didn't quite make the conformation standards, or does the breeder breed primarily for the kind of temperament and health in all the dogs that make for an excellent pet?

Also, any breeder who cares about where his or her puppies are going will make sure to emphasize the downsides of the breed (every breed has downsides). A breeder who only raves about and praises the breed and his or her own lines isn't giving you the whole truth. The breeder should also give you the downsides to owning a dog in general to make sure you know what you are getting into.

2. How long have you been breeding, and how many litters have you bred?

Although a breeder just starting out isn't necessarily a bad breeder, breeders with years of experience are oftentimes a better gamble. Experienced breeders have developed lines of dogs and have been able to really get to know and refine their dogs for the better. Breeders who are irresponsible, either in the breeding itself or the business end (or both), often don't last too long, so if a breeder has been breeding Labs successfully for twenty-five years, you can, to some extent, trust the test of time.

Number of litters is significant, too. If a breeder has been breeding Labs for twenty-five years but has only bred a few litters, that breeder will have far less experience. On the other hand, if a breeder has only been breeding Labs for a few years and has bred twenty-five litters, that's a red flag, too. That breeder is probably just trying to turn out as many puppies as possible to make a quick buck without taking the time to breed for health and temperament and without making any attempt not to breed dogs with genetic problems.

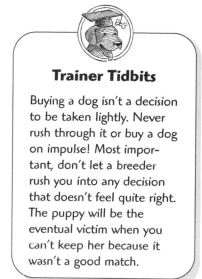

Trainer Tidbits

Buying a dog isn't a decision to be taken lightly. Never rush through it or buy a dog on impulse! Most important, don't let a breeder rush you into any decision that doesn't feel quite right. The puppy will be the eventual victim when you can't keep her because it wasn't a good match.

3. May I talk to your veterinarian, and can you give me any referrals?

Ask the breeder if you can talk to his or her veterinarian. Why wouldn't a breeder want you to talk to his or her veterinarian? If his or her dogs have a lot of health problems, or if the breeder rarely sees the vet unless the dogs have a health emergency, the breeder may not be eager to let you in on that information. But a good breeder who routinely takes puppies in to his or her vet and has healthy dogs should be happy to let you give the vet a call. A breeder's veterinarian should be able to give you a different perspective on the dogs coming from the breeder you are considering. The vet probably has an idea of the longevity of dogs from that breeder, of whether genetic abnormalities or other health problems tend to occur more often than should be expected and of any other medical problems or concerns.

As far as referrals, sure, your breeder will probably only give you the names of people who are happy with his or her dogs, not the names of any who have complained. But what's wrong with that? The red flag should go up if your breeder won't give you any names. Chances are, that means few if any are happy with their dogs, or the breeder is afraid you might find out about something he or she doesn't want you to know. It can be hard to pinpoint a breeder with a bad reputation if you aren't in the dog community, but getting a few referrals is one way to get the skinny.

4. Do you offer any guarantees?

Some breeders offer long written guarantees that state you can return the puppy if she develops any genetic problems, and she will be replaced by a puppy of equal value. This guarantee might give you some peace of mind that the breeder is doing a good job and is fairly confident the dog won't develop a genetic problem. But sometimes problems occur despite a breeder's best efforts. And think about this: Are you going to want to return a family member because she did not turn out to be perfect? (What family member is?)

All living beings have defective genes. Some of them are expressed, and some of them are not. You are looking for a breeder who is doing everything reasonable to produce pups that will have a full and healthy life. (It's a good sign if the breeder has very old dogs.) Longevity is very important. Some people have bred a litter and have not done any of the health checks (such as OFA for hip dysplasia and CERF for eye problems), yet they'll offer a written guarantee! If they don't know what they are doing, will they be around when your pup grows up? Probably not. Your guarantee might not be worth the paper it was written on.

Good breeders will openly discuss the possible genetic problems that may appear and how they can be dealt with. Such breeders may offer to help you if your dog does develop problems. A reputable breeder will want to know if one of his or her puppies has a genetic problem because that information should help determine future breeding strategies. Good breeders will sell their puppies that are not going to be shown in conformation under an *AKC limited registration*. Litters from these dogs are not eligible for registration by the AKC. An open dialogue with the breeder and taking the time to make sure your choice of breeder and choice of puppy are good ones are probably worth more than any health guarantee.

Lab Lingo

An **AKC limited registration** means that a dog is registered with the AKC as a purebred dog, but that no litters produced by that dog will be eligible for registration. Dogs with limited registrations are ineligible to compete in conformation, but they are eligible to compete in obedience and other types of competition, such as tracking and hunting tests.

That being said, however, any good breeder should be willing to take a puppy back and refund your money if a veterinarian says the puppy has a significant health problem; some breeders will offer more extensive guarantees. Take your puppy to the vet, preferably straight from the breeder, before you've had a chance to get too attached. The breeder may require that you take the puppy to a veterinarian sometime within the first seventy-two hours. (A leisurely vet inquiry three months after you've bought the puppy shows you aren't taking your puppy's health seriously.) A vet is the only person who can tell you whether you have purchased a healthy puppy.

Make sure you don't use the excuse of a written guarantee and/or falling in love with a cute puppy to avoid doing your job. What's your job, again? To identify a good breeder who is doing the proper health checks, raising the puppies in a family surrounding and screening *you* to make the best match.

5. How soon can I take the dog home?

In many states, the law requires that dogs can't be sold until they are a particular age, often 7 weeks old. Even that is a little young. According to many breeders, 8 weeks is the earliest a puppy should be taken from her mother. Puppies need the chance to learn from their mothers and littermates; this is one of the first steps towards socialization. If a breeder says you can take home that tiny, sickly looking 4-week-old puppy, run! Yes, the other way! (Before you look too closely and get too attached. You'll just be asking for heartbreak.)

Also beware the "bait and switch" con. If a breeder tells you over the phone that he or she has exactly what you're looking for and promises to reserve her, then when you arrive, says, "I'm so, so sorry! I just sold that puppy to someone, but I have this other puppy I know you'll just love. She may look small, but. . ." That breeder was probably trying to get you on the premises even though he or she never had what you were looking for and hopes that once you see the dog he or she is trying to pawn off on you (because the dog has some problem), you'll fall in love and won't be able to say no.

6. What do you do to keep your dogs healthy and happy?

Ask the breeder what he or she does to keep the dogs happy and healthy. This general question gives the breeder a chance to volunteer additional information about what he or she does to care for the dogs. Good breeders can feel free to brag about the quality of food they use, the degree of socialization they employ, how their dogs are a part of the family, extensive veterinary and/or preventive care and so on. Let the breeder brag. It will be an education on what you can do to continue your puppy's good health in the future. A red flag answer to this question is "Huh?"

Questions for You

But wait just a minute, the interview is far from over. In fact, before you have a chance to ask the breeder all of your questions, chances are the breeder will (and should) be asking a few questions, too. If a breeder doesn't ask you any questions about where you plan to keep the dog, why you want a dog, how much you know about Labs and other questions designed to determine whether that breeder's puppies will fit into your particular situation and home (and even match your personality), you should be hesitant to continue the deal. A breeder who isn't concerned about where the puppies are going probably won't be too likely to take them back if there is a health problem and probably isn't as conscientious as some of the other breeders out there who put the welfare of their dogs before profits.

The breeder will probably ask you some of the following questions (if you are a breeder reading this book, take note):

1. **What are you looking for in a dog?** This is a breeder's chance to make sure you want a Lab for all the right reasons. For instance, a good breeder wants to weed out people just looking for a guard dog to patrol the backyard. The breeder will want to know you are in it for the long haul and are looking for a dog to bring into your family. If you are interested in breeding and/or showing, the breeder will want to make sure you know what you are doing and, especially in the case of breeding, that you will proceed responsibly and in the best interest of the breed.

2. **Do you plan to spay or castrate this puppy?** Some breeders will require you to sign a *spay-neuter* (or spay-castrate) *agreement*, depending on the puppy you are taking home. Many others will rely on you to consult with your vet to determine the right time to spay/castrate your pup. If your dog is registered under an AKC limited registration, you should not breed your pup. The puppies can't be registered, not even under a limited registration. A veterinarian can tell you all the health benefits of spay/castration (plus, check out Chapter 12). Of course, if you are buying a puppy for showing/breeding, the breeder should know so he or she can advise you. In this case, spay/castration doesn't apply. Even if your puppy is not registered under a limited registration, you will still want to spay or castrate it if you aren't prepared to enter into the complex, expensive and difficult task of breeding quality dogs.

Lab Lingo

A **spay-neuter agreement** is a contract you sign that states you agree to have your dog spayed or castrated and that you will not breed that dog. Many breeders require these agreements for dogs they don't think should be bred, either because they don't meet the breed standard or because they have some genetic problem.

3. **Where do you plan to keep this puppy?** Breeders want to know if their beloved puppies will end up backyard denizens,

locked in a kennel for ten hours every day while you are at work or snuggled on the couch with someone who works at home or stays home much of the time. Of course, just because you have a job and have to work (don't we all?) doesn't mean a breeder will refuse to let you take home that practically perfect puppy. The breeder will want to know your plan, however. And you should have one! Will you come home for lunch to walk your puppy? Will someone else be there most of the time who is willing to take care of your new pet? Have you considered hiring a pet sitter or dog walker to do middle-of-the-day duty? If you live in a big city, you may even be close to a doggy daycare center; more and more are popping up all the time.

4. **Can you afford a dog?** We aren't just talking the cost of the dog, you understand. Dogs are an ongoing, continual expense that you must be ready to take on. What if your dog gets sick? What if she gets hurt? And don't forget vaccinations, rabies shots, heartworm pills, flea and tick control, a good quality food, training costs and supplies—the list goes on and on. A responsible breeder will think twice about selling a dog to someone who can just barely pay for the dog herself, keeps asking about price and trying to wrangle a deal or who gives the impression that he or she wouldn't be able to afford any unexpected veterinary care.

5. **How committed are you to being a good dog owner?** Some people visiting breeders are obviously dog people. They've owned and loved dogs before, or they just seem to have a natural rapport with the puppies. These people will get down on the floor, call the puppies to them and revel in puppy play. Inexperienced dog owners or people who aren't particularly comfortable with dogs may sit and wait for a dog to come to them. A breeder will be watching you and the way you interact with the puppies just as closely as you should be watching him or her. The breeder will also want to know that you understand the time commitment, financial commitment and even the emotional commitment involved in owning a dog.

6. **Do you and the puppy have a good rapport?** Even with dog people, certain human-dog combinations just don't click. Others are matches made in heaven. A breeder knows how to recognize those wonderful matches. You may have in mind that

If you're looking to add a puppy to your family, go to a good source and expect to ask a lot of questions and to be asked a lot of questions in return. All parties should want to make sure the match is a good one.

you absolutely have to have that female yellow Lab, but that chocolate male trying so hard to get your attention may think you're just about the greatest human being she's ever met in her life. Don't overlook it!

After you and a breeder have passed each other's interview, business can proceed. You're not through yet!

Health Tests and Guarantee

We mentioned health guarantees previously in this chapter, but we'll mention them again because they are important. Good breeders guarantee the health of their puppies and will take a puppy back and refund your money if there is something wrong with the puppy. The best way to tell is to take your puppy from the breeder's place immediately to the veterinarian; some breeders require you do this within seventy-two hours or less. Ask the vet if you should be watching for other problems that might show themselves later in your puppy's life.

63

To maintain the best odds for future health, you'll also want included in the health guarantee (or elsewhere) evidence that both parents of the litter have had their hips x-rayed and are certified free of hip dysplasia by the Orthopedic Foundation for Animals (OFA). You'll also want proof that both parents have had their eyes examined by a board-certified veterinary ophthalmologist to minimize the chance your puppy will develop inherited eye problems such as *progressive retinal atrophy (PRA)*. Many breeders register their dogs with an organization called the Canine Eye Registration Foundation (CERF) to certify that their dogs are free from genetic eye problems. This foundation works in conjunction with the American College of Veterinary Ophthalmologists (ACVO) to maintain a registry of purebred dogs that have been examined and found to be unaffected by any major inheritable eye disease such as PRA.

Lab Lingo

Progressive retinal atrophy (PRA) is a degenerative genetic eye disorder that causes eventual blindness. A veterinary ophthalmologist can detect the disease when a Lab is anywhere from 18 months to 4 years old. There is no treatment. Labs affected by this problem usually go totally blind at between 6 and 8 years old. However, blind Labs can function well in familiar surroundings due to their other keen senses.

You'll also want a record of how many vaccinations the breeder has given your puppy (she should have had at least one round), and the breeder should already have the puppy on a worming program.

The health of your puppy isn't all up to the breeder, of course. Once your puppy comes home with you, it is your job to keep her healthy. Although many breeders will take a puppy back if you neglect her and she gets sick (for example, your puppy could easily get heartworm if you neglect to give her heartworm pills), if the problem isn't genetic, don't expect to get your money back. If you aren't willing to pay for your puppy's medical care, many breeders would rather take the puppy back than have you take her to a shelter or worse (some breeders may actually require in writing that you return the dog to

This roly-poly, clear-eyed, alert puppy is the picture of health.

them). But breeders try to avoid selling puppies to people who would neglect them.

It your puppy does come down with a genetic problem later in life, however (such as hip dysplasia or any other problem that may be inherited), the breeder will want to know about it. He or she may take the dog back and refund all or part of your money. Chances are, however, that you'll be pretty attached to your dog by then, and maybe you'll be willing to see your dog through the crisis or stay with her to the end.

The breeder may, alternatively, pay for or help to pay for treatment, but if the breeder is going to do this, make sure it is stated in the original health guarantee. Whatever the breeder is or isn't willing to do should definitely be set down in writing before any puppies or money changes hands. After the guarantee is agreed upon, don't expect the breeder to do more than promised. A deal is a deal; make sure it's a good one and a fair one for both of you right from the start.

Let Your Breeder Help You Choose

But what if all the puppies in your breeder's litter look like textbook examples of healthy pups? What if they all dote on you? How on earth do you choose?

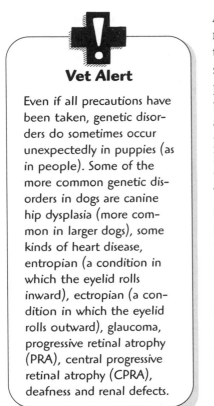

Vet Alert

Even if all precautions have been taken, genetic disorders do sometimes occur unexpectedly in puppies (as in people). Some of the more common genetic disorders in dogs are canine hip dysplasia (more common in larger dogs), some kinds of heart disease, entropian (a condition in which the eyelid rolls inward), ectropian (a condition in which the eyelid rolls outward), glaucoma, progressive retinal atrophy (PRA), central progressive retinal atrophy (CPRA), deafness and renal defects.

Ask the breeder! A good breeder does more than engineer the creation of those adorable little puppies. He or she also pays attention to each puppy and tries to determine inborn tendencies, energy level, personality and health. The breeder knows those puppies much better than you can know them all in a visit or two, so take advantage of that knowledge. Tell the breeder everything you can about your personality, situation and preferences in a dog. The breeder will then be able to help you choose the puppy that will best suit you (and you, her).

As we said before, the breeder will be looking for a puppy that seems to have that special rapport with you. Trust in the breeder to help you find your perfect match if you just aren't sure which one is best. (For more information on how to choose the perfect puppy from a practically perfect litter, see the next chapter.)

The Rescue Option

Maybe something is gnawing at the back of your mind. What is it? Could it be that you can't quite forget how many dogs are abandoned and euthanized each year? And could it furthermore be that you suspect lots of these dogs are Labrador Retrievers or Lab mixes? Could be!

For some people, purchasing a dog from a breeder, although a better risk as far as knowing what you are getting is concerned, just isn't the right way to go. Maybe you want to do your part to help at least one of the hundreds of thousands of dogs that are abandoned every year. Many of those dogs are euthanized. A few lucky ones are given a second chance, rescued by breed rescue groups and placed into good homes. Could a down-on-her-luck Lab be the perfect pet for you?

Adopting a rescued dog could very well be the best dog-related decision you ever make. On the other hand, it could also result in disaster. It all depends on how well you prepare (and on a little bit of luck, too). Many wonderful, friendly, well-trained, loyal dogs are given up to rescue groups because of circumstances having nothing to do with the dog, such as a divorce or a job that requires a move to a place where dogs aren't allowed. A family may be heartbroken to give up their beloved pet but may hope that a good rescue organization can place her with a new family where she will be just as loved.

On the other hand, some dogs are put into shelters because of behavioral problems or health problems, or because the owners just didn't want to spend the time or the money to take care of the pet they never should have acquired. Such people are often less than straight with rescue organizations. Rescue workers do their best to evaluate a dog's temperament and health, but the effects of past abuse or neglect may not always be immediately obvious. Even these dogs can eventually make wonderful pets, however. If you are willing to put some time, energy and money into these dogs, they'll know they owe you a huge debt, and they'll probably show you their gratitude every day for the rest of their lives.

Most rescued dogs are adolescent or adult dogs. These dogs can be excellent choices for someone who doesn't want to take on housetraining and all

Vet Alert

Before you take on a rescued Lab, spend some serious time getting to know the dog. Work with the rescue group to determine whether you and your potential pet are a good match. If the dog seems to have serious problems, enlist the help of a good canine behavior consultant. Be persistent. A good rapport can be an important step in overcoming problems, and many problem dogs have quickly become practically perfect dogs when they find the right human companion.

the other necessary duties of puppy raising. If you are patient, loving, understanding, gentle and consistent, a rescued Lab may well be your practically perfect Labrador Retriever.

Trainer Tidbits

Maybe you have your heart set on a puppy, but an older Lab can be the ideal dog. Older Labs generally require far less work than puppies and are likely already trained in good behavior. Sure, an older Lab may not have the life-span ahead of her that a puppy would, but the years she does have left can be filled with joy for both of you. Please consider adopting an older Lab that has lost her home.

Labrador Retriever Rescue Organizations

Labrador Retriever rescue organizations are run by people who love the breed and are committed to finding appropriate homes for dogs that have been abandoned. But breed rescue can become overwhelming. Breed rescue workers describe receiving several hundred e-mails a day and hundreds of phone calls every week from people who need to give up their dogs. Although a few saints out there have devoted their lives to rescue and have been doing it for years, many rescuers start with good intentions and soon burn out. As a result, any list of rescue organizations we provided here would probably soon be out of date.

To find a good rescue organization currently in operation near you, call the American Kennel Club or the Labrador Retriever Club, Inc. (See contact information in Appendix B.) Or search the Internet for *Labrador Retriever rescue.* You'll get up-to-the-minute information on who is doing Labrador Retriever rescue right now.

Other Rescue Groups

Even if you don't have a Labrador Retriever rescue organization near you, you may have an all-breed rescue group. Search *dog rescue* on the Internet, or talk to local veterinarians, dog trainers or even pet stores (those that don't sell dogs). Local breeders may even have good information.

Animal Shelters

Finding a Lab (or a Lab mix) at an animal shelter is another option. Animal shelters vary widely in quality, but an increasing number are either no-kill shelters or shelters that do euthanize but make every possible effort to place the more-adoptable dogs into good homes. Shelters may have stiff requirements for adoption (they want to make sure the dogs don't end up right back in the shelter!). Some don't allow students to adopt dogs under any circumstances. Some require written proof from renters that the landlord accepts dogs. Some interview prospective adopters to find a good match, and many require spaying or neutering (many also have the procedure done before you can adopt, or give adopters discount coupons for the procedure).

Adopting a shelter dog carries many of the same risks as adopting a rescue dog. Although shelter workers make every effort to evaluate the personalities of different dogs, they are often overburdened, overworked, understaffed and barraged with more animals than they can keep track of. But, again, with some time, effort and financial resources, including classes with a good trainer and sessions with a behaviorist, many shelter dogs, even with troubled pasts, can be successfully and lovingly rehabilitated into the ideal family pet.

Trainer Tidbits

Don't be surprised if rescue organizations return your message collect—that's common procedure for rescue due to the vast number of calls breed rescue organizations typically receive. Remember, these people do the work for free and purely for the love of Labs. The least you can do is pay your part of the phone bill.

Labs from Neighbors or Friends

Maybe your neighbor Mrs. Smith (or whoever) is a breeder. Maybe you are lucky, and she's a good breeder. But a lot of people (though certainly not all) breeding dogs in their backyards aren't doing it with specific goals such as health and temperament in mind. Dogs from breeders like these will often have more than their fair share of genetic and behavioral problems, and although they may be cheaper up front, they will be far more expensive in the long run. "But Mrs. Smith is such a nice lady!" you might protest. Go ahead and have coffee with her every Wednesday afternoon. Feel free to gossip over the fence together or swap recipes or power tools or whatever. But we suggest you get your dog from a more-reliable source.

If, on the other hand, your neighbor's Lab had a litter, you may be tempted to take one of the puppies off her hands so they don't end up euthanized. You are running a risk if you don't know the health, temperament or even the appearance or breed of the *sire*. Yet if you raise the dog well from puppyhood, don't care what she will look like and don't mind what size she will be, you very well might end up with a great pet. Plus, you can rest easy knowing you have rescued a Lab or Lab mix from possible destruction. But be ready for surprises, especially in the way of unexpected health problems.

Lab Lingo

The **sire** is the father of a litter of puppies, and the **dam** is the mother. Breeders use these terms regularly.

Classified Labs: The Newspaper

A lot of breeders advertise in the classified section of the newspaper, so this is one way to find breeders in your area. However, a classified ad in no way proves that the breeder is a good one. Go ahead and call a breeder listed in the newspaper, but don't forget to survey the premises carefully, interview the breeder and make sure they make an effort to interview you.

The newspaper is also the place to find dogs whose owners can no longer keep them. Maybe the dog is a gem, and the owner wants to avoid taking her to the animal shelter. On the other hand, maybe the dog is a big problem, and the owner has no intention of telling you that his 95-pound Lab, Skippy, has to find a new home because she has chewed her way through all the neighbors and is working on a serious criminal record. That "free to good home" dog may end up costing you a fortune. Spend adequate time with the dog and the previous owner to get a sense of the true situation before making a decision.

That Doggy in the Window: Pet Stores

Pet stores are the first place many people look when they are considering buying a dog, and lots of people have purchased great pets from pet stores. However, we feel that if you're going to pay a lot of money for a dog, you should be able to talk to the breeder and see the dog's parents. When you purchase a dog from a pet store, you have no access to the breeder, so you can't ask any questions or see the premises.

Pet store employees may or may not know anything about the breed, and although some pet store employees make a serious effort to sell dogs only to those who seem like they will provide a good home, others are more focused on their sales commissions. Also, pet stores often get their dogs from large-scale breeders who aren't necessarily trying to better the breed. These dogs may be cute, and they also might make perfectly fine pets. They also may be a bad health risk, they most certainly haven't been bred with any goals for bettering the breed in mind, and there's no telling what behavioral problems they may develop due to a rough start with no socialization. Again, we'll admit, lots of people have purchased great pets from pet stores.

Lab Lore

Because the Lab is the most popular dog in America, because many dog owners don't control their dogs and because many dog owners don't neuter their dogs, there are a lot of Lab mixes out there. Lab/Shepherd mixes, Lab/Rottweiler mixes, Lab/Hound mixes and Lab/Pit Bull mixes are all common (we've even seen a Lab/Dachshund mix—a full-sized Lab on short little legs), not to mention Labs mixed with other retrievers such as Golden Retrievers and Chesapeake Bay Retrievers. Unfortunately, many Lab mixes are unwanted "accidents" and end up in animal shelters. Lab mixes can be wonderful, intelligent, practically perfect pets and certainly can't be blamed for the indiscretion of the owners of their parents. If you are considering rescuing a Lab, don't overlook the Lab mixes. One may be perfect for you.

Now your plan is even closer to complete. You know what type of Lab you want and you know where to look. Keep reading for some straight talk about how to pick out the puppy made for you.

The Least You Need to Know

➤ A good breeder is an excellent place to find a Labrador Retriever, but don't assume all breeders are good. Evaluate the premises and interview the breeder before you buy.

➤ Rescuing a Lab that has lost her home can mean giving a second chance to a wonderful dog that will be forever grateful. Rescued dogs may also take a lot of patience and time to rehabilitate if they have been abused or neglected.

➤ Friends and neighbors, the classified ads and pet stores are also potential sources for Labrador Retrievers, although they each carry with them certain risks. Buyer beware!

Chapter 6

Picking Your Particular Puppy

> ### In This Chapter
>
> ➤ Are you sure you have your priorities and expectations in order?
>
> ➤ How to test for behavior, activity level and personality
>
> ➤ How to pick a healthy puppy
>
> ➤ How to avoid puppy-picking pitfalls
>
> ➤ Which advice to listen to and which to ignore
>
> ➤ What if you have second thoughts?

You're at the breeder's or the shelter, or you're getting ready to meet with a rescue representative. You'll probably meet several Labs, whether puppies or adult dogs. How do you pick which one is your Lab? Choosing your particular puppy involves a combination of factors: research, testing and good old-fashioned chemistry.

Refining Your Expectations

The first step in choosing your particular puppy is to have a clear idea what you want. We've tried to help you figure out your personal requirements for a puppy in the first few chapters of this book, but you can't spend too much time on this one. Now that you've read a little about Labs and some of the sources for good dogs, you should be able to refine your Labrador Retriever wish list a little. We'll help! Write out your answers to the following questions, as completely as possible:

1. Do you think you want a young puppy, an older puppy, a young adult dog or an older dog?

   _____

   _____

   _____

2. What positive behaviors are priorities for you in your new dog?

   _____

   _____

   _____

3. What negative behaviors are you particularly concerned about avoiding?

   _____

   _____

   _____

4. Describe the type of relationship you would like to have with your dog.

   _____

   _____

   _____

5. Explain your training plan. Will you train your dog yourself? Take him to obedience classes? Hire a professional trainer? A combination of all of these (the option we recommend)? A training plan is essential before you bring home your dog. Know how you will manage and educate your dog, so he knows how to behave. We'll give you extra space to answer this most important of all questions.

   _____

   _____

   _____

Look over your answers. You want a puppy that is housetrained, doesn't play-bite, doesn't chew the furniture, listens to you and does what you ask? Be ready to spend some time managing and training your pup.

Do you want a great family pet? What does that mean to you? A dog that lies on the couch and watches television with you, a dog that goes running with you every morning or a dog that accompanies you on your hunting trips?

You want a very trainable puppy? Find a breeder who practices the Start Puppy Training Procedure (see the next section) or something like it. You want a hunter or an obedience champ? Find a breeder who has had success producing dogs skilled in these areas, but also make sure the breeder breeds for the qualities necessary in a good family pet.

Do you have a clearer, more realistic picture in mind than you did when you first picked up this book? Perhaps the picture looks about the same. Either way, defining your expectations is important, and making them realistic is only fair to you and your dog.

Puppy Testing and Selection Procedures 101

There they are—a bunch of adorable little Labrador Retriever puppies rolling around and playing in the

Vet Alert

According to a study by Karen Overall in *Clinical Behavioral Medicine for Small Animals* (Mosby Year Book, 1997), a minimum of seven to eight million animals are euthanized for behavioral problems in animal shelters, and that number is probably equaled or exceeded in private practice. Don't let your dog become a statistic. Know what you are getting into and make a commitment to teach your dog good behavior.

Trainer Tidbits

If your one requirement for a puppy is "I want a dog that doesn't require any work," we strongly suggest you peruse your local department store's wide selection of stuffed toy dogs. Or consider a pet rock. Every real live dog requires and deserves good management, training, time and lots of love.

Refining your expectations about what you want in a Lab is a big part of making the best decision for both of you.

whelping box in front of you. They're all so cute! They're all so energetic! They all look healthy! How ever will you choose?

The first thing to do is to ask the breeder what kind of training he or she is doing on the pups. If the answer is none, ask to be able to see the pups when they are relatively hungry, so you can try what Joel has dubbed the Start Puppy Training Procedure. If the breeder has already begun this practice or something similar, ask to see a demonstration.

The Start Puppy Training Procedure

Joel developed the Start Puppy Training Procedure (SPTP) as an alternative to some of the methods many use to determine a puppy's personality. When a breeder begins to work with pups as soon as they are able to eat solid food, the puppies grow up already accustomed to this gentle *lure-and-reward training* method. But if your puppy hasn't been oriented yet, it isn't too late. Try the SPTP right at the breeder's and see how the puppies respond. One may stand out as being especially responsive to your efforts, and that puppy may be the one for you.

Set aside a small handful of kibble, and then take one piece in your hand. Bring the puppy to an area slightly away from his brothers and sisters (but not to an unfamiliar area—you want the pup to be comfortable and unafraid). Stand him in front of you, and then slowly raise the piece of food in an arc so that when the puppy follows the food with his nose, his rear end winds up on the ground. Did this 8-week-old puppy just perform a "sit"? Sure looks like it! Reward your puppy by giving him the food.

Lab Lingo

Lure-and-reward training is a method of training that has been used for many years by progressive trainers to teach puppies and dogs the meaning of simple commands. If you have any difficulty in using this method, there should be a trainer in your area who can teach you how to do it. If you cannot find a trainer, call the Association of Pet Dog Trainers at 1-800-PETDOGS and ask them to refer you to a lure-and-reward trainer.

With the pup in the sit position, take another piece of food, and while the puppy is still sitting, slowly move the piece of food away from the puppy at nose level until the puppy has to stand to get it. Did the puppy just perform a "stand"? Sure looks like it! Reward your puppy again by giving him the food.

When you have see-sawed the puppy back and forth for awhile, take another piece of food and slowly move it straight down from the puppy's nose to the floor. When the puppy follows the food, he will be performing a "down." Good dog! This is probably plenty for session one. When you bring your puppy home, you can begin to say "Sit" before you lure the puppy with the food and then "Yes" after he is sitting and before you offer the reward. Your puppy will learn to sit with one sweet request and a simple hand signal. The same applies for "stand" and "down."

Try this method with several of the puppies, and each may react in a different way. Some may ignore you. The test might not work if a puppy isn't hungry. After all, he is just a baby and he may take a bit of time to get through to him what you are asking of him. Some puppies may follow you for a minute or two, and then lose interest and go back to their siblings for another romp. But then, one puppy looks you in the eye and does exactly what you want. A-ha! Could it be you've found your perfect pup?

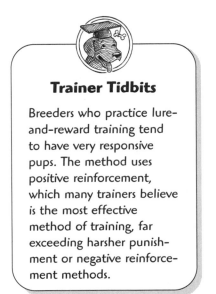

Trainer Tidbits

Breeders who practice lure-and-reward training tend to have very responsive pups. The method uses positive reinforcement, which many trainers believe is the most effective method of training, far exceeding harsher punishment or negative reinforcement methods.

The Personality Test

Trying out the SPTP on different puppies is a great way to get a glimpse at each puppy's personality potential, including his energy level and his general interest in you personally. On the other hand, a puppy that doesn't quite get it the very first time may be exceptionally bright, just exceptionally busy at the moment. A dog that does hone in on you and seems particularly eager to get it right and understand what you say may have just the personality you want.

As you test for personality using the SPTP, remember your refined list of expectations and use it to judge the actions and reactions of the puppies. Does that one seem as though it might make a great hunter? Does this one seem particularly interested in learning tricks? Is this one a little less active? In particular, evaluate these puppy qualities:

➤ Activity level

➤ Shyness or boldness

➤ Interest in you

➤ Interest in the SPTP

➤ Appetite (dependent on when he had his last meal)

➤ Tendency to play-bite (normal behavior in most pups)

➤ Distractibility (a quality in all puppies, but in some more than others)

➤ Overall appearance of health

Take notes if it will help you to remember: "The black one wouldn't sit still long enough to see I had food in my hand. The yellow one slept the whole time. The chocolate one loved me!" Now you have some idea about whom you're dealing with!

The Healthy Puppy Test

You'll want to determine, to the best of your ability, how healthy the puppies are in your pool of potential pups. You probably aren't a vet and, as we said before, you must have a vet check out your puppy as soon as possible. You can look for a few obvious signs of good or poor health, however. Take this checklist along with you:

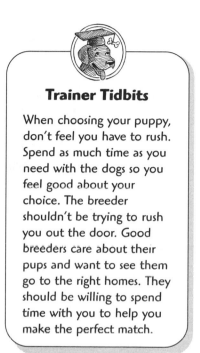

Trainer Tidbits

When choosing your puppy, don't feel you have to rush. Spend as much time as you need with the dogs so you feel good about your choice. The breeder shouldn't be trying to rush you out the door. Good breeders care about their pups and want to see them go to the right homes. They should be willing to spend time with you to help you make the perfect match.

☐ Look at the puppy's eyes. Are they clear, bright and clean, or are they runny, weepy looking or caked with goo?

☐ Look at the puppy's ears. Are they clean both inside and out, free of ticks and free of bald patches?

☐ Look at the puppy's mouth. Are his gums and teeth clean, the proper color and free of sores, plaque and food? Check the roof of the mouth—is it clean and without sores? Is the tongue clean? Does the breath have that sour milk puppy smell, or does it smell rotten?

☐ Look at the puppy's coat. Is it free from mats, dirt and feces, especially around the rectum? Is it clean and very soft? Or is it patchy with bald spots (possible sign of a skin infection)? Is there any evidence of ticks or fleas? (Small black spots and/or raised red bumps are evidence of fleas. Ticks are easier to spot, but they may range from the size of a pinhead to the size of a big marble.) Does it smell bad?

Try some of the puppy personality tests described in this chapter to help you choose your puppy.

☐ Look at the puppy's paws. Are they clean with clipped nails and nothing lodged between the pads? Are the pads clean and intact or scraped up? Does the puppy walk easily or does he limp?

☐ How does the puppy act? Is he energetic, curious, interested in you and eating well? Or does he seem to be lethargic, not to want to eat, to have trouble defecating or not to notice you even when you try to get his attention?

If the puppy you are beginning to fall in love with is clean, pest-free, odor-free and free from any evidence of skin infections, and if he acts energetic, curious, hungry and fascinated by your very presence, you have a winner!

Basic Chemistry

Even though we advocate choosing your puppy carefully by considering many factors about the breeder (or other source), we certainly wouldn't discount the power of chemistry. Sometimes, a match is right. All the other factors are, ideally, right as well. But when you are looking at a litter of healthy, active, interested pups that all pick up your training suggestions and seem to think you hung the moon, chemistry may be all you have to select one over the others.

Which dog keeps drawing your attention? Which one seems particularly fascinated in you? Which one looks you right in the eyes as if to say, "I know you! You're the one I've been waiting for!" This is where love at first sight kicks in. Try not to let it kick in before you've objectively eliminated certain puppies that wouldn't be good choices for other reasons. But when it does kick in at the appropriate time, go with it. This is what dog ownership is all about. This is the fun part, the rewarding part and the part that makes you feel good.

Trainer Tidbits

Good breeders will have taken the whole litter of pups to their vet for a complete physical before you pick up your puppy.

"But He Picked Me!"

Avoiding puppy-picking pitfalls is just as important as remembering all the right things to do. One of the biggest mistakes potential owners make is letting the dog do all the choosing. Whether actively or passively, puppies can sway you. Did that adorable yellow Lab run right up to you as soon as you entered the room? And even though his eyes were a little runny, did he just want to curl up in your arms and sleep? Thinking a dog is asking you to save him or picked you, even when other signs indicate he may not be healthy or well-bred, is asking for heartbreak. Be realistic about the dog you choose.

"But My Friend Told Me Never To . . ."

The world is full of people who think they know it all and are happy to impart their vast knowledge to you. Sure, sometimes people give good advice, but other times, they are simply repeating what they've heard from some other advice giver. Don't let anyone influence you besides the members of your own family and the breeder you trust, especially if you've heard anything like the following:

➤ Big dogs are nothing but trouble. (A larger dog that is well-trained is a joy!)

➤ You should never get a dog if you have to work all day. (You can always make arrangements to come home for lunch or hire someone to check on your dog during the day. Larger cities even have doggy daycare.)

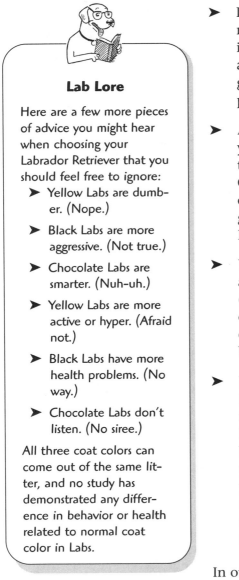

Lab Lore

Here are a few more pieces of advice you might hear when choosing your Labrador Retriever that you should feel free to ignore:

➤ Yellow Labs are dumber. (Nope.)

➤ Black Labs are more aggressive. (Not true.)

➤ Chocolate Labs are smarter. (Nuh-uh.)

➤ Yellow Labs are more active or hyper. (Afraid not.)

➤ Black Labs have more health problems. (No way.)

➤ Chocolate Labs don't listen. (No siree.)

All three coat colors can come out of the same litter, and no study has demonstrated any difference in behavior or health related to normal coat color in Labs.

➤ Purebred dogs are bound to have major health problems. (If a dog is bred responsibly with health as a priority, chances are very good that your dog will be the picture of health.)

➤ An older dog will never bond to you because he already bonded to somebody else. (Ridiculous! Older dogs can be excellent companions that are forever grateful to you for loving them. Labs are especially adaptable.)

➤ You'll end up giving that puppy away. They're too much work. (Puppies are a lot of work, but a dedicated and loving owner can quickly guide the puppy to good behavior.)

➤ Now you'll be tied down for life! (Having a dog does mean you'll need to plan for vacations and long periods away from home, but it certainly doesn't mean you can't ever leave home. Take your dog along, hire a pet sitter or board your dog at a good kennel. See Chapter 15 for more on traveling with your dog.)

In other words, every dog is an individual, and every family is unique. No one knows you like you, and no one knows your dog like the breeder. Working together, you can ensure the perfect match. No outside advice required!

How to Avoid Second Thoughts

Planning and preparation are the keys for avoiding second thoughts. If you know exactly what you are getting into and what degree of time, effort and financial commitment to expect, you won't experience any rude awakenings. You'll have realistic expectations, and you'll be able to provide a consistently loving environment for your new friend.

That doesn't mean you won't get frustrated once in awhile. Puppies can be trying, and when you are standing in the middle of your front yard at 3:00 a.m. for the fourth night in a row as your puppy joyfully romps through the grass as if he has no intention of relieving himself for quite some time, you may think, "What was I thinking?" Just remind yourself what you were thinking: That you will make an excellent dog companion, and that you are committed to making your new Labrador Retriever the best dog he can be. Before you know it, your puppy will be able to make it through the night without having to go outside, so why not enjoy it while it lasts? How often do you get to enjoy the morning at 3:00 a.m?

The Least You Need to Know

➤ Continue to refine your expectations so you know exactly what you want in a dog before you bring one home.

➤ Trying out simple lure-and-reward training exercises at the breeder's place can help you to judge each puppy's personality and receptivity so you can choose the puppy that best suits you.

➤ Make sure to pick out a puppy that looks and acts healthy. Even so, don't neglect a vet visit on the way home from the breeder's place.

➤ Don't forget the importance of chemistry. You should feel a special connection to the dog you choose.

➤ Don't let the puppy pick you. You pick the puppy.

➤ Don't listen to the advice of friends who are so-called puppy experts. Listen to your own good judgment and the breeder's advice.

➤ You won't have second thoughts if you are properly prepared and fully committed.

83

Part 2

The MRE System: Teaching Your Lab to Be Practically Perfect

So you think training your Lab will be easy? While Labs are more train-able than some breeds, training any dog is a major commitment of time and energy. But this is a commitment well worth making, and we'll show you how to proceed.

First, we'll explain Joel's highly successful MRE System, then we'll break it down into its individual parts: Management, Relationship and Education. Next, we'll help you learn to successfully manage your Labrador Retriever, the first step to guiding your new pet towards a happy and rewarding life with you. Then we'll talk about the relation-ship between you and your Lab, and how to maximize it at every turn.

Last, we'll spend a good deal of space educating you about how to edu-cate your Lab. You'll learn everything from how to teach your brand new puppy to sit using the lure-and-reward method, to how to teach your older dog to understand and respond to more-advanced requests, includ-ing the all important "Come" command.

Chapter 7

Managing Your Lab

Once you've selected your Labrador Retriever, whether puppy, adolescent, adult or senior, you may feel you've cleared the first big hurdle, and indeed, you have. But the race is far from over, and you've got three hurdles yet to come. Get ready, because they are crucial hurdles if you want your dog to be the dog of your dreams.

After over a decade of training dogs and their owners, Joel has developed a three-point system that summarizes the most important considerations for becoming the excellent owner of an excellent dog. Joel calls the system the *MRE system*, which stands for Management, Relationship and Education.

Dogs are dogs. They aren't people. Therefore, they come programmed with certain doggy behaviors that humans don't always find particularly appealing. They can't help it—as we said, they're dogs! But that doesn't mean these behaviors can't be managed. In fact, managing your Lab's behavior is the most important part of the MRE system.

Lab Lingo

The **MRE system** was developed by Joel Walton to demonstrate the three most important aspects of handling dog behavior: proper Management, a good dog–owner Relationship and continual training or Education.

The Importance of Management

Just about everyone has come into some kind of contact with a misbehaving dog. Maybe a neighbor dog liked to dig up your flower beds and chase your cat. Maybe you had a puppy as a child, and your parents ended up sending her to a farm or giving her away one day because she caused too much trouble. Maybe the dog sitting at your feet as you read this is doing her best to eat the soles off your slippers (and you're still wearing them).

But you never dreamed that uncontrolled rocket of black, chocolate or yellow fur tearing through your home, stopping only to deposit a, um, mishap on your carpet would belong to you. Dogs like that are other people's dogs, aren't they?

We've said it before, and we'll say it again: No dog comes preprogrammed with knowledge of how humans want her to act. Your puppy doesn't have a clue why you would care where she relieves herself or how fast she bolts through the house or what she chooses as a chew toy. No matter how nice or respectable or giving or affectionate a human you are, unless you manage your new dog, that adorable ball of fur with the melt-your-heart eyes will probably turn out to be more trouble than fun. Your new Lab means well, but she also means to be a dog (as well she should).

Management is the key, after which comes the development of the right relationship with your dog (see the next chapter, where we'll talk about what the right relationship is) and training or educating

Dogs are dogs and will behave like dogs. Understanding and accepting them as such, using the MRE program, will make a huge difference in your relationship.

your dog (see Chapter 9). How you manage different behaviors varies, so we'll break it down for you, but here's the key—remind yourself of it frequently: To properly manage your dog, don't let her get into trouble in the first place.

Lab Lingo

Management is the part of the MRE system involving guiding your dog towards good behavior by removing the opportunities for unwanted behaviors.

Managing Puppy Behavior

Boy, is that new Labrador puppy cute! And boy, is having a new puppy difficult! New puppies are indeed a challenge. The first few

89

Lab Lore

According to three epidemiological studies conducted by the National Council on Pet Population Study and Policy, 62.5 percent of dogs surrendered to shelters were trained by the owner only. Only 4 percent had attended obedience classes, 1.2 percent had been professionally trained and 1.3 percent had obtained training through private lessons. Several separate statistics within each of the studies showed that approximately 97 percent of the dogs surrendered to animal shelters received no formal training, either a class or private lessons. Kind of makes you consider hiring a professional, doesn't it?

weeks with a new puppy aren't unlike the first few weeks with a newborn human. You probably won't get much sleep, you'll spend an inordinate amount of time cleaning up and you'll sometimes think the unthinkable: "What on earth have I gotten myself into?"

Never fear, the end of the new-puppy intensity is near if you manage your new little bundle in a way that allows her to easily behave in the way you expect. Puppies do lots of things we don't care for. They whine and cry when you'd rather be in dreamland. They use the world as their toilet. They treat your fingers like chew toys. And oh, the energy! Just watching a Lab puppy can give you an overwhelming desire to take a nap. Can you manage all that behavior? No problem. Start out with our easy management steps, before you move on to relationship and training aspects to further develop and refine the behaviors you desire.

Barking and Whining Management

How can such a tiny pup make so much noise? And why, oh why, must she make that noise at 3:00 a.m.? Even when you do everything right, you won't get much sleep the first few nights with a new puppy. For one thing, puppies don't have the bladder control of older dogs and will need to be taken out at least once during the night. For another thing, your poor puppy is confused, lonely and scared. After all, she has just been taken away from her mother and littermates and the only home she has ever known. Sure, she may have acted like you were the answer to her prayers at the breeder's, but she had no idea what was in store.

Take pity on your puppy and recognize that whining and crying through the night are only natural. Then—and this is the hard part—after you've taken your pup outside for her midnight bathroom break, put her back in her doggy den and (gulp) ignore her.

Easier said than done (and it wasn't even easy to say). We know you didn't get a puppy so you could ignore her, and that whining, crying, whimpering sound is almost unbearable to a confirmed dog lover. But you have to be strong. You have to stick to your guns. Why? Because your puppy has a very important early lesson to learn: How to be by herself.

If you respond to your puppy's cries during the middle of the night, your puppy will learn some lessons, all right:

➤ Whining works.

➤ She doesn't have to sleep through the night.

➤ She can manipulate you.

Those aren't the lessons you want to teach your puppy. You want to teach her that:

➤ You don't respond to whining unless it's for a good reason (the puppy needing to relieve herself is a necessity).

➤ Nighttime is for sleeping. Daytime is for playing.

➤ You cannot be manipulated, because you are the coach in the household.

Actually, letting your puppy whine it out is easy (if you have a good pair of earmuffs). It requires no action whatsoever on your part, and after a night or two, the puppy will realize that her strategy isn't working. Sooner or later, she will realize she is tired, and she will go to sleep. Before you know it, your dog will eagerly hustle into her den come bedtime or whenever she wants to escape the family and take a little personal time.

Of course, reinforce your nighttime management with daytime management. When your puppy has slept well and quietly with only one or two trips outdoors during the night, take your pup out, have a training session, and praise her.

Trainer Tidbits

Remember, the doggy den is a place for your puppy to sleep. It needs to be just big enough for her to stand up, turn around and lie down. If you start feeling that you are putting your pup in the doggy den too often, make sure you are spending lots of time doing positive lure-and-reward training. Remember, pups sleep a lot, and it is more humane to do a time-out than to be yelling at the puppy for being overactive and overtired.

One last point about nighttime management: We strongly recommend the use of a doggy den, which is a nicer name for a crate or kennel. Doggy dens are wire or plastic enclosures used to give your puppy a safe, secure place to go. Dens also keep your puppy out of trouble at night and when you aren't home.

Lots of people think doggy dens are cruel and will tell you so if you mention that your dog has one. The opposite is true. Dogs are den animals and need a small enclosed space to feel safe. Without one, they may feel anxious and insecure. You can often find den-less dogs underneath tables, chairs or desks, looking for a place to call their own. Make it easy on them. Give them a den just big enough to sit, stand and lie down in comfortably.

Introduce the den in a positive manner, and your dog will likely love to sleep, rest or just hang out in there. Dogs normally don't soil the space where they sleep unless they absolutely can't hold it any longer. Plus, it is certainly kinder to keep your dog out of harm's way when you can't be around to supervise. A den for your new pup is one of the most important accessories you can buy.

Housetraining Management

Doggy dens are important for another reason. They are a great management tool for housetraining puppies and even adult dogs that haven't yet been taught the skill. When you first bring home your new puppy, watch her carefully. When she looks ready to relieve herself, whisk her outside. When she urinates and/or defecates, praise her gently and sincerely. When you can't watch your puppy continuously, put her in her den (not for more than four to six hours when your puppy is younger than 12 weeks, including at night). As soon as you take her out of her den, take her outside. Puppies won't soil their dens unless they have no other option, so keeping your puppy in her den will teach her to exercise bladder control.

After you get to know your puppy a little better, you'll recognize the signs that she is ready to relieve herself. Some puppies start to sniff the carpet, some will wander away from you, some will just get that look. Catching the signs every time will make for a smooth housetraining transition because your dog will soon learn that outside is the acceptable place.

Another way to manage housetraining is to be familiar with the *gastrocolic reflex*. This reflex (which human babies also experience) causes defecation to occur approximately 30 minutes after a meal. If you feed your puppy at consistent times each day then take her out 20 to 30 minutes later, you may be successful in preventing an accident every time.

Of course, accidents do happen. You look away from your puppy for just a minute to read the mail and uh-oh! If your puppy does urinate or defecate in the house and you catch her in the act, immediately pick up the puppy and take her outside. If she continues to eliminate outside, praise her.

If you don't catch your puppy in the act, never punish her and never, ever rub her nose in the waste. Your puppy didn't make a mistake—you did. But don't feel you have to punish yourself, either. Just resolve to do better next time.

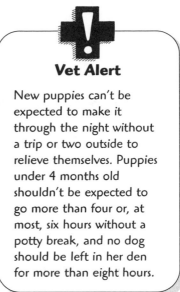

Vet Alert

New puppies can't be expected to make it through the night without a trip or two outside to relieve themselves. Puppies under 4 months old shouldn't be expected to go more than four or, at most, six hours without a potty break, and no dog should be left in her den for more than eight hours.

Trainer Tidbits

Puppy owners always want to know, "When will my puppy be housetrained?" It would be nice to be able to give an answer like "two weeks and three days," but here is the straight scoop: Your puppy will be housetrained just as soon as possible, if you do everything right.

Lab Lingo

The **gastrocolic reflex** is a physiological process in young mammals that results in defecation a short time after a meal. In dogs, feeding at regular times will usually result in defecation at regular times, making housetraining easier.

Trainer Tidbits

Immediately and thoroughly clean indoor accidents with an active enzyme cleaner (ask your local pet supply store manager for the best brand). Dogs tend to eliminate in places where they smell previous elimination, and enzyme cleaners will remove the scent. If you don't want to spend time mixing concentrate when you are in a hurry to clean up a mess, buy the slightly more expensive ready-to-use variety.

Play-Biting Management

Puppies bite. Not to be nasty, mind you. For puppies, play-biting (sometimes called mouthing or puppy biting) is a way to explore the world. Just as a human baby grabs with her hands and explores with her mouth, puppies explore and grab through biting. They play with their siblings using their teeth, and their siblings hardly notice. Play-biting is not a sign of aggression; it is a sign of play, and puppy play is good. Puppy play is how puppies learn.

But to humans, puppy bites hurt. Those tiny teeth are as sharp as needles. The puppy doesn't know that, of course. She doesn't have any idea that you aren't covered in tough canine skin. You need to do two jobs while the puppy is mouthing: First, teach the puppy not to bite hard. Second, teach the puppy not to bite at all.

Your puppy must learn that human flesh is much more sensitive than the flesh of puppies and dogs. This is one of the most important things that you will teach your pup. An adult dog may bite if she has pain inflicted on her. Just imagine your beloved, well-behaved dog is asleep on the family room floor. A 3-year-old child comes running over, falls on your dog and sticks a finger in the dog's eye or ear or causes pain to your dog in some other fashion. If your dog bit the child at this point, that would be normal behavior. If you were sleeping on the sofa and someone woke you up by slapping you hard on the face, you would wake up in an aggressive fashion, and nobody would say you have bad temperament! Teaching the puppy that human flesh is sensitive (bite inhibition) is like buying insurance. You will be glad you did it, and hopefully it will never be tested.

One way to help your puppy learn is not to give her the opportunity to bite you. Don't hold out your fingers or feet for your puppy to bite! When your puppy does bite you (because she will find those fingers despite your efforts), say "Ouch!" sharply to startle the puppy into recognizing that you are reacting. Immediately withdraw your hand or whatever the puppy is biting. Then immediately train your puppy or do a time-out. Do this consistently, and your puppy will learn that she needs to be careful when playing with humans. You may have to endure a few uncomfortable nips during this process, but isn't it worth it? See Chapter 9 for more on how to train your puppy not to play-bite.

Chewing Management

Puppies also chew to explore the world, and they chew like a wood chipper when they are teething. In Chapter 10, we'll talk in more detail about how to teach your puppy what is appropriate to chew, but the best way to manage chewing is to limit your puppy's access to things she isn't allowed to chew.

Just as you child-proof a home against a toddler, you should puppy-proof your home against a chewer. Before you bring your new puppy home, walk through each room of your house trying to see with the eyes of a puppy. Then take the following precautions:

Trainer Tidbits

Labrador Retrievers seem to have a particular penchant for chewing. Even adult Labs will chew destructively if not given a proper outlet for their energy and if left unsupervised for long periods of time. An adult Lab can easily destroy large items of value, such as bicycles, swing sets and even parts of your car. Better to teach your Lab early on about chewing etiquette.

➤ Hide or tape up all electrical cords.

➤ Keep shoes in closed closets.

➤ Secure cords from window blinds so puppy can't reach them.

➤ Keep garbage out of reach.

➤ Police the floor on a daily basis for choking hazards such as paper clips, rubber bands and pieces of string.

➤ Keep everything of value to you that could possibly be destroyed by chewing out of puppy's reach.

➤ If you have stairs in your home, make sure everyone in the family knows to keep the door at the top of the stairs closed. If you don't have a door, keep a baby gate in place so your puppy won't fall down the stairs.

Because you will be watching your puppy 100 percent of the time when she is on the loose for housetraining purposes, also watch her for chewing tendencies. Whenever your puppy shows any indication that she is preparing to chew on something forbidden, remove the item and give your puppy a quality chew toy, preferably one that can be stuffed with treats.

Orbiting Management

Orbiting refers to the behavior of dashing wildly around the house. Older puppies and sometimes adolescent dogs orbit with joyful abandon, and nothing is safe that lies in the path of destruction. The bigger your puppy is, the more damage orbiting can cause.

But again, your puppy isn't trying to destroy your coffee table or your antique tea set. She is simply burning off some of that incredible supply of puppy energy. The key to managing orbiting behavior is to provide your puppy with plenty of opportunities for both physical and mental stimulation. For very small puppies, exercise in the house and the yard should be sufficient, but the bigger your puppy gets, the more she will need a daily brisk walk out in the fresh air. Tired puppies are happy puppies, and they're less destructive, too.

To further manage orbiting, pay attention to the time of day when and/or the types of situations in which your puppy tends to experience an energy overflow, and then apply the following techniques when the orbiting time or the situation approaches:

➤ Put a leash on your puppy in the house.

➤ Engage in a vigorous lure-and-reward training session (see Chapter 9), take your puppy outside to relieve herself and then put her in her den.

➤ Teach your puppy to come when you call (see Chapter 10). A puppy cannot come to you and orbit at the same time.

Control orbiting by rechanneling energy, and you'll soon have a well-behaved dog that knows when to romp and when to wait patiently for the proper time to romp.

Managing Your New Adolescent or Adult Dog

One of the advantages to bringing an older dog into your family is that she may already be trained in certain desirable behaviors. On the other hand, many adolescent and adult dogs have developed undesirable behaviors because their owners didn't train them and then gave up on them. Therefore, the best way to manage a new older dog is to treat her just like a puppy. Don't assume your dog will know better. She may not have any idea what you expect. If you manage her in the same gentle, positive manner you would apply to a puppy, she will soon learn the house rules and how to stay out of trouble.

Consider that you have been blessed with a dog that wasn't handled correctly in the past. A dog treated with love and supported in the managing and education process is similarly blessed and will return your caring management and education with years of love and devotion. We've seen it happen again and again. And if you find during the management and education process that your adult dog already has many skills and positive behaviors? Then you are doubly blessed.

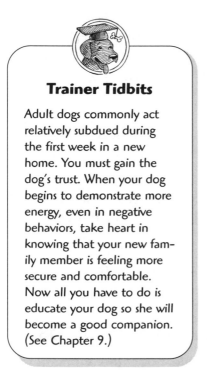

Trainer Tidbits

Adult dogs commonly act relatively subdued during the first week in a new home. You must gain the dog's trust. When your dog begins to demonstrate more energy, even in negative behaviors, take heart in knowing that your new family member is feeling more secure and comfortable. Now all you have to do is educate your dog so she will become a good companion. (See Chapter 9.)

Managing the Transition

Adult dogs may come with some additional challenges not present in puppies. For one thing, dogs are creatures of habit. If they are used to being in one place for several years and are suddenly moved, or if they have been shifted around a lot, they may come to you full of insecurities and anxiety. Begin good management and positive training immediately, so your dog has the chance to learn the rules and expectations as soon as possible. Show your dog that she can be happy and successful in her new home and that this home is a home for keeps.

Separation Management

You may have heard a lot about separation anxiety. Separation anxiety is actually a clinical diagnosis that isn't as common as people think. Most trainers refer to barking, digging and other destructive or annoying behaviors a dog exhibits when the owner is away as learned behaviors that can be modified by good, positive training. Rather than experiencing anxiety, your dog may just be bored out of her mind. In Chapter 10, we'll show you how to train your dog about what she is and isn't allowed to do when she's home alone.

Here are some good ways to begin to manage this type of behavior:

➤ Come home for lunch to walk your dog if you work all day long (or hire someone).

➤ Provide your dog with lots of stuffed hollow chew toys (see Chapter 10) to chew and play with in your absence.

➤ Spend a lot of quality time practicing lure-and-reward training with your dog when you are home.

➤ Don't leave your new dog too often or for too long a stretch until you have solidified your relationship (see Chapter 8).

With proper management and training, your dog will be well-behaved, even when you aren't looking.

Like a Puppy Managed for the Very First Time!

Overall, the key to managing any dog of any age is to treat her like a puppy. Throughout this book, whenever we offer tips, hints and training methods for puppies, feel free to apply these to your new dog of any age. Every dog is a puppy to some extent when she enters a new family. Treat your dog as you would a baby. She deserves no less.

Vet Alert

True separation anxiety (in which a dog becomes extremely distraught when the owner leaves) is sometimes exhibited by adult dogs that have had insecure or abusive pasts. It may also be caused by a medical problem. The dog may become extremely destructive, even injuring herself, and may require medication and behavioral treatment. If you suspect your dog suffers from true separation anxiety, see your vet.

The Least You Need to Know

➤ Management is the first and most important step to keeping your dog out of trouble and guiding her toward good behavior.

➤ Many undesirable puppy behaviors are completely natural and need only be modified.

➤ Prevent your puppy from getting into trouble or from behaving in an undesirable way rather than allowing her to get into trouble and then punishing her.

➤ Treat your new adult dog like a puppy, and life will be easier and happier for all.

Chapter 8

Relating to Your Lab

In This Chapter

➤ Getting to know your new Lab

➤ The Ten Commandments of a good dog-human relationship

➤ Maintaining your relationship

➤ How to be a good puppy parent

➤ The many faces of discipline

The second part of the MRE system is the relationship between you and your Lab. Good relationships between dogs and humans don't just happen. Sure, you can have great chemistry to start with. You can adore each other. But before you really know each other and develop a rapport based on mutual trust and communication, you won't have a true relationship.

Unfortunately, there are many ways to compromise your relationship with your Lab, and most of them happen completely unintention-ally. You might not have any idea why your Lab puppy suddenly stops listening to you or doesn't greet you with affection when you return home. Relationships take work. You probably knew that about human relationships, but human-dog relationships aren't that much different. What can you do to get the most out of the relationship between you and your new friend? We're here to tell you!

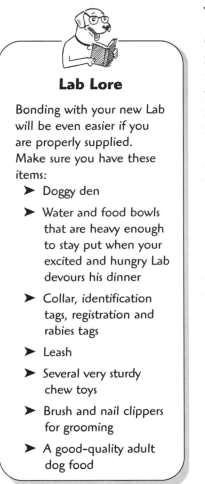

You and Your Lab

Once you get your new dog home, it's time to get acquainted. You surely have some first impressions of your Lab, and he probably has some first impressions of you, too. It is important for you to spend a good amount of time with your new dog during the first few weeks he comes to live with you. You'll both have adjustments to make, but you also need to bond in order to build the foundation of a relationship you hope will last for a very long time.

The day you bring your Lab home, begin observing him. Notice how he acts when you behave in certain ways. Notice when he gets tired, when he gets hungry and when he needs to go out. Notice what he seems to enjoy and what seems to scare him. As you play with him and cuddle him, notice when he enjoys it and when he seems ready to be left alone. In other words, tune in to your dog. This is the only way to really know him.

After your dog has been with you for a few days, answer the following questions to get a clearer picture in your mind of your dog's personality. (Writing often helps to clarify what you already know.) This information can also be transferred into your pet records for future reference (or just keep this book with your pet's vaccination and other health records).

1. My Lab is _____ months/years old.

2. My Lab eats _____ times per day. I feed him _____. His appetite is _____.

3. At night my Lab sleeps for about _____ hours before he needs to go out. I would characterize his sleep patterns as

   _____.

4. My Lab's overall health seems _____.

5. Something the vet said about my Lab:

   _____.

6. My Lab's favorite toys are _____.

7. My Lab is most active in the _____.

8. I think his favorite thing to do is

   _____.

9. He seems to have a tendency to _____.

10. He is very good about _____.

11. Something I think we'll need to work on is

    _____.

12. When it comes to teaching my Lab what is expected of him, my confidence level is _____.

13. I'm a little worried about handling _____.

14. I don't think I'll need to worry at all about

    _____.

15. We are spending _____ minutes per day on training exercises.

16. My Lab reacts to training sessions by

    _____.

17. My Lab's favorite reward for doing a good job seems to be

    _____.

18. When it comes to training, I'm very comfortable about

    _____.

19. When it comes to training, I need to work on my tendency to

    _____.

20. He's a typical Lab when it comes to

    _____.

21. He doesn't seem so Lab-like when it

    _____.

22. I'm good at managing him when I don't give him the opportunity to _____.

23. I've slipped up a few times by letting him

    _____, but I

    plan to avoid that in the future.

24. One thing I can't resist letting my Lab do is

    _____.

25. I'd also like to remember the following story or stories about my Lab's first few weeks with me:

    _____

    _____

    _____

    _____

    _____

    _____

    _____

    _____

    _____

    _____

    _____

Feeling bonded yet? We hope so! But as you know by now, bonding is only the first step toward relationship success. You also have a few more responsibilities, and they are your responsibilities, not your

The bottom line is your relationship with your Lab. Keep the MRE principles in mind, and it'll be a great one.

dog's. Dogs are pack animals by nature and are hardwired to get along with other living beings they consider their pack or family. The dog is doing his part. The rest is up to you.

How to Have a Good Relationship

If you have just brought a dog home or are getting ready to bring one home, you are smack in the middle of a great opportunity. You have the chance to forge a wonderful and rewarding relationship with a loving pet that can bring you years of happiness and devotion.

But how do you make it happen? Think about the good relationships with others in your life. Do you tend to have better relationships with the people who praised and rewarded you when you did something right? Did these same folks keep you out of trou-

Trainer Tidbits

Your relationship with your dog will be stronger and more stable if you can keep in mind one cardinal principle: Bad behavior is never the dog's fault. Dogs don't misbehave on purpose. Revenge or ill humor doesn't motivate them. They want to please you, and they depend on you to show them how.

105

ble while you were learning what was expected of you? When you misbehaved, did these people show you how to behave correctly?

Trainer Tidbits

This little trick will help to reinforce good behavior in your dog. When he is behaving the way you want him to behave, look at him. When he is doing something you don't like, don't look! (You probably don't want to see that trash spread all over the kitchen, anyway!) Dogs notice where your attention is directed and even looking at your dog can be a form of reinforcement.

Now, think about the people with whom your relationship isn't so great. Did these people punish you harshly when you made a mistake? Did they punish you even when you weren't sure what you did wrong? Do they tend to ignore you, or put you at the bottom of their priority lists, or act irritated by you?

In many ways, dogs are like people. They tend to prefer the people who are kind, affectionate and keep them out of trouble. They like to know the rules, and the people who make the rules clear without harsh or cruel punishment are the people to be trusted. Dogs won't behave as well if they are treated meanly, punished excessively or punished when they don't know what the punishment is for. They don't like to be ignored or treated like an irritation. They want to be loved. Don't we all?

A relationship is a relationship, whether with child, spouse, friend or dog. All our fellow sentient beings deserve our kindness and respect. Respect your new dog and pay attention to him so you can guide him in the best way. And always remember the Ten Commandments of Dog-Human Relationships:

I.   Thou shalt have fun with your dog. Dogs, and especially puppies, relish fun. Play with your dog, walk him, romp with him and make training sessions fun, too. The couple that has fun together stays together!

II.   Thou shalt allow your dog to be good at something. Give your dog something to do. Whether it's training sessions, obedience classes, fun tricks, hunting or running in the park with you each morning, dogs like to have a purpose and a task at which they can succeed. Let your dog excel at something, and he'll love you for it.

III. Thou shalt give your dog companions. Dogs are social animals, and although some dogs do well alone all day, most dogs like to have someone to see every few hours. Come home for lunch if no one will be home all day. Have friends, relatives or a professional pet sitter visit and walk your dog when you won't be around much. If you can handle the added expense, commitment and training time, you could also consider bringing home another dog to keep your dog company.

IV. Thou shalt keep your dog out of trouble. Your dog can't misbehave, by chewing your new shoe or forgetting his housetraining, for example, if you don't give him the opportunity.

V. Thou shalt teach your dog what you expect. How can your dog know those new shoes aren't chew toys if you don't show him, in ways he can understand, that some things are off limits for chewing, but other things are okay for chewing? Similarly, how will he know where it is acceptable to relieve himself unless you show him?

Vet Alert

Never get a second dog just to keep your first dog company. Every dog deserves love, attention and proper care. If you can't afford two dogs, find another way to give your dog something to do. On the other hand, if you can afford it and are willing to spend the time training both dogs, a second dog can be fun for the family and a great pal to your first dog.

VI. Thou shalt not reward your dog for doing something you don't like. Even if you don't realize it, your reactions to your puppy's behaviors could be reinforcing the behaviors you dislike the most. For example, if you don't pay attention to your dog very often, he may discover that an accident on the carpet is the only way to get your attention, even if the attention involves getting yelled at. (See Chapter 9 for more on how not to reinforce objectionable behavior.)

VII. Thou shalt praise and reward your dog when he does something right or well. Praise is the big payoff for good behavior as far as your dog is concerned. When he pleases you, let him know it.

VIII. Thou shalt know what you want your puppy to do. You can't show your puppy what you expect if you don't have your expectations clearly in mind.

IX. Thou shalt confine your dog in his doggy den or some other safe area when you can't pay attention to him. This is not cruelty, but kindness. You are keeping your dog out of trouble and letting his energy and hunger renew so that the next training session will be productive. (And sometimes your dog needs a rest from you.)

X. Thou shalt not ever yell at, jerk, hit, grab, pinch, shock, squirt or kick your dog. Not ever. There is always a better way. Labs were not bred to take abuse; no dog is bred to take abuse.

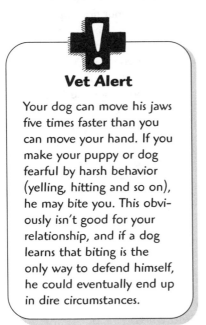

Vet Alert

Your dog can move his jaws five times faster than you can move your hand. If you make your puppy or dog fearful by harsh behavior (yelling, hitting and so on), he may bite you. This obviously isn't good for your relationship, and if a dog learns that biting is the only way to defend himself, he could eventually end up in dire circumstances.

Following these ten simple commandments in conjunction with the training explained in detail in Chapter 9 will ensure a wonderful, warm and companionable relationship between you and your dog that will last a lifetime.

How to Keep That Relationship

Forming a solid bond with your dog and teaching him the ropes and the rules are an important beginning, but if you want to maintain that relationship, remember that dogs are a lifelong commitment. You can cement that commitment if you:

➤ Remain consistent in the way you relate to your dog.

➤ Remain consistent about what your dog can and can't do.

➤ Provide a home full of rewards, benefits and good things for your dog. (We don't mean you should spoil him. We mean you should create an environment in which he is happy to be.)

➤ Continue to educate your dog so he can enjoy a lifetime of learning and has continual chances to please you.

➤ Keep loving him!

That's all it takes. Not so complicated, is it?

Be a Good Puppy Parent

Even if you aren't a parent, you had parents or parental figures in your life. Parents are important for children in their roles as lawmakers, guidance counselors, moral supporters, disciplinarians and sources of unconditional love. And these are just the roles you'll play with your new puppy! You make the rules and teach your puppy how to follow those rules, all the while offering your unconditional love.

Trainer Tidbits

Dogs take a cue from your body language. When you want your dog to relax and calm down, act relaxed and calm yourself. Don't run around frantically, waving your arms and screaming, "Down! Stop it! Calm down!"

But what about discipline? Discipline can mean many things to many people. Let's look at it from a learning viewpoint. You want your puppy to learn to behave in a certain way and also to learn how not to behave. There is a well-established scientific learning theory involving two types of discipline: reinforcement and punishment. Using this theory can help you understand how to help your pup be a good citizen.

Reinforcement makes behaviors more likely to occur:

➤ Positive reinforcement is doing something pleasant or nice for your pup right after he does something good for you. For example, if you say, "Sit," and your pup sits, you give him a treat.

➤ Negative reinforcement is stopping something bad when the dog does something for you. For example, you stop constricting the choke chain on your dog's neck when you ask him to sit and he sits.

Most progressive trainers prefer to use positive reinforcement and little or no negative reinforcement. Why would you want to cause discomfort to your puppy if you don't have to?

Punishment is something that makes a behavior less likely to occur:

➤ Positive punishment means that you add something unpleasant when your dog does a behavior you want to decrease. For example, if your dog barks at another dog, you give him a leash jerk. If the positive punishment works, he may be less likely to bark at that dog the next time he sees it. Positive punishment may sound sensible, but it is always risky. What if your dog interprets your action to mean that in the presence of that other dog, you become nasty? You may help your dog to learn to dislike other dogs. Joel has seen this happen time and time again.

➤ Negative punishment means taking away something good to decrease the likelihood of the behavior. For example, to help your dog stop barking at other dogs, you could immediately turn around and walk away from any dog that is the object of his barking. If your dog likes to meet other dogs, taking away his chance to meet them will be negative punishment and will make him less likely to bark at dogs in the future.

Trainer Tidbits

If your new puppy or dog hides a lot under a table or a chair or in a distant room, he probably needs more time in his doggy den where he can feel safe and secure. Also, try to subject him to a little less stimulation and chaos until he is better adjusted.

Positive reinforcement and negative punishment are the preferred methods because they don't involve doing anything nasty to your dog. Even if you think withholding reinforcement is a little nasty, it only makes sense. If you don't work or obey the law, good things are taken away from you. Your dog can learn that basic principle, too.

On the other hand, negative reinforcement and positive punishment are best avoided. Why do something aversive to your dog if you don't

This puppy feels secure underneath a chair, which he's using as a doggy den.

have to? Remember, if you do choose to use negative reinforcement and positive punishment and you do not see positive results at once, then you are not using the learning theory correctly. Even if you don't intend it, you are being abusive.

Also remember that aversive action toward your dog can have many unpleasant and even tragic side effects. It can ruin your relationship. It can make the dog fearful or aggressive. You certainly will not be as happy a person if you are causing discomfort to a beloved family member.

Focusing your parenting efforts on the positive rather than the negative is the sure way to teach your dog right from wrong and good from bad. It will also cement your relationship for good. Your dog will know that good things come from you, and who wouldn't want a relationship with someone like that?

The Least You Need to Know

➤ Relating to your Lab is an important step in helping your dog be the best dog he can be.

➤ You can be a good puppy parent by learning the best way to teach your dog what is good behavior and what is bad behavior.

➤ Positive reinforcement means rewarding your dog when he does something good.

➤ Negative reinforcement means removing an unpleasant condition when your dog does something well.

➤ Positive punishment means doing something your dog doesn't like in order to decrease a behavior.

➤ Negative punishment means taking away something your dog likes in order to decrease a behavior.

Chapter 9

Educating Your Lab, Part One

In This Chapter

➤ Do puppies need to meet lots of people? Aren't they naturally friendly?

➤ What is lure-and-reward training, and how do you do it?

➤ What is reward training, and how do you do it?

➤ How to teach your dog not to bark, play-bite or have accidents in the house

---

Can you imagine what you would be like if your parents had lain around on the couch looking at you until you were 18 years old just to see what you would pick up on your own? No, your parents spent a lot of time training (educating) you, so you would know the house rules and the rules of life, too. Your parents also sent you to school so experts (teachers) could further educate you.

Imagine, too, the absurdity of the argument, "This kid doesn't know how to do anything! Must be bad breeding." Of course, you wouldn't know anything if your parents didn't teach you anything. You might figure out some basic survival tactics, but you certainly wouldn't be very good at anything, let alone have any manners.

But that little puppy or dog you have just brought home has a smaller brain than you do. How could you expect her to figure out everything on her own? Dogs need our guidance so they know what to do and how to act. Puppies are more self-sufficient when it comes to survival than human infants, but they certainly aren't preprogrammed to be housetrained, let alone to heel on a leash or to sit at your feet at your request.

And that brings us to part three of the MRE system: Education. It is your responsibility to educate your dog if you want her to be a good companion. Education isn't as hard as it might seem. You need to know what you are doing, make a plan and know when to ask for help.

Your Canine Eliza Doolittle: Socialization

Socialization is a fancy term that simply means this: Your pup has to meet every kind of person that you want her to accept as an adult, starting when she is a little puppy and continuing until she is an adult. If you properly socialize your pup, there is a very good chance that she will not be fearful or aggressive to all of the nice folks she meets as an adult.

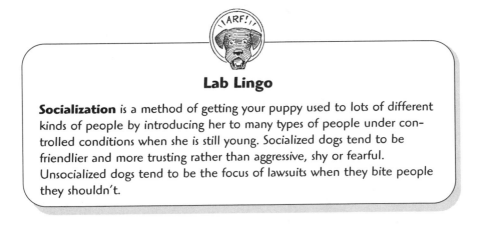

Lab Lingo

Socialization is a method of getting your puppy used to lots of different kinds of people by introducing her to many types of people under controlled conditions when she is still young. Socialized dogs tend to be friendlier and more trusting rather than aggressive, shy or fearful. Unsocialized dogs tend to be the focus of lawsuits when they bite people they shouldn't.

You not only have to socialize your pup with lots of folks, you also need to manage the interactions so that they are positive for your puppy. You have to be able to control what the people your pup meets are going to do. Bad experiences with strangers can teach your puppy that some folks are not acceptable.

Danger: Kids Ahead

If you are a couple without children and you get a Lab puppy, you'll want to look ahead to the time when you will have children (even if you aren't planning to have children, you never know what the future holds). If you are trying to socialize your puppy to children but you do not control the interactions, your pup may very well learn that children are loud, obnoxious and downright dangerous.

Socializing your pup to children doesn't mean leaving her alone in a room with seven toddlers. Young children aren't any more well trained to handle a puppy than the puppy is trained to handle them. When socializing your puppy to young children, hold the puppy and control the interaction by carefully monitoring how and how much the children touch the puppy and how much noise they make while doing it. Just as you would be very careful with a baby or a toddler around a strange dog, you must be careful with your puppy to make sure that the vast majority of her interactions with children, and with adults, too, are positive.

Preventing problems is much easier than solving them. A dog that wasn't socialized well can still be trained, but it is a much longer road. In any situation where your pup is going to meet someone new, make sure you can control the situation. It is better to pass up the chance to socialize

Vet Alert

Young puppies are very susceptible to certain diseases, especially before they have received all their vaccinations, and humans can subject puppies to diseases. You don't need to keep your puppy isolated, however. When having people over to meet your new puppy, simply have them remove their shoes at the door and wash their hands before they hold the puppy.

Trainer Tidbits

If you don't have the kind of house where people are frequently coming and going, consider having a few puppy socialization parties. Invite friends over, have everyone remove their shoes and wash their hands and then have people approach your puppy one at a time and introduce themselves. Let your puppy get to know each party guest. In return, you provide the snacks.

115

your puppy if there is any chance that he is going to be frightened by the new person, such as a screaming child, a person with a cane or someone who might tend to grab the puppy unexpectedly. Just make a note to find the same kind of person to socialize your pup in the future.

The ABCs of Socialization

When socializing your pup to someone new, try the following steps:

1. Make sure the puppy is hungry and the new person is seated in a comfortable chair with treats you know your puppy likes.

2. Wait for the puppy to approach the person, and then have the person silently offer the puppy a treat.

3. Once the puppy will readily take treats from the new person, the person can gently talk to the puppy while she takes the treat.

4. Next, the person can lure the pup into various positions (you show him or her how), and then reward the pup.

5. If you want your pup to learn to obey other people, you could have the person give the same commands you use.

6. Petting the puppy gently on the head or chest is a good reward after she obeys a command. Sometimes, however, petting will activate a Lab pup, and you may see some jumping up or play-biting.

Earliest Lessons

Training your new puppy doesn't start at 6 months of age. It starts the minute you bring your puppy home. If you show your pup right from wrong at the very beginning, it won't feel as if you are suddenly changing the rules just when she gets to know you!

You want the pup to relieve herself outside? As soon as you get out of the car after that very first drive home, take your puppy to the designated bathroom location outside. Set her down and watch her, but do not interact with her. She'll probably sniff around for a minute or more. When she starts producing urine or feces, gently praise her. Congratulations! You just took that important first step in the house-training process.

After your puppy is finished relieving herself, take her into the house to the room where you are going to spend most of your time together (usually the living room, den or kitchen). This should be a room where you feel comfortable, too, so that you will enjoy being in here with your puppy.

Let your puppy do some exploring on her own. During her explorations, she will probably come back to you periodically. Gently pet and praise her. Reassure her that she is in a safe and wonderful place. If she starts to chew on something off-limits, give her a safe object to chew like a sturdy, hollow chew toy and then gently praise her when she chews it. If she shows no interest in the chew toy, stuff it with a few safe goodies (puppy treats), and she'll quickly get interested. Congratulations! You just took that first important step in teaching your puppy what is and isn't okay to chew!

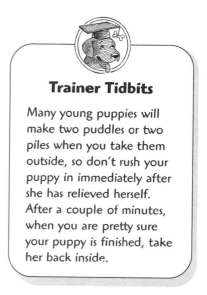

Trainer Tidbits

Many young puppies will make two puddles or two piles when you take them outside, so don't rush your puppy in immediately after she has relieved herself. After a couple of minutes, when you are pretty sure your puppy is finished, take her back inside.

Young puppies are easily excited, and when they get excited, they have to urinate. Always keep this fact in mind as you vigilantly watch your puppy play and explore. Whenever your puppy starts to get excited, take her outside to her special spot so you can praise her again when she urinates there.

Watch your pup for signs of fatigue. Like young children, young puppies will play like mad, and then suddenly collapse. Don't let your pup overtire herself. After about ten or fifteen minutes of exploring and/or chewing, take her outside to her spot and then bring her back in. Toss a few pieces of her dry dog food in her den and gently place her inside.

Your pup's doggy den is the safe place where she will hang out when you cannot watch her. Dogs are den animals, so forget the idea that you are being cruel by caging her. It would be much crueler to let her get in trouble or injure herself by chewing inappropriate objects.

Trainer Tidbits

Remember to puppy-proof your house, doing the most careful job in the room where you and your puppy will spend the most time together. You want your new puppy to be able to explore the room without the chance of injuring herself by chewing on an electrical cord or by swallowing a rubber band. Remove or put everything out of puppy's reach that she could possibly damage or destroy.

You now have the easy yet challenging job of getting your puppy used to spending time in her doggy den. This is as easy as training gets: Put her in her den, and then do nothing. Oh, how badly you'll want to take her out when she begins to whine! But do nothing! If you respond to her vocalizations, she will train you to let her out, and she will not get used to her den.

Many of Joel's clients ask, "How do I know whether the pup is fussing because she has to go to the bathroom?" It's pretty simple. Always take her outside just before you put her in her den. If you just took her out to the potty, then she is not fussing because she has to go to the bathroom.

After she has been asleep in her den for awhile and wakes up, take her outside before she starts fussing. The key is to keep a watchful eye on your puppy at all times, even when she is in her den. If you anticipate her elimination needs, training her to love her doggy den and to be housetrained will both be much easier.

Later in this chapter we'll go into more detail about training, but when it comes to teaching your pup to love her den, your daily schedule should go something like this: In the morning, take your puppy out of her den and immediately take her outside to relieve herself.

During the day, keep her out of her den when you are ready to train her, play with her and watch her 100 percent of the time. When one responsible person can watch the pup every second to make sure she isn't getting into trouble and to watch for signs that she needs to be taken outside to relieve herself, she can stay out of her den. When no

Like young children, young puppies like to play. Nap time will be necessary afterward.

one is available to play puppy watcher (which could be a full-time career), put the pup in her den.

At night, your puppy should get used to going to sleep before or when you go to sleep. Put her in her den at night, set your alarm if necessary for the middle-of-the-night potty run (especially if your puppy sleeps in another room and her cries won't wake you) and let her cry it out. It isn't cruel. The sooner she learns that night is for sleeping and day is for playing, the better off you'll all be. Labs are social animals and will be most comfortable sleeping near you. That doesn't mean you have to let your Lab sleep in the bed with you, but if you can keep your Lab's doggy den in the room where you sleep, your Lab will probably rest easier.

How Dogs Learn

Knowing how your dog learns is an important part of knowing how to teach your dog. Knowing one key truth about dogs will help you in almost every aspect of training: Dogs do what benefits them right now. If your puppy comes to you and you talk sweetly to her, gently stroke her and give her a piece of her food, she will be more likely to come to you in the future. If she comes to you and you ignore her or,

119

worse, yell at her when she tries to get your attention by jumping on you, she may not be as likely to come to you next time. If she jumps up on you and you smile and laugh and say, "What a cute puppy!" she will be more likely to jump up on you next time. It's that simple. When it comes to dogs, you reap what you sow.

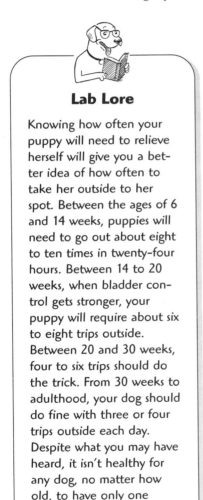

Lab Lore

Knowing how often your puppy will need to relieve herself will give you a better idea of how often to take her outside to her spot. Between the ages of 6 and 14 weeks, puppies will need to go out about eight to ten times in twenty-four hours. Between 14 to 20 weeks, when bladder control gets stronger, your puppy will require about six to eight trips outside. Between 20 and 30 weeks, four to six trips should do the trick. From 30 weeks to adulthood, your dog should do fine with three or four trips outside each day. Despite what you may have heard, it isn't healthy for any dog, no matter how old, to have only one chance in twenty-four hours to eliminate.

Dogs are motivated by rewards. They are social animals and have a very predictable list of things they find rewarding:

➤ Comfortable temperature

➤ Water to drink

➤ Attention

➤ Food

➤ Air to breathe

➤ Sex (when they mature, females for a few weeks each year and males any time)

Knowing what pleases your dog is the first step in training. The second step is using those rewards in a method. The two best and nicest methods for training any puppy or dog are:

➤ Lure-and-reward training

➤ Reward training

Lure-and-Reward Training

If your puppy is both hungry and well rested, you can hold a piece of food in front of her nose and use it to lure her into various positions (the basis of the Start Puppy Training Procedure described in Chapter 6). Here's how it works:

➤ **The Sit.** When your pup is standing, slowly move the lure up and slightly to the rear, and she will sit. Say "Yes" and give her the food reward.

➤ **The Stand.** When your pup is sitting, slowly move the lure straight away from her, far enough so she has to stand up. When she stands, say "Yes" and give her the food reward.

➤ **The Down.** When your pup is sitting, slowly lower the lure straight down from her nose to the floor. When she lies down, say "Yes" and give her the food reward.

When you are ready to bet $100 that you can lure your puppy into a position, you are ready to start giving the positions names and teaching the pup to perform them on request.

➤ Say "Sit," lure the dog into position; say "Yes," and then reward the dog.

➤ Say "Stand," lure the dog into position; say "Yes," and then reward the dog.

➤ Say "Down" (from sit), lure the dog into position; say "Yes," and then reward the dog.

➤ Say "Sit" (up from a down), lure the dog into position; say "Yes," and then reward the dog.

The beauty of the lure-and-reward method is that the breeder can teach it to pups by the time they start eating solid food. You as the new owner can start this type of training on the very first day you bring your puppy home. Why wait? It's fun for you and the puppy. You immediately start to request things of your puppy and reward her, rather than letting her decide what she wants to do (which will inevitably get her into trouble).

Here are a few tips for lure-and-reward training:

➤ Always practice lure-and-reward training when your puppy is hungry.

➤ When your pup is following the lure (the piece of food), don't say anything. If you talk, you'll distract your puppy from the task at hand.

121

Joel demonstrates how easy lure-and-reward training can be by teaching this pup the Stand while sitting in a chair.

➤ Make sure the pup is paying attention to the lure before you move it, and then move it very slowly.

➤ Hold the lure with two fingers and your thumb. You want the pup to see, smell and be able to touch the lure, but not to be able to take it away.

➤ At first, use your puppy's regular dry dog food as a lure. If she loses interest, move on to something more exciting, such as tiny pieces of bland cheese or low-fat meat slices. If you use anything besides the pup's dry dog food, just flavor the dry food with the cheese after the pup catches on and gradually switch back to the dry dog food.

➤ If you try all of these tips and still can't get lure-and-reward training to work, find someone skilled in this type of training to help you.

Reward Training

For most puppies and dogs, lure-and-reward training is the best way to teach your dog to follow commands that are easily lured. But some behaviors or commands aren't lurable. How do you use a moving

See how the puppy is paying attention to Joel while he gets the lure from his pocket?

piece of food to make your dog yawn, for example, or for housetraining? You don't. For these types of behaviors, reward training is best.

How can you use reward training to get your dog to perform a behavior on command? Suppose your dog yawns when she gets up from her nap, and you think it would be great to get your dog to yawn every time you say, "Bored?" The first step is to let your dog know that, whenever she hears a specific word or sound, she will get rewarded. The reward could be a verbal "Yes" followed by a treat or a click from a *clicker* followed by a treat. Practice this whenever you can. Say "Yes" or click the clicker throughout the day, and then offer your dog a treat afterwards.

Trainer Tidbits

Using pieces of your dog's regular food for training is the best way to avoid excess calories. Take the training allotment out of your dog's regular ration of food.

As soon as your dog figures out that when you say "Yes" or click the clicker, she gets a treat, she'll start coming to you when she hears the praise or click, looking for her treat. Now you can begin to associate the praise/reward with a behavior.

123

To teach your dog to yawn on command, you will need to wait for her to wake up (knowing her typical schedule will make this a lot easier). Whenever your dog wakes up and yawns, say "Yes" or click the clicker, and then give her a treat. After you practice this for awhile, your dog will start yawning more often because she has figured out that yawning results in a reward. You may be amused by how much she yawns!

Lab Lingo

A **clicker** is a simple device that makes a click when you press it. It is a plastic box with a thin metal tab in it that makes the clicking sound. You can buy them in some pet stores, and Joel says they used to come in Cracker Jack boxes. (Sort of dates Joel, doesn't it?)

When you are willing to bet $100 that your dog is going to yawn (by watching your dog, you'll learn the signs), begin to say, "Bored?" just before she yawns. When she does yawn, say your "Yes" or click your clicker, and then give her her reward. Keep practicing! Before you know it, your dog will be yawning on command.

Lab Basic Training

Reward training is the best way to approach the elimination of undesirable behaviors, as well as the addition of desirable behaviors. But knowing some other techniques will help, too. The following sections describe some of the most common behaviors in puppies that we humans tend to dislike and how you can teach your dog better ways to spend her time.

Whenever your pup is behaving unacceptably, the right thing to do is train her or do a time-out (put her in her doggy den). Punishment hurts the relationship and isn't very effective. Letting your pup continue the behavior will make it worse and hurt the relationship, as well.

Barking

"Help, Joel! My puppy barks!" "Joel, what do I do? My dog barks!" Well, of course she does. Dogs bark. When you were a child and first began to figure out that you could communicate verbally, did your mother shriek, "Doctor! Help! My child talks!" Of course not! She probably bragged about you, proudly declaring, "My child can talk!"

Talking and barking aren't exactly the same, of course. But people talk and dogs bark for some of the same reasons. Sometimes your dog barks to communicate something to you. For example, your puppy may bark when you leave her alone in her doggy den. She is used to spending most of her time with her littermates, and it is perfectly normal for her to protest, "Hey! Where is everybody? I'm lonely!"

As much as you love your puppy, however, you must teach her how to be alone some of the time. The best way to do this is to ignore the barking. This is both good management and good education. You took her out to relieve herself before you put her in the den, so you know she isn't barking for that reason. Let her bark. Behaviors that are not rewarded decrease in frequency. Puppies and dogs are smart enough to know that if the barking doesn't work, it is better to conserve energy for more important things. It may take your dog a little while to figure this out, but she will figure it out eventually.

When your dog does stop barking, she'll take a nap. Be sure to be there when she wakes up so you can take her out of her den and outside before she starts barking. She will have to go out, and you want to make sure you take her out, but you don't want to combine this necessary action with an inadvertent reward for barking.

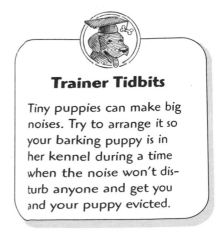

Trainer Tidbits

Tiny puppies can make big noises. Try to arrange it so your barking puppy is in her kennel during a time when the noise won't disturb anyone and get you and your puppy evicted.

Some folks confine their pups only when they leave the house. This usually results in a puppy or dog that will bark if she ever does have to be confined when the owners are home. It makes housetraining more difficult than it has to be, and it takes away a great management tool to prevent mouthing, jumping up and other behaviors. Teach your pup that it is normal to be confined in

125

her doggy den occasionally when the family is home. It doesn't mean she will be confined all the time. She can be out whenever she will be watched so that she doesn't get into trouble.

Play-Biting

Play-biting is normal puppy behavior and the method by which puppies explore their worlds. Puppies play by grabbing each other with their teeth; such biting isn't a result of aggression or fear. If you watch your puppy when she is play-biting, you'll see that she is relaxed, not fearful or aggressive. She's having fun!

Trainer Tidbits

In the wild, puppies and dogs have two peak activity periods: dawn and dusk. These correspond with the times when you tend to be home: in the morning and in the evening after work. You will probably notice a lot more play-biting during your puppy's peak activity period. Be prepared to tell her "Off" and then either train her or do a time-out (put her in her den).

However, just because play-biting is normal doesn't mean you should let your puppy bite anything she wants. Most humans find play-biting obnoxious at best and painful at worst. Yet you must avoid punishing this behavior. You do not want to take a puppy that is playing and turn her into a fearful or aggressive dog.

A two-step approach to play-biting is usually the best approach. First, teach your puppy that human flesh is very sensitive by saying "Ouch!" sharply every time your pup's teeth make contact with your skin. Every puppy/human pair requires a different tone and volume that will be effective for getting the puppy's attention. You may need to experiment to find yours. Your goal is to startle and momentarily stop the play-biting. It is important to understand that you will be doing this for weeks and that you will probably not see immediate results as far as a decrease in the frequency and the force of the play-biting. Be patient. Over a period of weeks, you'll see a change.

You are teaching your puppy bite inhibition, a fancy term meaning you are teaching your dog not to bite too hard. All dogs will bite as adults if they are given the right (or sometimes the wrong) reason. Teaching them bite inhibition can avert disaster.

The second step is being able to tell your pup not to play-bite even before she does it. You accomplish this by teaching her the "Take it" and the "Off" commands:

1. Hold a small quantity of her dry food in your hand. Say "Take it" as you give her one piece.

2. Close the rest of the dog food in your fist and hold your fist right in front of her nose, about an inch or two away. Say "Off" in a sweet and gentle voice. She will mouth or paw at your hand to try to get the food.

3. Wait until she stops mouthing or pawing for three to five seconds. Then say "Take it" again and give her another piece.

4. Continue this process until her meal is done. By doing this, you are teaching her that "Off" means not to touch. After you see her responding well to this for a few days, you can start to tell her "Off" when she looks like she is going to play-bite you.

Housetraining

If you followed the management advice for housetraining in Chapter 7, your pup may already be housetrained. Lucky you! If not, however, have no fear. You can complete the process now.

The goal is to have your puppy at the preselected elimination spot when she has to relieve herself. These times tend to be:

➤ Whenever she wakes up

➤ After she drinks water (the younger the pup, the sooner after drinking)

➤ After she eats (the younger the pup, the sooner after eating)

➤ Whenever anything exciting happens (like five minutes of training)

➤ Whenever you play with her for five minutes (training is play; do it whenever you can)

➤ If she has not been out for awhile

➤ First thing in the morning

➤ Last thing at night

Trainer Tidbits

A good way to make puppy duty a family affair is to make a rule: Whoever gets up first in the morning has the job of taking the puppy out to relieve herself. Whoever is the last person to go to bed at night has the job of taking the puppy out to relieve herself.

Trainer Tidbits

If your puppy doesn't relieve herself within five minutes of being outside, take her back in the house. Train her if you can, watching her like a hawk, or return her to her den (watch her in there, too). The next time you take her out, she'll probably relieve herself right away. If she doesn't, that only means she can hold it longer than you thought.

Always take your puppy outside on a leash. It is very important that she learn to potty on a leash. You want to be able to take her with you on vacation and your other travels. Stopping at a rest area for both of you to potty can be very frustrating if she hasn't learned to potty on leash. And you certainly don't want her running loose near the interstate!

Just before you take her through the door to the outside, say "Let's go outside." Walk directly to the potty area. Stand there and do not interact with your pup. Watch her carefully. When she starts to give signs that she is going to urinate or defecate, say "Go potty," and then while the urine or feces is flowing, gently praise her: "Good potty!" (Not too loudly. You don't want to scare her into stopping!) Make sure you give her an extra minute or two in case she needs to go more.

When your pup is back inside, don't forget: One responsible person must watch her 100 percent of the time, or she should be in her doggy den. When Joel tells this to his clients, they usually nod their heads, "Yes, yes, 100 percent of the time." Joel likes to stop them and explain that housetraining a puppy requires full-time attention. We can't emphasize this enough! It isn't easy to be so vigilant, but it is by far the fastest and easiest way of getting your pup housetrained. If she never has a chance to have an accident in the house, she'll learn very quickly.

Also, remember to say "Let's go outside," just as you open the door to take the pup out. She will soon catch on to the meaning of these words. While you are watching your pup in the house, if she starts to sniff or circle or goes to the door, put on her leash immediately and take her outside at once. You and your puppy are doing a great job!

If your pup starts to squat in the house, say "Go outside" with a slight edge in your voice, and then whisk her outside at once. If she has done anything in the house at this time, or if you find a little puddle or pile that you didn't see her make, wait until after you put her in her den to clean it up. Remember, punishment would be pointless. She obviously hasn't learned where her potty location is yet, and it was your job to take her outside on time. Don't blame her, and don't punish yourself. Just do your best to avoid a future incident through better management. Don't forget to clean up the mishap with a good enzyme cleaner to eliminate the smell that might signal your dog to eliminate in the same spot again.

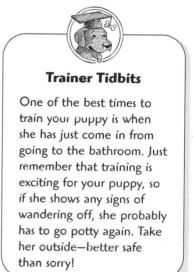

Trainer Tidbits

One of the best times to train your puppy is when she has just come in from going to the bathroom. Just remember that training is exciting for your puppy, so if she shows any signs of wandering off, she probably has to go potty again. Take her outside—better safe than sorry!

Don't worry, we have lots more to tell you about how to train your dog to do what you want her to do and not to do what you don't want her to do. Just keep reading. A subject this good takes two chapters.

The Least You Need to Know

➤ Socializing your puppy, or getting her used to lots of different kinds of people, is an important way to teach your puppy to be friendly rather than shy, fearful or aggressive.

➤ Lure-and-reward training is a great way to teach your dog certain simple commands such as sit, stand and down.

➤ Reward training is another great training method designed to reward your dog for doing the right thing rather than punishing her for doing the wrong thing.

➤ Using a few simple techniques, you can teach your dog not to bark when in her doggy den, not to play-bite and how to be housetrained.

Chapter 10

Educating Your Lab, Part Two

In This Chapter

➤ Teach your dog not to chew things he shouldn't and not to jump up on people

➤ Teach your dog to sit, stand, lie down, take things from your hand, leave things alone and come when called

➤ Hiring a trainer or behavioral consultant

You aren't done training your dog yet—not even close. In fact, training your dog and giving him new things to learn and do are a life-long process. But we've still got more to tell you about the education part of the MRE system. Positive training does more than help you with barking, play-biting and housetraining. It can also help you teach your dog what he can and can't chew, not to jump up on people, how to listen to you and a whole range of typical dog commands: sit, stand, down, take it, off, come, long sit, long down, walking on a loose lead and heel. Are you ready? Take your pup out for a potty break, bring him back in, get your treats ready and let's go!

More Good Behavior

If you have been consistent in your management of your new puppy and especially if you have also been trying some lure-and-reward training, your puppy is behaving better and better. He has more to learn, however, and positive training is the key.

Chewing

Chewing is perfectly normal puppy and dog behavior. Puppies and dogs chew for many reasons, such as:

➤ Teething

➤ Boredom

➤ Exploring a new object

➤ Stress

➤ Because it's fun

It makes sense to teach your puppy or dog what to chew rather than not to chew at all. To do this, you need to use chew toys. The best kind to use is a sturdy, hollow, rubber one. Some puppies/dogs will chew these toys the first time they get one. If your puppy or dog doesn't seem interested in chewing his toy, you can stuff it with tasty treats, which will certainly pique his interest.

Trainer Tidbits

Joel's favorite chew toy to use is the Kong chew toy, a virtually indestructible object perfect for the bois-terous chew sessions for which Labs are notorious. Joel's friend Jean Donaldson has an excellent section in her CD-ROM, "Dogs Behaving Badly," which shows you exactly how to stuff a Kong.

When you stuff a hollow chew toy, the idea is to put in something desir-able that your puppy or dog will have to work for to get out. Wedging in a hard treat such as a big dog bis-cuit works well. Then put in a few smaller pieces that your dog can get out with some work. Last, put in a small handful of his dry food that will fall out as soon as he touches the chew toy. You can also add a small amount of peanut butter, if neces-sary, for an even bigger incentive.

After you have a chew toy that defi-nitely interests your dog, hold it in your hand and say, "Chew your toy," and then give him the toy. Praise

A stuffed chew toy can keep your puppy occupied for some time and can teach him that this is a good thing to chew.

him for chewing the toy. By teaching him to chew his toy every day, you will help him develop a strong preference for chewing his chew toy rather than the furniture, your shoes, your children's toys or whatever else you would prefer didn't make contact with doggy teeth. Always make sure you have a chew toy handy (it pays to keep several around the house). If your dog begins to chew anything else, say "Chew your toy!" Then make sure he does.

Keep the stuffed chew toys for when your puppy or dog is out of his den. When your dog is in his den, a regular, unstuffed chew toy will do for when he has the urge to chew.

Jumping Up

Most people don't like it when a dog jumps up on them, although with a puppy, the behavior is easy to forgive. You may even feel flattered. "Oh look, he likes me! Good dog!" Silly human! You just reinforced a behavior that won't be so cute when your dog weighs 75 pounds and comes barreling across the kitchen to greet you.

Puppies and dogs jump up on people because they want to look into our faces. Dogs can tell what mood we are in and whether we are in the mood for fun by looking at our expressions. But the poor dogs

133

are way down there on the floor! You can't blame them for jumping up to get a better look. After all, they can't ask you, "How are you feeling today? Are you going to play with me or would you rather I left you alone just now?"

Jumping up is another one of those normal doggy behaviors that you can manage through positive training. It helps to look at it from a human point of view. Imagine coming up to a good friend and putting your arm around him or taking his hand and giving it a friendly squeeze. Now imagine that in return, he slapped you in the face. That would probably hurt your relationship. Would you do such a thing to your best canine friend? To your dog, jumping up on you is the equivalent of a friendly hug. Don't punish your dog for being friendly!

That doesn't mean you can't teach your dog, however. Little puppies almost have to jump up so they can see what is going on. Most people will pet a little puppy that puts his little paws on their legs, wags his tail and looks up with love in his eyes. Six months later, someone will be advising you to knee your dog in his chest or try other silly, unpleasant or even nasty things.

But you don't have to solve the problem in six months. If you put a buckle collar and a leash on your pup, you can make sure he doesn't jump up on people. You can get him to sit first, and then the person he wants to get to know can gently stroke his chest in a calm manner. If you practice this management and training method, you will wind up with a dog that sits to greet people. If sitting gets him the reward of lots of attention and petting, he'll be glad to sit for you and anyone else who will give him affection.

"My Lab Won't Listen!"

As a trainer, Joel hears a lot of people complain that their Lab won't listen. Do you have the impression that your puppy or dog doesn't listen to you? Before you throw your hands up in despair, ask yourself just what you want him to listen to. It would be wonderful and convenient if dogs understood English (or any human language). Then we could just explain to them what we wanted them to do. That's what you do when human children finally learn to speak, right?

Of course, puppies and dogs don't understand English, but they do read you in other ways. They interpret your facial expressions, your body language, the tone of your voice and some of the words you say, after you have carefully taught them the meaning of those words through training. Dogs get to know you and how you tend to act in different situations. They watch you for cues. They want to please you, so they are paying attention. You can take advantage of all this attention by learning how to communicate in a way your dog understands. And as we've been saying all along, your dog understands rewards.

Command Central

When we say your dog can't understand English, we mean he'll never be able to understand English in the complex way humans understand it. You can teach him the meaning of certain words, however. These words, often called commands, are most effectively taught as requests. Why command when a request will do? A request is all you need, if you ask in just the right way. You remember the old saying: You catch more bees with honey than with vinegar!

Sit

Although we described how to teach your dog some basic commands using lure-and-reward training, we'll review the methods here because they are important. "Sit" is probably the first command that comes to mind when people envision training their dogs.

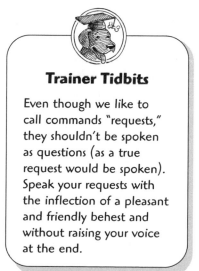

Trainer Tidbits

Even though we like to call commands "requests," they shouldn't be spoken as questions (as a true request would be spoken). Speak your requests with the inflection of a pleasant and friendly behest and without raising your voice at the end.

To teach your dog to sit using lure-and-reward training, first make sure your dog is well rested and hungry. Using his dry dog food as a lure (or another more-tempting treat such as low-fat cheese sandwich slices if dry food isn't enough of a lure), grasp a piece of food with your first two fingers and your thumb. When your pup is standing, hold the piece of food directly in front of his mouth, almost touching his lips. Very

135

slowly raise the piece of food so it moves in an arch from in front of his lips to slightly above his head. Most pups will follow the food with their noses and will wind up with their rears on the ground. That is a sit! Well done!

After you do this a few times, you can add the verbal request:

1. Say "Sit" in a sweet tone of voice.

2. Lure your dog into the sit position with the food.

3. Say "Yes" in a sweet tone of voice.

4. Give your dog the piece of food.

Vet Alert

Some people dislike the idea of training with food, claiming that praise is adequate reward for any dog. Sure, praise is nice. You like it when your boss praises you for a job well done. But a raise is a lot bigger motivation, isn't it? Your dog loves praise, but when you back it up with a little gastronomic "raise," you'll be speaking your dog's language!

Stand

Lots of dogs pick up the sit command fairly easily, but many dog owners don't think to teach the stand command. The "Stand" command is handy when you want to groom your dog, when you want him to get ready to go out or when you want to try a new training exercise.

When your pup is sitting, hold the lure so it is almost touching his lips, and then draw it forward, parallel with the ground and far enough so the pup has to stand up to get it. Make sure you do not lower or raise the treat. When the pup stands up to get the treat, he is doing a stand. When he's got it, add the verbal request:

1. Say "Stand" in a sweet tone of voice.

2. Lure your dog into the stand position with the food.

3. Say "Yes" in a sweet tone of voice.

4. Give your dog the piece of food.

Down

"Down" is a great command when you want your dog to lie at your feet and behave himself. Everyone will be impressed with how well your dog is controlled, but you and your dog both know you have a mutual understanding about when to play and when to lie down and relax.

When your pup is sitting, hold the lure directly under his nose. Slowly lower the lure straight down to the ground under his nose. Do not move the lure forward. Most pups will follow the lure down and get into the down position. If your pup does not lie down after a few tries, make sure you are moving the lure as slowly as possible. If he still doesn't lie down, you may have to move the lure slightly towards him or slightly away from him. Experiment and see if you can find a place that works.

If you still can't lure your dog into a down, move on to other commands and then go back to the down on another day after he has a better idea about what it means to follow the lure (in other words, it means reward). If it still doesn't work, seek out a good, positive dog trainer or canine behavior consultant to help you.

Once your dog has the idea, add the verbal request:

1. Say "Down" in a sweet tone of voice.

2. Lure your dog into the down position with the food.

3. Say "Yes" in a sweet tone of voice.

4. Give your dog the piece of food.

Take It and Off

"Take it" and "Off" are two wonderful commands you can use to teach your dog to take something from your hand or not to touch something.

To teach your dog to take anything from your hand, use the take it command. You can also use the take it command to ask your dog to pick up anything off the floor. Drop your keys? Ask your dog to "Take it!" Labs love to carry anything around in their mouths. That's what they were bred to do. Use your imagination, and you will have

137

a companion to help carry things for you. Remember a dog with something in his mouth cannot pick up a forbidden object.

You can manage many normal doggy behaviors with the off command. Play-biting, mouthing, jumping up, picking up forbidden objects (such as people food), nose prodding, licking and other behaviors all respond well to a properly timed off command.

You can teach your pup the take it and off commands together. Take a small handful of the pup's dry food. Say, "Take it," and give your pup one piece of dry food. Close the rest of the food in your fist and say, "Off," in a nice tone of voice. The pup will probably lick, gnaw or paw at your hand. Such temptation so close at hand! But stick with the technique.

Hold your hand steady and wait for him to stop touching your hand for three to five seconds. Then say, "Take it," and give him one piece of food. This process works almost like magic. The pup learns that if he stops touching you when you say, "Off," he will get the take it command and then a food reward. And he learns this amazing feat without a single harsh word from you.

Come

The "Come" command is among the most important. If you can get your dog to come on command, you may someday be able to avert danger or even save his life. A dog that comes to you is also much easier to manage, and that improves your relationship.

Teaching your pup to come to you using the lure-and-reward method is fun and easy. Make sure your pup is hungry and rested and that you are holding a desirable treat. (Your pup's regular dry food should be your first choice.) Train your dog to come in a safe location where there is nothing more rewarding than you and the treat (no tempting squirrels to chase, kids to play with or other dogs to visit with).

Hold the treat with two fingers and your thumb, with the back of your hand resting against your thigh, near the centerline of your body, with the food towards the pup. Smile at the pup and say, "Come," in a sweet tone of voice with just a hint of excitement (don't overdo it, but don't sound bored, either). If your pup doesn't come running over to you, look down at the food treat and wait for one minute. Almost all hungry puppies or dogs will come running over to you at once. If not, you might show him the treat. If he still isn't interested, try a more-rewarding treat.

If he still refuses to come, squat down (or sit in a chair you have placed right behind you). Your pup will be much more likely to come to you when you get down to his level. Wait another minute. If he still hasn't come, walk away from him. When he follows you, lure him into a sit and reward him while touching his collar and saying, "Yes," just as if he had come right away.

When the pup does come to you, slowly lure him into a sit, give him the treat with your right hand and slowly caress his neck with your left hand, very near his collar. Say "Yes" as you do this. If your puppy or dog gets away from you in an unsafe area, calling him to you will become very important. You don't want him to shy away when you reach for his collar because you will need to do this to get him on his lead and under control. So always gently put your hand on your dog's collar when he comes to you.

We will work on speed later, but remember, getting him to come is the important job at this point, even if it takes a minute or two. Every time you get him to come and he gets rewarded, he will be more likely to come the next time.

Trainer Tidbits

After going through reward-based training, if your dog does not obey a request the first time it is asked, he probably doesn't understand your request. If you repeat the request before the dog has a chance to do it, you may condition your dog to obey the second or fifth command. Instead, train that request in a positive manner until he wants to do it the first time.

Long Sit

A long sit is a sit that your dog holds for an extended period of time. In Joel's experience, people tend to use the stay command with a puppy, punishing him as soon as he moves. But this is hardly fair! Your pup doesn't know what "Stay" means.

139

Instead, use this nice and very positive way to get your pup to stay in the sit position. After you have taught your dog to sit, you can start teaching him that "Sit" means he should remain in a sit position until you give him another request or a release. Before you try the long sit, make sure your dog knows how to do the sit command well.

Here's how to train your dog to do a long sit:

1. Begin with a small handful of treats in your left hand behind your back. Always have one treat in your right hand when you are ready to give your pup a reward. Remember, you have taught your pup to follow a treat with his nose and body (this is what the lure-and-reward method is based upon). If you have more than one treat in your right hand and you give him one and then move your hand away while still holding a treat, he will follow your hand. It's what you've taught him to do!

2. Give your dog the sit command, and then after a few seconds, say, "Good sit," and give your pup one treat.

3. Have your pup sit several more times, gradually increasing the amount of time between when your dog sits and when you say, "Good sit." Give him the reward immediately after saying, "Good sit."

You will probably want to work up to a two- or three-minute long sit. Use the long sit while waiting to cross a road or while talking to a neighbor on your daily walks. If you want your puppy or dog to remain in one place for a long time, use the long down command, which is more comfortable for your dog.

Long Down

The long down is like the long sit. It means your dog will lie down and wait for a long period until you release him or give him another request. The long down is taught the same way the long sit is taught. You say "Down," wait a few seconds, and then say "Good down" and offer the reward. Gradually increase the time between saying "Down" and saying "Good down." This method is so much better than commands taught with reprimands or worse punishments when the pup gets out of position.

Greg Goebel

Greg Goebel

Greg Goebel

Greg Goebel

Philip Steinkraus

Philip Steinkraus

Philip Steinkraus

When a puppy is rewarded for doing something you want and doing it well, he'll be happy to comply, and you'll be happy with the results.

You can work up to thirty minutes or more on the long down. Joel uses this request with his pups when he is at the computer working. They will happily remain lying next to him for as long as he likes. They often gaze up at Joel fondly, and he can see them thinking, "Joel is going to give me another treat, sometime."

You can use any release word you want for the long sit and the long down. Joel likes to say, "Go play," and toss a treat. Remember the release word is just that. It means your dog can go do whatever he likes. If your puppy or dog wants to keep lying next to you, that's his choice. You should feel flattered!

Trainer Tidbits

While being trained in the long sit, your pup may get out of position. If he gets back into position within thirty seconds, wait five seconds and then say, "Good sit," and reward him. Make sure you wait, or he may learn that getting up and then getting back down is what you want. If your pup doesn't get back into position within thirty seconds, say, "Sit," and lure him back into position.

141

Walking on a Loose Lead

One of the biggest problems dog owners have is walking their dogs on a loose leash. You can see puppies and dogs pulling their owners down any street. Why do dogs do this? Because it works. When they are young, they pull on their leads, and their owners go where they want to go. What a great system! Why would a pup stop?

Joel devised a simple method for training dogs to walk on a loose leash years ago. He calls it the Zen method of walking on lead. Follow these steps:

1. Stand outside with a buckle collar and a 6-foot lead attached to your dog, whom you have put into a sit.

2. Pick a path that is a straight line leading to some landmark (a tree, for example), and start walking towards it.

3. If the lead is slack, continue to walk. If the lead becomes tight, stop and become a tree. "Becoming a tree" means you stand with your knees slightly bent and the end of the lead (the loop) in both hands at your waist. You are going to stand there until the puppy sits, lies down or gives you slack in the lead. Then you start walking again.

The logic behind this method is that the dog is getting continuous positive reinforcement by keeping slack in the lead (he gets to walk with you). If he tightens the lead, he gets continuous negative reinforcement (it's no fun to be tied to a tree-like owner; it's boring).

If your dog lags behind, just keep walking. He will almost always decide to go with you. If you find yourself dragging him across the ground, change the area or direction you are walking. If he still won't go with you, try using a tasty lure.

If you can't seem to make this method work, either because you can't get yourself to be a tree for a longer time than your dog can wait or because you can't help dragging your dog in frustration, stop and consult with a positive dog trainer or canine behavior consultant who can demonstrate the right way to teach your dog to walk on a loose lead.

Heeling

After you have taught your dog sit, down and stand using the lure-and-reward method, you are ready to teach him to heel off-lead. Yes, off-lead! You do not need a lead when the puppy wants to work with you. He wants to work with you because you are very rewarding!

Hold one treat in your left hand in front of your dog's nose after you have him sitting on your left side. Say "(Your dog's name), heel." Then step off on your left foot, take four-and-a-half steps, lure the puppy into a sit, say, "Yes," and give the pup a treat. If you have trouble getting the pup to go with you, make sure he is hungry and use a more-attractive treat. Keep trying. Eventually he'll figure out what you want and be happy to oblige (and to follow that treat).

Vet Alert

Practice heeling off-lead in a safe location. No busy streets or distractions! Keep the conditions safe for your dog.

Finding a Good Trainer

Sometimes, your dog just won't behave the way you expect, no matter how closely you follow the training instructions. Whether your dog has had a difficult past or is just very independent, you may need to consider hiring a good dog trainer or canine behavior consultant who uses positive methods. An expert can demonstrate techniques and help you to establish an effective line of communication with your dog.

Finding a good trainer or behavior consultant may be more difficult than finding a good veterinarian. Veterinarians are licensed and have a well-defined education. Dog trainers and canine behavior consultants are not licensed (although some are certified), and you cannot be sure what kind of education they have.

When looking for a trainer or canine behavior consultant, find someone who has these characteristics:

➤ Understands how dogs learn. This well-defined science is not in the realm of speculation.

➤ Will train you to train your puppy or dog in a positive and non-confrontational manner.

➤ Is familiar with and uses lure-and-reward training and/or clicker training.

➤ Understands that 8-week-old puppies are fully capable of learning all of the requests that will make them good companions.

➤ Understands that you need help managing your pup and keeping him out of trouble while you train him in a positive manner.

➤ Is familiar with the work of pioneers in the field of positive reinforcement training, such as Dr. Ian Dunbar and Karen Pryor.

➤ Is a member of a professional organization, such as the Association of Pet Dog Trainers.

➤ Offers private lessons and/or classes.

➤ Can offer references. Make sure you check these references. References from veterinarians are ideal, and your vet may be able to refer you to a trainer or behavior consultant.

Trainer Tidbits

Joel is often amazed when people say they have taken their dog to an obedience class but don't know the name of the trainer. You know the names of your children's teachers, don't you? Develop a relationship with your dog's trainer to better develop the relationship between you and your dog.

Obedience classes are less costly than a private trainer. There are benefits to both methods. Many behaviors are best dealt with by a qualified canine behavior consultant who can come to your home and help you with housetraining, jumping up, chewing, play-biting and other issues. If your dog has exhibited any aggressive or fearful behavior, you will certainly want to find a well-qualified behavior consultant who has a good record dealing with these problems.

Ignore trainers and books that suggest you wait until your puppy is 6 months old before you can expect much. What a waste of precious learning and bonding time! These sources often advocate the use of choke collars and other punishments, and this age requirement is given only because such harsh punishments might be dangerous for young puppies.

Does Your Lab Need a Behavior Consultant?

If you aren't sure whether your dog and your situation warrant professional guidance, ask yourself the following questions. If you answer yes to even one, you could benefit from a professional behavior consultant or animal behaviorist:

Vet Alert

When looking for a trainer, always inquire into the methods used before you sign up. Sadly, abusive training methods do work with some dogs, so some trainers continue to use outdated, punishment-based methods.

➤ Have you had your puppy or dog for more than a few months and is he still urinating and/or defecating in the house?

➤ Is your dog having behavior problems that are getting worse?

➤ Are you seeing any signs of fearful behavior? For example, has your dog become afraid of something, such as the mailman, delivery men or family members, that he wasn't afraid of in the past? Or maybe he just looks afraid. You are the expert when it comes to your dog's behavior.

➤ Are you seeing any submissive urination or urination due to excitement?

➤ Is your dog behaving aggressively? Is he barking aggressively at people, growling at you or biting?

➤ Are you having serious problems managing your dog's behavior?

➤ Are you finding yourself wanting to punish your puppy or dog?

➤ Is your relationship with your dog getting worse?

➤ Is your dog risking his life (and/or your possessions) by indiscriminate chewing?

Calling a professional does not mean you have failed at anything. Good professional behavior consultants and animal behaviorists have years of experience in handling problems that you may never have encountered before. They can make your job much easier and your relationship with your dog much better. So why not pick up that phone today? If you follow the advice in this book and the advice given to you by a professional dog trainer or behavior consultant, your dog's behavior should continue to improve until he is practically perfect!

Remember that behavior is always changing, either improving or getting worse depending on what is happening in the dog's life. If you have followed the advice of using rewards to improve your dog's behavior, chances are, the behavior will improve. If some behaviors are getting worse, you need to work specifically on those behaviors. Be vigilant and committed. Dogs, like humans, need to learn as long as they are alive. Keep it fun and keep it up! We're right here with you.

The Least You Need to Know

➤ By using reward training, you can teach your pup not to chew things he isn't allowed to chew and not to jump on people.

➤ Lure-and-reward training is the best way to teach your puppy to sit, stand, lie down, take something from your hand, leave something alone and come to you.

➤ Don't be afraid to hire a good dog trainer or canine behavior consultant who uses positive training methods.

Part 3

Keeping Your Lab Healthy

That little puppy may be the picture of health, but keeping your Lab healthy takes some care, including preventive measures and plenty of preparation. In this section, we'll begin by showing you how a Lab is "built." Although Labs are generally an extremely robust breed, we'll warn you about some of the health problems some Labs may experience.

We'll go on to recommend some preventive approaches to health care, from an appropriate vaccination schedule to a great diet and plenty of exercise. We'll also help you to prepare for any emergencies by assembling your own canine first aid kit.

Last, we'll help you to choose a practically perfect veterinarian, and even make suggestions for other professionals to include on your Lab's health care team. Although choosing a great vet involves more than just flipping through the Yellow Pages, it is an effort that will pay off time and again over the course of your Lab's life.

Chapter 11

Healthy Lab 101

> ### In This Chapter
>
> ➤ Name that dog part
>
> ➤ Know your Lab's genetic tendencies
>
> ➤ What to feed your dog (and how much and how often)
>
> ➤ Keeping your dog fit through exercise

Now that you've brought home your practically perfect pet, you'll want to keep her healthy. Maintaining a healthy Labrador Retriever is a relatively easy task, especially if you focus on preventive maintenance. Health problems, just like behavior problems, are a lot easier to prevent than to fix!

Labrador Retrievers are a particularly healthy and robust breed with few genetic abnormalities (although genetic problems do occasionally crop up in any breed). Labs are the prototypical medium-sized dogs and are often the breed used to illustrate a typical dog in all kinds of books, magazines and other publications. Of course, your Lab is anything but typical—she's special! And you want to know everything about her.

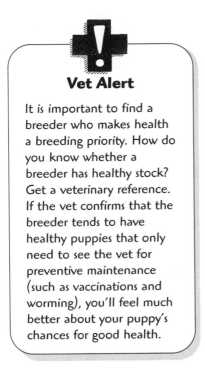

Vet Alert

It is important to find a breeder who makes health a breeding priority. How do you know whether a breeder has healthy stock? Get a veterinary reference. If the vet confirms that the breeder tends to have healthy puppies that only need to see the vet for preventive maintenance (such as vaccinations and worming), you'll feel much better about your puppy's chances for good health.

Lab at a Glance

When you look at your Lab, what do you see? You see those loving eyes and that playful demeanor, but do you know the signs of good health? Are you familiar with basic canine anatomy? And do you know what your dog's genetic tendencies are in terms of health? You'll be better able to maintain and preserve your dog's health if you know what to expect, what looks and feels normal and what signs to watch for that might indicate a potential problem.

Each day during your dog's grooming session, move your hands over her coat. Get to know how your Lab feels. If you are familiar with your Lab's normal condition, you'll recognize any changes, such as lumps, bumps, dry skin patches, hair loss, weight loss, weight gain or sores. The sooner you alert your vet to problems such as these, the better they can be resolved.

As you get to know your dog, you may wonder what all those body parts are called. Knowing a little bit about canine anatomy helps you to know your dog better and also to be able to talk to your vet in a more-specific and informative way. Let's start with a mini anatomy lesson, so you'll know a little more about what makes a dog a dog.

Anatomy of a Labrador Retriever

Do you know a hock from a stifle? The withers from the croup? Check out the illustration on the tearcard at the front of the book for a complete rundown of the body parts of your Labrador Retriever:

➤ The skull consists of the bone components of the head.

➤ The crest is the upper rear arched portion of the neck, just below the occiput (base of the skull).

➤ The neck is the area between the head and the shoulders.

➤ The withers are the highest points of the shoulder blades.

➤ The back is the long plane between shoulder blades and hips.

➤ The loin is the area between the back and end of the rib cage and the croup, or pelvic girdle.

➤ The croup is that portion of the body above the hind legs and extending from the loin to the base of the tail and the buttock area.

➤ The hock joint is the lower joint on the rear leg between the lower thigh and the rear pastern.

➤ The stifle is the knee joint located between the upper and lower thigh.

➤ The elbow is the joint between the upper arm and forearm.

➤ The dewclaw is a vestigial claw on the pastern of the front legs; it's often removed on puppies.

➤ The pastern is the region between the wrist and forefoot.

➤ The wrist is the joint connecting the forearm and the pastern.

➤ The forearm is the region between the elbow and the wrist.

➤ The shoulder is the shoulder blade, or scapula, and associated muscles.

➤ The muzzle is the foreface or forward portion of the upper and lower jaw and the nose portion of the head, in other words, the portion of the head in front of the eyes.

➤ The stop is the dividing point between the muzzle and the skull. It marks a change in the profile line between the muzzle and skull.

Labrador Retriever Health in Brief

Because there are so many Labrador Retrievers, breeders have a large gene pool to draw from. That translates into healthier dogs.

151

Knowledgeable breeders do health checks and everything else they can to avoid genetic disorders. However, because breeding is not only a relatively new science but also an art, it isn't possible to completely avoid all genetic problems. Science is continually developing better tests to pinpoint genetic diseases, sometimes before the dog shows any symptoms. Yet there still is much work in this area to be done.

Lab Lore

Labrador Retrievers come in all sizes, from very small (around 35 pounds) to very big (over 100 pounds). Although the breed standard (the standard used to judge purebred show dogs) calls for a dog between 21½ and 24½ inches and weighing between 55 and 80 pounds, that doesn't mean your practically perfect Lab will necessarily fall into that standard. Most breeders would agree that form follows function, and because Labs do so many diverse jobs, it only makes sense that they come in many different sizes. A friendly, eager and intelligent character is a more-consistent quality of the Labrador Retriever than size.

As we said, Labs tend to be very healthy, but some genetic disorders do occasionally occur. These are some of the more-common genetic disorders in Labrador Retrievers:

➤ **Hip Dysplasia.** This is the most common orthopedic problem in Labs (and in many larger dogs). Although not congenital (it isn't present at birth), hip dysplasia is probably due to a combination of genetic and environmental factors. If your dog develops hip dysplasia (the condition can be seen on an x-ray), she may suffer no symptoms at all. Or she may eventually experience severe pain and even lameness. Some Labs require no treatment, but if your Lab develops hip dysplasia and does require treatment, many excellent management strategies, treatments and surgical options exist.

➤ **Progressive Retinal Atrophy (PRA).** This degenerative eye disorder eventually results in your dog becoming blind. A board-certified canine ophthalmologist can examine your dog's eyes if you suspect she is having any vision problems. PRA is a genetic problem involving a recessive gene. If a puppy receives the gene from both parents, she will develop PRA. If she receives the gene from only one parent, she will be a carrier and should not be bred to another Lab that is also a carrier. The location of the gene that involves PRA has been determined in Labs, and a blood test should be developed in the near future to determine whether your dog is affected, a carrier or clear. Yearly tests are necessary to maintain a clear status that can be registered with CERF, the Canine Eye Registration Foundation. If you buy your Lab from a breeder who is diligent about eye testing, you probably won't encounter PRA.

➤ **Epilepsy.** If your Lab has epilepsy, that means she will have seizures. Epilepsy can be due to environmental or genetic factors and will probably show up relatively early if inherited. Seizures can be frightening for your Lab and for you. The most important thing to do for your Lab during a seizure is to keep her from hurting herself. Talk to your vet about the best strategies for managing seizures if your Lab has epilepsy. Depending on the frequency and severity of the seizures, your vet may recommend medication.

For more information on your Lab's health, see Chapters 12 and 13.

Nutrition Basics

One of the most common questions new dog owners ask veterinarians is, "What should I feed my dog?" Simply perusing the aisles at your local pet store or grocery store may only confuse you further. The choices are seemingly endless, and the range in price is dramatic. Is a basic, inexpensive food good enough? Are so-called premium foods worth the price? Can't you just throw your dog a bone?

Pet nutrition is a big industry right now, and it pays to know what is hype and what is important information. Although the science is constantly changing and the press releases from the various big-name dog food companies are relentless, we'll give you our down-to-earth take on the matter.

Be a Label Reader

The dog food name, company reputation and the nicely decorated package often influence which brands people tend to buy. Only one thing should influence you, however: the label. No matter the price,

Lab Lore

Should you feed your dog a homemade diet? Homemade diets are particularly good for those few dogs that don't do well on commercial dog foods, either due to allergies or sensitivity to certain ingredients. However, homemade diets must be scrupulously prepared, and you have to know what you are doing. They take a lot more time to prepare than it takes to scoop out commercial dog food, and a diet lacking in any important vitamins, minerals or other nutrients can seriously compromise your dog's health. For instance, your dog could become very sick on an all-meat diet. If you like the idea of making your own dog food, read up on the subject, and then don't skimp on ingredients. A few excellent books show you how to prepare a homemade diet that is nutritionally complete.

no matter how clever or cute the television commercial and no matter what your friends or neighbors say, the label is the only thing that will tell you how good a dog food is.

What should you look for? First, look for approval by AAFCO, the Association of American Feed Control Officials. All dog foods must be approved by AAFCO if they advertise as an acceptable diet. Only supplemental foods such as treats don't require an AAFCO statement, so most dog foods have it. But if the one you're looking at doesn't have it, put it back on the shelf. It isn't nutritionally adequate.

But you don't want a food that is merely adequate, do you? You want a food that is good, a food that will help your dog be as healthy as possible. Many companies also have their own feeding trials so they can best refine their foods to help dogs thrive. Look for evidence of feeding trials on the label.

Take a look at your dog's teeth. Are they a little different from your own teeth? You bet they are! Dogs are carnivores. Sure, they can eat grains and vegetables (in the wild, they eat whole animals, including the animal's stomach contents, which often consist of grains and vegetables). But dogs need a higher level of protein than humans. Although grains and vegetables contain protein, it isn't in a form as digestible as meat. Therefore, we recommend looking for a food that lists at least two sources of meat in the first five ingredients.

Labs love to eat, and they have a tendency to be overfed. Find out about your Lab's nutritional needs so she gets what she needs—and no more.

Most dog foods will list a few grain sources in the first five ingredients as well. That's fine. Grain is a protein source, too, although a few dogs will have allergies to certain grains (try out a lamb and rice or other anti-allergenic dog food if your dog has trouble digesting her food). Just be sure grains aren't the only protein source. Grains are high in carbohydrates, and dogs don't digest carbohydrates as well as humans do. Too much of some grains may also hinder the absorption of other important nutrients. For example, iron absorption is hindered by diets high in soy protein.

Lab Lore

Although some people advocate giving dogs raw meat bones, we don't recommend it for Labrador Retrievers. Labs are chewers extraordinaire and even large raw bones can splinter in their powerful jaws. Bone splinters can cause internal injuries, so forgo the raw bones for your Lab and stick to sturdy chew toys for chewing.

AAFCO-approved dog foods will also contain an array of vitamins and minerals. If the food is approved by AAFCO and especially if it has successfully passed feeding trials, the vitamin/mineral ratios should be adequate.

155

Next, look for how the food is preserved. Most foods these days are naturally preserved with vitamin E and sometimes vitamin C. Chemical preservatives such as ethoxyquin (a known carcinogen) could harm your dog's health and are best avoided.

In general, we suggest looking for three things in dog food:

1. The food should be approved by AAFCO and, ideally, should have passed feeding trials.

2. The food should have at least two sources of meat in the first five ingredients.

3. The food should be naturally preserved.

After you find foods that meet these basic requirements, the rest is up to you. You can find all kinds of fancy foods out there. Some are loaded with delicious-sounding ingredients, lots of natural and organic vegetables, herbs, fancy oils and high-protein grains. Others are strictly no-frills. As long as the food you choose meets the three standards we set out, it should be fine for your dog.

Vet Alert

If your dog refuses to eat her food, she may be sick, or the food may be spoiled. If it smells of rancid fat, throw it out. Always check the food for expiration dates and bugs, and don't feed your dog expired or infested food. To avoid spoilage, keep dog food sealed in an airtight container and don't buy more than a month's supply at one time.

The last, and perhaps most, important consideration: Your dog should think the food you feed her is yummy! If your dog eats the food you've chosen eagerly (and most Labs will eat just about anything eagerly!), you have your dog food.

Puppy Nutrition

Puppies eat puppy food, don't they? You may be surprised to learn that we don't recommend puppy food for your Labrador Retriever puppy. Although great for small dogs, the high protein and fat content of puppy food may encourage your Lab puppy to grow too fast. Several studies in the early 1990s demonstrated that larger breeds, including Labrador

Retrievers, that grow too rapidly as puppies are at a higher risk for orthopedic problems such as hip dysplasia later in life.

A high-quality adult maintenance diet, however, is perfect for a Labrador Retriever puppy. Just be sure you feed her enough. Your puppy should grow at a steady rate, stay slim and well muscled (roly-poly puppies may look cute but are headed down a long road of health problems) and have plenty of energy.

How often should you feed your ravenous little puppy? We don't recommend making food available all day long (free feeding). Labs love to eat, and even on an adult maintenance diet, a puppy could become overweight. Instead, feed your puppy three times per day for the first three or four months. Then, you can usually switch to a twice-a-day diet.

Avoid feeding your Lab, even when she is an adult, just once per day. Labs love to eat, so let them enjoy it twice each day. Just be sure to adjust portions accordingly so your Lab doesn't get too fat!

How much should your puppy eat? That depends on how active she is, how often she is outside in cold weather and how old she is. The portions on the dog food bags may not be right for your dog. For puppies, we recommend starting with 1 cup of dry food three times per day. Take the food away after fifteen minutes. If your puppy doesn't finish her food, adjust the daily portion down by ¼ cup or so. If your puppy acts frantically hungry, adjust the daily portion up by ¼ cup or so.

Vet Alert

A number of recent studies have suggested that deep-chested dogs such as Labrador Retrievers may be more prone to bloating or stomach torsion, an extremely painful and life-threatening condition, if they are only fed once per day. Once-a-day feeding encourages faster, more frantic, eating, which may contribute to bloating.

Take time to experiment. Don't overfeed your puppy, but don't starve her, either. In general, if your Lab is energetic, looks healthy, has bright eyes and a shiny coat and eats with relish but not so desperately that she acts as if she is starving, you have the right portion. Also, do a rib test once every month or so. If you can see your dog's ribs, she may be too thin. If you can't feel her ribs when you run your hands gently along your dog's rib cage, she may be too fat. If you can feel them under a light layer of flesh but they don't have a pronounced appearance, your dog is probably just right.

When your dog becomes more or less active, when she reaches adult height or when the weather changes, you may need to adjust the food portion once again. The trick is to stay tuned in to your dog.

Adult Nutrition

If you've been feeding your puppy a high-quality adult maintenance dog food, you don't need to switch foods when she reaches adulthood. Labs continue to grow for two years or so, but nothing matches the growth rate of that first year. When your puppy reaches her first birthday, you can probably decrease portions slightly. But again, the best way to know how much to feed your dog is to pay attention to the way she looks and acts and to gauge her individual energy needs. The more energy she uses, the more quality protein and calories she requires.

Geriatric Nutrition

Just because your dog is getting older doesn't mean she is getting sicker, slower or any less hungry. The old school of canine nutrition once believed that older dogs (over the age of 8) should automatically be switched to a lower-protein diet. Now nutrition scientists are discovering that unless a dog already has a kidney problem (the kidneys process protein), senior dogs need just as much, if not more, protein than younger adult dogs.

Older dogs tend to lose lean body mass (muscle), so they need plenty of protein to stay strong. Protein doesn't cause kidney problems (some evidence points to too much phosphorous instead), although protein can aggravate an existing kidney problem.

If your older dog has become less active, she may require fewer calories than before. Decreasing portions slightly may be all you need to do. On the other hand, if your dog becomes very inactive due to a health problem such as hip dysplasia, you may need to switch to a nutritionally dense food that offers more nutrition in each bite. Older dogs may not be as hungry, either, so nutritionally dense food could

158

become important. If your dog's appetite changes or you feel she needs a dietary adjustment, see your vet for advice.

On the other hand, if you keep your Lab healthy and active, she may not show a single sign of slowing down even into her second decade of life. If your dog remains active and retains her appetite, there isn't any reason to change her diet.

Your Active Dog

Some dogs are extra rambunctious. Other dogs are true working dogs, whether avid hunters, trackers or obedience champions. These very active dogs need extra protein and calories to give them enough energy and to maintain their muscle mass. If your dog is very active, you can feed her more than you would feed a normally active or sedentary dog.

The food you choose can be a high-protein food, as long as the protein is from a good source (in other words, meat). You may also want to supplement your active dog's diet with a little extra fat, especially during the winter months if your dog is often outside in very cold temperatures. One tablespoon of canola or safflower oil mixed with your dog's food and a scrambled or boiled egg once or twice a week will give your active dog a dietary energy boost. Remember to keep monitoring your dog. If she is getting too thin (if you can see her ribs), gradually increase her portions.

Lab Lore

Should you give your dog vitamin/mineral supplements? Most canine nutritionists say no, as long as you are feeding your dog a dog food that is nutritionally complete. Oversupplementation can compromise your dog's (and especially your puppy's) health by skewing the balance of nutrients. Unless your vet recommends supplements to address a particular health problem, stick to your regular dog food.

Can Your Dog Pinch an Inch?

Labs certainly tend to be active, but because they love to eat, they also tend to get overweight. Some Labs prefer a relatively sedentary life that, coupled with the typical Lab appetite, can translate into extra pounds that may eventually compromise your dog's health. Overweight Labs are more prone to hip dysplasia and other bone and joint problems. They are more likely to suffer from heart disease (just like overweight humans), and many other bodily organs and systems will wear down faster in an overweight dog. As we mentioned before, it is particularly dangerous to overfeed a puppy because a too-fast rate of growth can seriously compromise bone and joint strength later in life.

Lab Lore

Although we don't generally advocate adding people food to your dog's diet, consider adding about ¼ cup of plain yogurt with active cultures mixed into your dog's food a few times a week. Yogurt helps to replenish your dog's intestinal flora and improve her digestion. Just don't use the sweetened kind. You may not like plain yogurt, but your dog may find it an interesting addition to her regular kibble.

One of the main reasons Labs (and other dogs) get to be overweight is from too many treats and/or table scraps. It's tempting to give your Lab the rest of that cheeseburger and french fries or the last of the vanilla pudding or meatloaf or lasagna. But once you begin feeding your dog just one bite of your dinner, extra feeding can easily get out of hand. Instead, make it a rule never to feed your dog any of the food the family is having for dinner, especially not right from your plate (unhealthy, and it encourages bad manners!). If you absolutely must feed her some people food, mix a cooked egg or some cooked vegetables into her regular food, in her regular food bowl. Remember, obesity is one of the most common health problems in dogs. Too much extra food, even healthy food, is bound to end up around your dog's middle.

How can you tell if your dog is too fat? First, look at your dog from above. Her waist should be narrower than her ribcage. If she looks like a barrel, she's probably overweight. Next, feel your dog's ribs. If they feel as if they are padded with a mattress (in other words, if you have difficulty finding them at all), your dog is probably overweight. Check with your vet if you suspect your dog has been packing on the extra pounds, and then work together to manage your dog's weight problem through a combination of dietary adjustments and exercise.

Diets for Ailing Dogs

Certain health problems, such as kidney disease, diabetes and heart disease, call for dietary alterations. Your vet can best advise you on how to change your dog's diet to best manage a particular disease. If your dog is diagnosed with any disease or condition and your vet doesn't mention your dog's diet, be sure to ask if you should be making any changes in your dog's diet. And be forthcoming. If you've been feeding your dog pepperoni pizza four times a week, tell your vet. It may help him or her diagnose a problem.

Trainer Tidbits

To avoid your dog becoming overweight from too many training treats, use pieces of regular dog food taken out of your dog's daily allowance of food for training sessions. Reserve extra dog treats for special occasions.

Get Moving!

Dogs need exercise, just like humans. Obese dogs need it, slim dogs need it, puppies need it, adult dogs need it and senior dogs need it. Exercise keeps your dog's muscles strong and her heart fit and provides a release for all that Lab energy! Labs that don't get enough exercise may wind up engaging in destructive chewing, or they may become jittery, nervous and/or hyperactive. One or two nice long daily walks, at least twenty to thirty minutes, is all it takes, and you'll benefit, too! If you have a large fenced yard, don't think that is a substitute for a daily walk. Walking your dog is a great way for the two of you

Vet Alert

Don't share that chocolate bar with your dog! Some dogs are allergic to chocolate and even a little can kill them. Don't risk trying to find out whether your dog can handle chocolate. Even if your dog isn't allergic, chocolate has no nutritional value and is bad for your dog's health.

to engage in an activity together. This will improve your relationship. Extra time romping in the backyard is great for Labs, too.

Vet Alert

Puppies and older dogs alike can experience joint injuries and foot pad injuries from running on concrete. If possible, allow your dog to walk on grass, dirt or any surface softer than a hard street or sidewalk. If you must walk your dog on concrete, slow the pace.

Puppy Exercise Needs

Lab puppies can be quite active. They need to have lots of outlets for that energy. If you expect them to lie at your feet all day, you'll probably end up getting the shoes chewed right off your feet! The fact that excess weight is particularly bad for puppies is another reason to make sure your pup gets lots of exercise.

Get your puppy used to walking on a leash right away. Put a collar and leash on your puppy as soon as you bring her home and keep it slack while following the puppy around in a safe area. Then follow the directions in Chapter 10 to teach your puppy to walk on a slack lead. Soon you'll be walking together like pros and getting the exercise your puppy needs.

Adult and Senior Exercise Needs

When your Lab is no longer a puppy, she may settle down a bit and require less exercise. On the other hand, she may not. Some Labs are highly energetic and enjoy lots of activity all the way through old age. Don't slack off on the walks just because your dog is no longer a puppy. Keeping your dog fit requires exercise every day, no matter your dog's age. Many old Labrador Retrievers are still happy to go on long, brisk walks, catch a Frisbee or retrieve game on an all-day hunting trip.

However, if your dog begins to suffer from bone or joint trouble in old age, you may need to slow things down a bit. Swimming is an excellent exercise for dogs that have hip dysplasia and other bone disorders. Take the cue from your dog and be sensitive. Labs love to please, so they may push themselves too hard if they think you really want to run that extra mile. Be in tune to signs your older dog needs to slow down: panting, limping, slowing the pace or signs of extreme exhaustion

With the help of a trusted veterinarian, your Labs will live long, healthy lives.

after exercise, such as sleeping for an unusually long time. Also, don't forget to check your dog all over during your daily grooming sessions. If touching certain areas elicits a yelp or a whimper, your dog is probably in pain. See your vet and take it easy on your dog, at least for awhile.

Couch Potato Owners Have Couch Potato Dogs

If you are the sedentary type but you have your heart set on a Lab, con-sider an older Lab that doesn't have the energy level of a puppy. Some older Labs love to sit around all day, although they should have at least one daily walk to keep in shape. If you never get any exercise, however, and can't even make yourself take that daily walk, either consider another type of dog (many small dogs can get enough exercise just running around the house), or hire someone to walk your Lab for you. Otherwise, you'll end up with a couch potato dog that may suffer from serious health problems as she ages.

Last of all, this chapter wouldn't be complete without a few words about choosing the right vet for you Lab. Don't just go with the first

Lab Lore

People who call themselves veterinarians must have a veterinary medical degree. These degrees are designated as DVM (Doctor of Veterinary Medicine) or, in the case of those who graduated from the University of Pennsylvania School of Veterinary Medicine, VMD (Veterinary Medical Doctor). DVMs and VMDs are the same thing, but accept no other substitute. A vet by any other name just isn't a vet.

vet you find. Be a little choosy, shop around and bring along this checklist:

☐ Were you easily able to make an appointment for an introductory visit?

☐ Does the reception area look clean?

☐ Does the reception area smell clean?

☐ Is the staff friendly and polite?

☐ Is your dog curious and unafraid in the reception area?

☐ Do you have to wait longer than twenty minutes to see the vet?

☐ Is the vet friendly?

☐ Do you feel unrushed, as though you have as much time as you need with the vet?

☐ Is the vet willing to answer your questions about qualifications, experience and philosophy of pet care?

☐ Does the vet seem genuinely to like and be interested in your Lab?

☐ Does your Lab seem genuinely to like and be interested in the vet?

☐ Do you get a good feeling about the practice and the vet?

Notes:

_____

_____

_____

_____

_____

Holistic Health Practitioners

In case you haven't noticed, there is a movement in both human and animal health care. It's big, it's a moneymaker and there just may be something to it. It's *holistic* health care, and it is increasingly recognized as a real alternative or, ideally, a complement to conventional or *allopathic* medicine.

Lab Lingo

Holistic health care treats the body as a whole, considering all possible factors that might contribute to a physical or emotional problem. **Allopathic** medicine seeks to relieve symptoms and focuses treatment on the problem itself. Most advocates of complementary medicine agree that holistic health care can be effective for many chronic or long-term problems, but allopathic care is best for acute or emergency situations.

Holistic health care takes the view that any illness, including emotional or behavioral upsets, is due to imbalances in your pet's whole self or life-force energy. A holistic health care practitioner will ask you many questions about your pet that may seem unrelated to the problem at hand, such as what your pet eats, what her habits are, where she lives and sleeps and her relationships with other pets and with people. Holistic healing seeks to balance the system as a whole, rather than treating individual symptoms, so the body can best heal itself.

The Least You Need to Know

➤ Get to know your dog's basic anatomy and what looks and feels normal for your dog so you can spot health problems if they occur.

➤ Although Labs are generally very healthy, they are prone to certain genetic health problems such as hip dysplasia, progressive retinal atrophy and epilepsy.

➤ Feeding your dog a food with quality protein sources and the right amount of calories for your dog's individual needs will help to ensure good health.

➤ Make sure your dog gets enough exercise to further ensure good health. If you exercise with your dog, your relationship will improve, and you'll both be healthier!

➤ Choose a vet you and your Lab feel good about.

Chapter 12

An Ounce of Prevention

In This Chapter

➤ Do you really have to get all those vaccinations for your dog?

➤ What about breeding? Wouldn't it be fun?

➤ Why you should sterilize your Lab

When it comes to health, nothing beats the effectiveness of prevention. Incorporating a few basic routines into your life for the sake of your dog's health can go a long way toward minimizing health problems in the future. Even minor neglect and forgetting to pay attention to subtle cues from your dog can result in a lot of pain and suffering, not to mention financial cost, down the road. Establish a preventive routine when you first get your puppy and consider the small amount of extra time a worthwhile investment in your dog's future health (and your future financial security).

Vaccinations

Perhaps the most important thing you can do to prevent health tragedies is to have your puppy vaccinated. On that very first vet visit, your vet can provide you with a vaccination schedule for your puppy's first year. The purpose of vaccinations in the first year and slightly beyond is to gradually build up a puppy's immune system for when he is no longer nursing and gaining immunities from his mother.

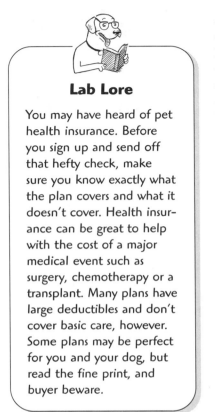

A vaccine introduces a very small bit of a disease into your dog's system so he can build up an immune response to it. Later, if the dog is ever exposed to the disease, his body will be prepared to fight it off. The typical vaccination mix protects your puppy from several dangerous diseases and should be administered about once per month from about 6 weeks to about 17 weeks (certain vaccines may have different schedules; check with your vet). Most vaccine mixes protect your Lab from the following diseases:

➤ **Canine Distemper Virus (CDV).** This upper respiratory viral infection causes severe vomiting, diarrhea and fever and used to be a leading cause of death in dogs.

➤ **Adenovirus-2.** This virus causes abdominal pain, jaundice and clouded corneas.

➤ **Canine Infectious Hepatitis.** This liver virus causes fever, vomiting and loss of appetite.

➤ **Leptospirosis.** This bacterial infection can be transmitted to you. It affects the liver, kidney and bladder, causing fever, vomiting, loss of appetite, abdominal pain and eye inflammation, among other symptoms.

➤ **Canine Parainfluenza.** This is the flu virus in dog form.

➤ **Canine Parvovirus.** Often called *Parvo*, this gastrointestinal virus can be deadly, especially for puppies. Some breeds (Dobermans and Rottweilers) are particularly susceptible, but any puppy can catch it. Parvovirus can enter your home in a number of ways, including shoes, which are best left at the door in homes with puppies. Parvovirus causes diarrhea, fever, severe stomach pain, vomiting and, when it isn't caught in time, death.

➤ **Coronavirus** (the coronavirus vaccine isn't in all combinations; the virus is more common in some areas of the country than in others). This intestinal virus is similar to but less serious than parvovirus. It causes vomiting, diarrhea and fever.

You can also elect to vaccinate your puppy against other diseases and conditions, depending on where you live and how often your dog is outside. These include bordatella (kennel cough), a respiratory virus, and Lyme disease. The bordatella vaccine is often required for any dogs being boarded in a kennel because bordatella is so easily spread through kennels. Lyme disease, spread by ticks, is a good vaccine to get if your dog is often outside in wooded areas, especially in the northeastern area of the country. Lyme disease causes lameness, fever, loss of appetite and swollen joints.

Vet Alert

If you decide to administer your Lab's vaccinations yourself by buying the vaccines at a feed store, be aware that some vaccination mixes and different brands can differ in quality and in contents. Also, if you don't keep your receipts and careful records, you may not be able to convince a vet, a boarding kennel or anyone else who needs to know that your dog has indeed been vaccinated. Taking your Lab to the vet for his vaccinations leaves a more reliable paper trail, and you can be assured of getting a quality vaccine.

Your puppy should also receive his first rabies shot at around 6 months of age, and many vets will charge less for this shot if you have your puppy spayed or neutered by this time. Unlike the other vaccinations, rabies shots are required by law (although some cities have local laws requiring distemper vaccines). Rabies is always fatal for dogs. Please don't neglect your dog's rabies vaccinations.

The Great Vaccination Debate

After that first crucial year, should you continue to have your dog vaccinated every year? Some say yes; some say no. If you have your dog boarded in a kennel while on vacation or take him to obedience classes, you may need to require proof of current vaccinations. But if you don't, what will happen if you don't vaccinate your dog? And what will happen if you do?

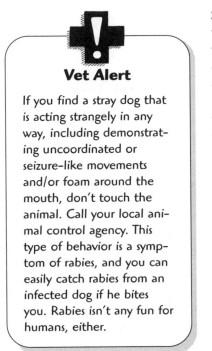

Vet Alert

If you find a stray dog that is acting strangely in any way, including demonstrating uncoordinated or seizure-like movements and/or foam around the mouth, don't touch the animal. Call your local animal control agency. This type of behavior is a symptom of rabies, and you can easily catch rabies from an infected dog if he bites you. Rabies isn't any fun for humans, either.

Some people believe that vaccinations are overadministered and unnecessary and may even cause chronic health problems in some dogs. Others disagree, citing the low incidence of negative effects from vaccines and arguing that annual vaccinations will help to eliminate dangerous canine diseases from the population.

Both sides have convincing arguments, but we tend to agree that doing your part to eliminate disease from the general population is important. Vaccinating your dog is like vaccinating your child. Yes, there is a very small but real risk of a serious reaction and a slightly larger risk of a mild reaction. But vaccinations have drastically or totally eliminated some serious childhood diseases and have dramatically improved the health of children in general.

We've seen a similar occurrence in the dog world. One of the leading causes of death in dogs used to be distemper, but thanks to the distemper vaccine, few dogs die from it anymore (the leading cause of death in dogs is now death by car, but more on that later). If your dog has a reaction to a vaccine or is in poor health, you have a good argument for choosing not to vaccinate your dog. If your dog is healthy and has never reacted to a vaccine, however, we encourage you to continue to vaccinate your dog, although you may be able to vaccinate only every two to three years after the first year. Ask your vet.

If you do decide to vaccinate less often than annually, don't let that be an excuse to ignore your dog's annual checkup. This checkup is an important preventive measure; it allows your vet to monitor your Lab's health, make sure you are doing all you can to keep your Lab healthy and catch any problems before they turn serious.

What's Optional; What's the Law

Although standard vaccinations are legally optional, law requires rabies vaccines. Rabies can be transmitted to humans and can be fatal. It is always fatal to dogs. Although some dogs do experience reactions to the rabies vaccine, refusing the vaccine is a greater risk than a reaction to the vaccine. Keep your dog up-to-date on his rabies shots and always keep a current tag on your dog's collar showing that your dog has been vaccinated for rabies. In the unlikely event that your dog escapes and bites someone, there won't be any doubt that your dog is rabies-free.

To Breed or Not to Breed?

Another big issue in canine health is whether to breed your dog. People used to believe that a female dog would be healthier if she gave birth to one litter of puppies before being spayed. Another common misconception is that a female dog must experience one heat before being spayed. But experiencing one heat means risking a pregnancy.

Lab Lore

Recent research has argued that annual vaccines may indeed be overkill. At a recent conference of the Ohio Veterinary Medical Association, it was reported that vaccines probably have a longer term of effectiveness than once believed and that a two- or three-year interval between booster shots may be more appropriate than a one-year interval. Studies demonstrating how long immune effects from vaccines last are only required for the rabies vaccine. The protocol of the annual booster shots for other vaccines isn't based on research. Talk to your vet if you are concerned about overvaccinating your Lab. The two of you may be able to develop an alternate schedule of vaccinations every two to three years instead of once a year.

We don't mean to discourage potential breeders who are interested in learning everything they can about the hobby and engaging in dog breeding in a responsible, informed and devoted manner. But for those of you trying to decide whether it might be fun to breed your dog, we have a simple and heartfelt request: Don't!

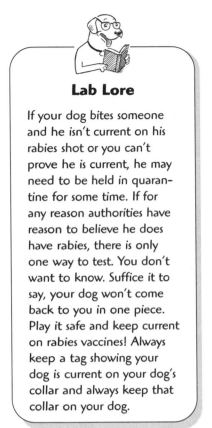

Lab Lore

If your dog bites someone and he isn't current on his rabies shot or you can't prove he is current, he may need to be held in quarantine for some time. If for any reason authorities have reason to believe he does have rabies, there is only one way to test. You don't want to know. Suffice it to say, your dog won't come back to you in one piece. Play it safe and keep current on rabies vaccines! Always keep a tag showing your dog is current on your dog's collar and always keep that collar on your dog.

When in Doubt, Don't!

Breeding is a time-consuming, expensive and sometimes heart-breaking endeavor (puppies don't always make it). For truly devoted, die-hard dog lovers who are willing to do everything possible to ensure healthy, well-trained, well-socialized pups and who are willing to make the effort to place those pups in good homes by screening and educating potential buyers, breeding can be a labor of love. But it isn't going to make anybody rich, and your female Lab certainly doesn't need to give birth to a litter or even go through a single heat to be healthy.

We are in the midst of an epidemic of unwanted pets. Each day in the United States, 10,000 new humans are born, and over 70,000 puppies and kittens are born. Shelters euthanize over 13 million dogs and cats every year in the United States. Unless you have a really, really good reason for bringing more puppies into the world, please consider finding another way to experience the miracle of birth.

Breeding Cons and Pros

Although breeding has many cons, it also has some pros for the right kind of person. If you still think you have the right stuff to be a great breeder, survey our list of breeding cons and pros. (Yes, we put the cons first—we want you to know what you are getting into!)

Breeding Cons

Breeding is expensive. You have to feed and house one or both parents and all the pups, get regular veterinary care for all, including shots and worming, heartworm prevention and pest prevention. You have to pay to advertise the puppies, which can be quite an expense. No matter how great your dogs are, you won't get rich breeding dogs. You might make enough to pay for your breeding expenses.

Breeding is time-consuming. You have to care for, socialize and begin training for all those puppies. Puppies need round-the-clock care, and you'll lose a lot of sleep when you have a new litter in the house.

Plus, you'll have to learn something about genetics and how to breed to best prevent genetic disease. You'll need to learn all about the process of pregnancy and birth in dogs, how to assist with the whelping, how to prevent health problems in pregnant dogs and in puppies, how to keep conditions sanitary, what kind of equipment you'll need—the list goes on and on. Prepare to do a lot of reading and a lot of networking with other breeders.

Vet Alert

If you think your children should witness the birth of puppies as an educational experience, consider this: A routine birth can quickly turn into a scary emergency situation. Puppies are sometimes born dead, and the birth experience sometimes proves fatal to the mother. Do you want your kids inadvertently to view the death experience when you had intended for them to see the birth experience?

Your time may often seem like it is no longer your own. You have to be prepared to answer the phone at all hours of the day and night when you have an ad in the paper for your pups (and people will call at all hours). You will need to be ready to answer the many questions people have, and you'll answer many of the same questions again and again.

You'll want to spend the time to screen potential owners of your pups on the phone. Then you have to invite the small minority of folks you think might make good homes for your pups to your home. You should take at least a couple of hours of your time with each potential client or client family to show them the parents or parent of the pups, show them the pups and give them all the information they will need to make a good decision.

Some people just like to drive around and look at puppies. After all your time, you may find out they have no real intention of buying. If and when you finally find good homes for all your puppies, you have to be prepared to be a continual source of information for the new puppy owner.

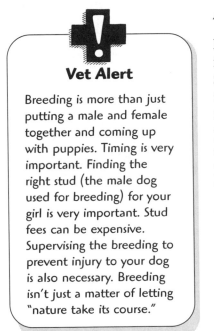

Vet Alert

Breeding is more than just putting a male and female together and coming up with puppies. Timing is very important. Finding the right stud (the male dog used for breeding) for your girl is very important. Stud fees can be expensive. Supervising the breeding to prevent injury to your dog is also necessary. Breeding isn't just a matter of letting "nature take its course."

Are you ready for all that?

Finally, breeding can be heartbreaking. Sometimes, the mother Lab dies. Sometimes puppies die. Sometimes they are born with serious genetic faults and have to be euthanized. If you can't even bear to watch a dog experience misfortune in the movies, you probably shouldn't take on the task of breeding.

Breeding is a big responsibility. You are bringing life into the world. It is up to you to see that those puppies have proper care and socialization and go into homes that will provide them with a secure and happy existence.

Breeding Pros

If you love Labs and are ready to devote all your extra time to developing healthier, more beautiful and better strains of Labs that make wonderful pets and can wow 'em in the show ring, go for it! You'll find there is a lot to learn. Hook up with experienced breeders, read every book you can find on the subject (see Appendix B for some suggestions) and learn everything you can.

The Importance of Spaying/Neutering Your Lab

Altering your dog, as sterilization is sometimes called, has lots of benefits and very few negative aspects. Here are some of the pros of sterilization:

➤ You won't risk bringing an unwanted litter of puppies into the world, contributing to the epidemic of pet overpopulation.

➤ You will reduce your female dog's risk of breast, ovarian, uterine or cervical cancer and your male dog's risk of testicular cancer or prostate infection.

➤ Your dog may become a little calmer and less agitated and less likely to escape in desperation to breed.

➤ Your male dog may become less aggressive toward other dogs.

➤ You'll never have to worry about the mess of menstruation in your female dog.

➤ Your female will be less likely to have mood swings.

The cons? There aren't many. You have to pay for sterilization surgery, but the cost is far less than the cost of taking on a litter of puppies or paying to have your dog treated for cancer. Many humane societies offer vouchers for significant discounts on sterilization that most vets will accept. In some areas, if cost is a problem, humane societies may even pay for the operation (although if you can afford to take on a dog, you should be able to afford to have it sterilized).

Dogs recover from the surgery in a few days to a week or two, and then they'll be back to their normal selves, although sometimes they'll seem a little more at ease and less agitated. Male dogs may be less aggressive towards other dogs and less likely to mark their territory with urine.

Contrary to popular belief, sterilization won't change your dog's personality, make him fat or lazy or take

Lab Lore

The latest controversy in the spay/neuter arena is how early to sterilize your dog. Although it was once believed that dogs shouldn't be neutered until they are finished growing so they can fully develop their bones and muscles, more and more vets and especially humane societies are advocating early sterilization (at 3 months of age or even earlier). Some vets still prefer to wait until 6 months, when a dog's bones are pretty much done growing, and research is still uncertain as to whether sterilization before 6 months affects growth in any way. Dogs can impregnate and get pregnant before 6 months of age in some cases. Talk to your vet about when he or she believes is the optimal time for sterilization.

away his guarding instinct. Nonsense! All sterilization does is take away that sometimes uncomfortable and overwhelming need to breed. Give your dog a break! If you aren't going to breed him responsibly, don't subject him to the urge to breed.

The Least You Need to Know

➤ Prevention is the best medicine; keep your dog healthy to prevent health problems in the future.

➤ Vaccinate your dog against serious illnesses.

➤ Don't breed your dog unless you are sure you are ready for the commitment.

➤ Have your dog sterilized to prevent unwanted breeding and to give your dog relief from the natural, uncontrollable urge to breed.

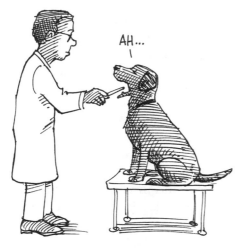

AH...

Chapter 13

Prevention, the Sequel

> ## In This Chapter
>
> ➤ Keeping bugs off your Lab
>
> ➤ Grooming your Lab from head to toe
>
> ➤ Using the daily grooming routine and Lab log to maintain your Lab's good health

Vaccinations and sterilization are great ways to prevent serious disease in your pet, but you can do much more. Parasite control and good grooming are two crucial preventive measures every responsible dog owner should take. A monthly dose of flea spray and an occasional brushing aren't enough if you really want to maximize your pet's health. A little knowledge about the latest technology and a little time each day with your pet are all you need to keep your dog happy, healthy, itch-free and beautiful.

Don't Bug My Dog!

No matter where you live and no matter how seldom your dog goes outside, chances are at some time or another she'll encounter a flea or two. And it only takes two fleas to generate hundreds and hundreds of fleas. Parasite control is an important consideration for dog owners. Many dogs are extremely allergic to flea bites and can develop flea-bite dermatitis, a painful skin condition that is difficult to resolve. Fleas can cause anemia and tapeworms in your dog, and in rare cases, they can even transmit bubonic plague to you! Not to mention their nasty habit of infesting your house and living and breeding in your carpets, furniture and bed mattress. Yuck!

Lab Lore

Some frightening flea facts: Only 1 to 5 percent of the flea population in an environment such as your home consists of adult fleas living on your dog. The remaining 95 to 99 percent are eggs, larvae and pupae living in your carpet, furniture and yard. Ten adult fleas can become 250,000 in thirty days under good conditions.

Ticks are another parasite common to dogs, and they are more than just a nuisance. Ticks can cause Lyme disease and many other diseases in your dog (and in you if you are bitten by the tick). For some diseases, including Lyme disease, the tick must remain attached to your dog (or you) for 72 hours to transmit the disease. But if you aren't checking your dog regularly for ticks, 72 hours can pass before you know it! Although many tick-borne illnesses are treatable, avoiding ticks is a more sensible, less costly and less-painful approach.

Worms and mites are other parasites you need to watch out for. Your dog can pick up these critters by sniffing the feces of another dog, eating fleas, getting bitten by a mosquito or even by walking, because some worms can be absorbed through her feet (and yours, too). Always keep your dog on heartworm preventive medicine, even if she doesn't often go outside. Heartworms can kill. Your vet can test your dog for worms at each annual checkup, as well. Mites can cause *mange*, a very itchy and uncomfortable condition that can eventually be fatal if untreated. See your vet if your dog is very itchy or losing patches of hair.

Checking for Parasites

During your daily grooming sessions, check your dog for parasites. Because Labs have short coats, fleas are relatively easy to spot, although they are of course more difficult to see on black Labs. Keep a flea comb handy and run it through your dog's coat. If you come up with nothing, great! If you find little black specks on the flea comb that jump back off, your dog has fleas. If you come up with little black specks that don't jump off, put them on a wet piece of white paper. If they turn reddish, they are flea dirt. Yuck! Your dog has fleas. Another way to check for fleas on your Lab is to run your finger through her coat so you can see her skin. If you see little black specks on her skin, you probably have a flea problem.

Ticks are larger, so they are easier to spot, but if you don't catch them and they remain attached, they can transmit diseases. The longer a tick is attached, the bigger it gets, because it becomes swollen with blood. Ticks aren't pretty. Removing a huge, swollen tick can be pretty grotesque and dangerous, too, if the tick pops. That tick bacteria can be absorbed through the skin, so always keep things sanitary when removing ticks.

If you do find a tick on your dog, remove it properly to avoid infecting your dog or yourself. Here is the best way to manage ticks:

Lab Lore

Dogs can get several kinds of worms. Tapeworms and roundworms are easy to see in your dog's feces. Tapeworms look like moving grains of rice and roundworms look like spaghetti. Dogs get tapeworms from eating fleas, which carry them. Roundworms are common parasites and are contracted when a dog sniffs the feces of an infected dog. Hookworms are passed via the feces of roundworms. They burrow through skin, and then move into the intestinal tract. Heartworms are transmitted by mosquitoes and are most common in warm climates where mosquitoes live year-round. Prevention is important because treatment is dangerous; many dogs don't survive the treatment.

➤ Avoid places that could be infested by ticks, such as wooded areas. If you periodically take your dog to a wooded area, keep yourself well covered (wear a hat, long sleeves and long pants) and check your dog immediately after your walk for ticks. You may be able to catch ticks on your dog before they have attached themselves.

➤ Keep the grass mowed in your yard and clear away brush.

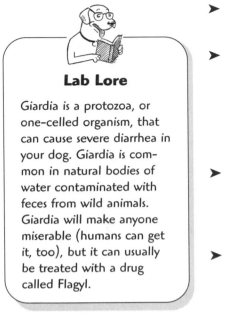

Lab Lore

Giardia is a protozoa, or one-celled organism, that can cause severe diarrhea in your dog. Giardia is common in natural bodies of water contaminated with feces from wild animals. Giardia will make anyone miserable (humans can get it, too), but it can usually be treated with a drug called Flagyl.

➤ Remove ticks as soon as possible after you discover them.

➤ To remove a tick, wear rubber gloves, and use a paper towel, tweezers or another device made for removing ticks. If the tick breaks, the bacteria could infect you.

➤ Grasp the tick close to the skin and pull straight up. If part of the tick remains under the skin, it could become infected.

➤ Always wash your hands thoroughly after removing a tick, even if you used gloves or tweezers, and disinfect the area where the tick was attached with alcohol.

➤ Never cover ticks with petroleum jelly, nail polish or other home remedies. Never burn a tick.

➤ Flush the tick down the toilet or drown it in alcohol. If you want the tick analyzed for Lyme disease, seal the tick in a bottle with moist paper and call your vet to find out where you can have the tick tested.

Vet Alert

Be very careful about mixing too many flea products. Check with your vet before you use more than one type at a time (such as a flea shampoo followed by application of a spot-on).

Preventing Infestations

The easiest way to get rid of a flea infestation is to prevent a flea infestation. Fleas are stubborn little critters, and they don't take kindly to being asked to leave. So don't invite them in!

We suggest a three-pronged approach to preventing a flea infestation:

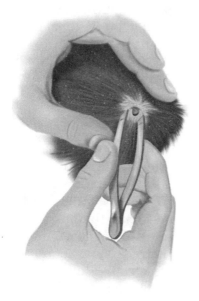

Use tweezers to remove ticks from your dog.

1. Keep your pet on an insect growth regulator (IGR) all year long. Available in pill form or in spot-on forms (you apply a spot of liquid between the dog's shoulder blades and sometimes also at the base of the tail), IGRs don't kill fleas, but they affect either flea eggs or the larvae, preventing them from hatching or developing into adult fleas. Eventually, the fleas will die out. With an IGR, if your dog does get a few fleas, they won't be able to breed, and you won't end up with an infestation.

2. During flea season (which might be in the summer or, in warmer climates, year-round), also keep your dog on an adulticide. We recommend the spot-on treatments rather than the flea sprays and dips, which tend to be more toxic. Spot-on treatments move out, through different methods and across the skin and coat, and kill any adult flea on contact. Used in conjunction with IGRs, adulticides don't give fleas a chance!

3. During flea season, designate one day of each week as Flea Control Day. Wash all bedding (human and canine), vacuum all carpets and furniture (paying special attention to areas your dog frequents), clear all brush and pet waste from your yard (these attract fleas), groom your dog with a flea comb and, if necessary,

181

spray an IGR spray made for carpets and furniture in your house and one made for yards in your yard (a professional can do this, too). However, if you have been vigilant, you probably won't need to spray anything anywhere. Modern flea control products work very well.

Lab Lore

Technically, the fleas plaguing your dog are probably *Ctenocephalides felis*. Non-technically, they are called cat fleas because cats are their preferred hosts. Cat fleas are extremely adaptable, however, and are quite happy to dine on your dog. The dog flea, *Ctenocephalides canis*, is rare in the United States. It's more common in the United Kingdom.

Tackling Infestations

If you do wind up with an infestation, you'll know it. Your dog will be scratching constantly, perhaps even waking you up at night with that thump-thump-thumping. She may end up with hot spots, those painfully itchy, red areas of skin that have reacted harshly to a flea bite or to the subsequent scratching. You may see fleas on your furniture or your bed. (If you let your dog sleep with you—it's okay, lots of us do it!) They may jump onto your arm and jump off again before you can catch them, and if you do catch them, you'll find them virtually indestructible unless you flush them.

Don't despair. Although it isn't easy, you can get the upper hand, but you need to get serious. First, secure your dog outside and clean house. Vacuum every possible surface and vacuum well, including under furniture and furniture cushions. Dust all surfaces well. Wash all bedding in hot water, including your dog's bedding. Spray the areas of carpet and furniture your dog frequents with a flea spray safe for use indoors and meant for furniture and carpets. The best kinds contain an adulticide and an IGR.

Next, it's your dog's turn. If you haven't been treating her with an IGR and an adulticide, now is the time to start. After a good bath, keep your Lab outside until she dries but keep her from rolling around in the grass, where she might pick up more fleas. Groom her with a flea comb, apply the proper spot-on and if you are giving her an oral IGR, give it to her right away. Then bring her into the clean house.

Continue to apply the adulticide and IGR according to the package directions and be vigilant about your weekly housecleaning sessions (but don't apply indoor flea sprays more often than recommended on the label). Don't bathe your pet again for three or four weeks, until the spot-on is ready to be reapplied. If you keep up the effort, your house and your dog will soon be free of fleas.

If your dog is experiencing a reaction to flea bites, such as flea bite dermatitis, or if she is acting sick and you think she might have developed another flea-related problem such as tapeworms or anemia, take her to the vet as soon as possible.

Some Beauty *Is* Skin Deep

The last important aspect of preventive care for your Lab is the daily grooming session. Labs are easy to groom and don't take much effort; there's no long coat to untangle or strip, for example. Daily grooming is important nonetheless. It is an important way for you and your Lab to bond, improving your relationship. It is also your chance to monitor your dog for any physical or behavioral changes. Consider it a chance to touch base with your best friend. Your dog will come to depend on it, and so will you.

Lab Lore

If you are interested in taking the "natural" route to flea control, the only products scientifically proven to work are limonene and borate powder products. You can also purchase homeopathic flea sprays, herbal flea dips, food supplements (such as Brewer's yeast and garlic) meant to make your pet taste undesirable to fleas, sulfur-based products, citronella-based products, B vitamin supplements, pennyroyal oil (highly toxic if ingested), Fleabane and Wax Myrtle branches and leaves. Not much research supports the effectiveness of these products, but testimonials abound. Never try to make your own natural products; use products already formulated for pet use.

Good Grooming for Health and Beauty

Good grooming involves more than a clean coat. It also involves foot and nail care, eye and ear care and a health check. A well-groomed

183

dog is clean and beautiful. An ungroomed dog looks (and is) neglected. Keep your dog healthy and looking her best through vigilant grooming.

Your Lab's Skin and Coat

Every day, begin your grooming session by giving your Lab a good going-over with your bare hands. Massage her head, face, neck, back, chest, legs and tail with your fingers, feeling for any lumps, bumps, dry patches, hair loss or anything else abnormal. The more you do this, the more you'll get used to the feel of your Lab and the better you'll be able to notice when something changes. You'll also loosen dead hair and skin so that it can be brushed away. In addition, your Lab will become accustomed to such a once-over and will be much easier for a vet to handle, when necessary.

Next, brush your Lab with a natural bristle or nylon brush. Although Lab coats don't require a daily brushing (they can get by with a weekly brushing), daily brushing feels great to your Lab and will keep her coat immaculately clean, free from shed hairs and shiny. Last, go over her coat with a flea comb, removing any dead fleas and checking for signs of infestation.

Vet Alert

Labs don't need to be bathed frequently, and too-frequent bathing can dry out their skin, stripping it of natural oils. Instead, make sure your Lab has plenty of time outdoors each day (outdoor air is good for keeping the skin moist) and stick to a good brushing for cleanliness. Only bathe your Lab if she gets really dirty; sometimes plain water will do the trick.

Your Lab's Eyes and Ears

It's time to play vet. Check your Lab's eyes and ears so she becomes used to having them looked at. Again, your vet's job will be much easier if your Lab is used to this kind of prodding.

When you look at your Lab's eyes, check for runniness or irritation. If they look like they need it, you can clean gently around your Lab's eyes with a cotton ball soaked in boiled and cooled saltwater (use about a ¼ teaspoon of salt per cup of water). If you have a yellow Lab and the area around her eyes becomes stained due to normal tearing, rest assured that this problem is natural and not really a problem. It doesn't hurt your dog. If you want to remove the stains, ask your vet to do it or very carefully remove them with a cotton ball soaked in hydrogen peroxide. Always put a drop of mineral oil in each of your Lab's eyes first, however. If you get hydrogen peroxide in her eyes, it will hurt.

If your dog's eyes look irritated, she could have a blocked tear duct, an overactive tear duct, conjunctivitis or something in her eye. Call your vet for advice. If your Lab is showing signs of vision loss or if her eyes look cloudy, she could be developing cataracts. As long as you have been taking your dog for annual appointments, your vet can probably catch cataracts early, but don't hesitate to take your dog to the vet if you suspect anything is wrong with her eyes. Never put anything into your dog's eye.

Your Lab's ears should be clean and free of ticks and fleas (of course). If your Lab's ears look dirty or waxy, you can clean the outside only with a cotton ball or cotton swab. Never put anything into your dog's ear canal. If your dog is scratching or shaking her ears quite a bit but you don't see any pests, or if you notice redness or a bad smell, take your dog to the vet. She could have mites, a yeast infection or a bacterial infection.

Your Lab's Feet and Nails

Foot care for Labs is as easy as coat care. Continue to play vet by picking up each foot, moving each toe and pressing lightly on each foot pad to accustom your dog to having her feet examined. The most important thing to do in your daily grooming session is to make sure your Lab's nails aren't getting too long. Long nails force the footpads apart on hard surfaces, making it difficult for your dog to walk correctly. Bone and joint problems may result if your dog's nails remain untrimmed for long periods of time.

To trim your Lab's nails, use a trimmer made for large dogs, never a human nail trimmer. Trim your Lab's nails frequently so you never have to trim off too much. This trimming will train the *quick*, the vein that runs through the nail, to recede. In nails that are never trimmed, the quick extends farther into the nail, and if clipped, they will bleed. (Keep a styptic pencil nearby to stem any bleeding just in case this happens.) You can see the quick in Labs with light-colored nails, but in black Labs, you have to guess. Just don't clip too far up.

Clip off the nail tips, just where the underside of the nail starts to curve. Trimming your dog's nails every three to four weeks should be sufficient to keep them in good condition.

Some Labs develop cysts between their toes. A topical antibiotic ointment may help, or your veterinarian may choose to lance the cysts. Labs prone to cysts tend to develop them periodically, and a cyst takes about a week or a little longer to resolve. If your dog is prone to cysts, make sure they remain clean and uninfected. See your vet if you think a cyst between your Lab's toes has become infected or if you aren't sure what to do about it.

Those Pearly Whites

The last important part of your daily grooming session should be a good teeth-brushing. Yes, dogs should have their teeth brushed, too! Dental plaque can get into your dog's bloodstream and into her heart, causing heart disease and dramatically shortening her life! If your dog has a serious problem with plaque or tartar buildup (that brownish yellow gook that sticks to her teeth), you can pay a vet to remove it. Sometimes this procedure requires an anesthetic. To avoid this problem, begin brushing your puppy's teeth on the first day you bring her home, and do it every day.

You can purchase a special long-handled dog toothbrush and toothpaste made for dogs at your local pet store (never use human toothpaste on dogs). Dog toothpaste tastes yummy to dogs, so at first, just let your dog lick the toothpaste off the brush. After a day or two of this, you can start carefully introducing the brush to her teeth. Don't expect to be able to do a full, thorough brushing at first. As your dog gets used to the toothbrush, she'll eventually let you scrub away, revealing those pearly whites in their full glory.

Your Lab's Daily Routine

Labs love routine, so try to hold your daily grooming session at the same time each day and do each task in the same order. Consider the grooming session a special time for you and your Lab to bond. Try to keep distractions to a minimum. You can't expect your Lab to stay put if you keep running off to answer the phone or check the food cooking on the stove. Reserve about fifteen or twenty minutes for your Lab and your Lab alone.

Vet Alert

Canned dog food is more likely to cause dental problems than dry dog food. The greater moisture content makes canned dog food stick to teeth. Your dog will love dry dog food if she is hungry. Dry dog food is not only equally nutritious, but it cleans teeth and is more cost-effective. We suggest avoiding canned dog food.

What this grooming time will do is send your Lab the message that she is important enough to warrant your full attention during this special time. If you do devote your full attention to her, you'll also be better able to notice any changes in her behavior or demeanor, and you may be able to catch health or behavioral problems early.

If you have decided to bring a dog into your life, devoting this daily time is an important part of that commitment. A dog isn't a decoration or a piece of furniture. She is a living, breathing, thinking animal that wants and needs a relationship with you. This is just once more chance to further and nurture that relationship.

Keeping a Daily Lab Log

As a final activity in your daily grooming session, we'd like to suggest you keep a Lab log. A simple notebook, datebook or calendar will do. Keep this log with your other grooming equipment. After you have groomed your dog, write down anything you noticed. For example, "Jen seemed tired today," "Nolan was very excited to be brushed today," "Zeke seemed depressed. Could he be getting sick?" or "Henry seemed thirstier than usual."

You can also use your log to record any vet visits, directions from your vet, medications prescribed and every time you administer medication (which you can do during or just after your grooming session). You'll find your Lab log invaluable when you need to answer questions from your vet, such as "When did your Lab first act sick?" or "When did you first notice that lump?" Bring your Lab log along to every vet visit, and don't forget to write in it every day. You'll be glad you did.

Is Your Lab Healthy? A Checklist

Just so you don't forget anything, we've provided you with a Healthy Lab checklist. You can copy it and post it by your grooming area so you can go through it each day. Whenever you notice anything that might indicate your Lab is less than healthy, call your vet.

Today, my Lab had:

☐ A shiny, clean coat

☐ Smooth skin without dry patches

☐ Clean, bright eyes

☐ Clean, pest-free ears

☐ Short nails

☐ Healthy foot pads, no cracks

☐ Clean, white teeth

☐ No fleas or ticks

☐ A normal energy level

☐ A good appetite

Be a Boy Scout (Prepared, That Is)

We don't like to think about terrible things happening to our dogs, and we're sure you don't either. But sometimes terrible things do happen, and you can minimize the tragedy if you are prepared.

If, despite your best preventive measures, your dog gets ill or injured, there are certain measures you can take to give your dog the best possible chance for survival and recovery. This chapter will help guide you toward the best healing strategies for those times when emergency strikes.

When your Lab is involved in an acute health situation, seconds count. Being prepared and knowing what to do can save precious time, even your Lab's life. Keep emergency supplies on hand and easily accessible at all times. Memorize what to do under certain emergency conditions and practice what to do. Your Lab is worth it.

Assembling Your Canine First Aid Kit

The first thing to do when preparing for potential emergencies is to assemble a canine first aid kit. Keep it next to the first aid kit you have assembled for the human members of your family (and if you don't have one of those, why not make them both up at the same time?). Make sure everyone in the family and any pet sitters know where the first aid kit is kept. Keep it well stocked at all times, and if you ever use up any of the supplies, replace them immediately. Your canine first aid kit should contain these items:

> ➤ Gauze pads and strips to use as bandages (tape doesn't stick to fur very well, so be sure you have strips long enough to tie a bandage around any part of your dog's body).

> ➤ Cloth strips strong and long enough to use as a muzzle. Practice wrapping the strips around your dog's muzzle a few times, and then tying them behind his head, but don't leave the muzzle on, of course. You don't want your dog to fear it. (An injured dog, no matter how well-trained, might bite out of pain.) Or you can buy a muzzle that fits your dog and keep it in your kit.

> ➤ A cloth strip and a wooden stick for use as a tourniquet or a tourniquet kit. (Use this only in cases of extreme bleeding or snake bite.)

Trainer Tidbits

A large plastic or metal tackle box or toolbox is an ideal container to hold first aid items for your dog. It is easy to carry, can be stowed in the trunk of your car on trips and keeps smaller items separate. Larger items, such as a blanket, jug of water and water bowl, can be kept separate, but don't forget them!

189

➤ A large sheet on which you could carry your dog, stretcher-style.

➤ A blanket big enough to keep your dog warm, in case of hypothermia.

➤ A tourniquet rod (only for emergency bleeding situations).

➤ Hydrogen peroxide, for cleaning a wound and to induce vomiting.

➤ Syrup of ipecac, to induce vomiting.

➤ Mineral oil, for use as a laxative. Give 1 teaspoon for puppies under 25 pounds, 1 tablespoon if your dog is 25 to 50 pounds and 2 tablespoons for dogs 50 pounds and over.

➤ An antibiotic ointment or creme (the human kind works for dogs, too).

➤ An antihistamine such as Benadryl that your vet approves for use on your dog, in case of an allergic reaction.

➤ Ice packs (keep accessible in your freezer) and heat packs (the kind you knead to generate heat are good).

➤ A snakebite kit, if you have an outdoorsy dog.

➤ Tweezers and pliers for removal of ticks, splinters, items on which your dog is choking, and porcupine quills.

➤ A thermometer appropriate for use on your dog (ask your vet which kind to buy and how to use it).

➤ Water and a bowl your dog can drink from.

➤ A spare collar and leash, in case his is lost, broken or you don't have it with you.

➤ A card with the number of your vet, an emergency center for pets and a poison center hotline that can answer questions about pets (call and ask).

Emergency Information: At Your Fingertips

That card we suggest you keep in your first aid kit can be a lifesaver if it has every number on it that you might need in an emergency and if you keep several copies in strategic locations: in the first aid kit, by each phone and in your wallet. This card is also great information for pet sitters.

Make up your own card after making the effort to find out and fill out all relevant numbers and information (see the following list). Some of the information we have in the following list may seem obvious to you, but you'd be surprised what you suddenly can't remember in an emergency. Also, if something happens to you, someone else might need some basic information, and pet sitters will want all the information handy, too.

Our Labrador Retriever's name is _____.

He is _____ years old and weighs _____ pounds.

He is allergic to _____.

His owners are _____.

We live at _____.

Our phone number is _____.

Our vet's name is _____.

The number is _____.

An alternate vet's name and number, in case ours is unreachable, is _____.

An emergency pet care facility number is _____.

Poison control hotline is _____.

A friend's name and number, to call in case we need help, is

_____.

Special information about our dog:

_____

_____

_____

_____

_____

_____

When Emergency Strikes

When your Lab is involved in an emergency, you need to act quickly. Knowing ahead of time what to do in any given emergency may save precious moments, even your dog's life. Keep that first aid kid handy, take it with you on camping trips and vacations when your dog accompanies you and always be vigilant. Keep your dog on a leash at all times, especially when near traffic. Always have your vet's number and an emergency number handy (memorize them!), and do everything you can to keep your dog away from hazardous situations and poisonous substances. Most importantly, if emergency does strike, try to remain calm. If you are frantic, you won't be able to help your dog.

The Least You Need to Know

➤ Keep your dog and your home pest-free to prevent skin problems and illnesses caused by fleas and ticks.

➤ A daily grooming routine and diligently kept Lab log is the best way to keep your dog in good health and catch any problems before they become too serious.

➤ Be prepared for emergencies by assembling a canine first aid kit and having emergency information on-hand.

Part 4

Your Lab, Your Life

If you are like us, your Lab is a full-fledged member of your family. But how often can you include him in your activities? More often than you think! This section will give you lots of suggestions for involving your Lab in your daily routine at home, at play and sometimes even at work.

We'll give you lots of hints and tips for travelling with your dog, whether around town running errands or including your Lab in your family vacation. People are doing it more and more often!

And if your life changes drastically, as many lives do, we'll help you to ease the transition for your pet, whether that transition involves the introduction of a new baby, a new pet, a divorce or the death of a family member. If you are there for your Lab, he'll be there for you.

Chapter 14

Your Lab at Home, at Work and at Play

In This Chapter

➤ You're busy. When can you fit in time with your Lab?

➤ You work. You can't bring your Lab along . . . or can you?

➤ Great ways to spend your leisure time with your Lab

➤ Kids and Labs: a match made in heaven, if you manage it right!

As your Lab puppy becomes less demanding, you may be tempted to spend less time with him. Now you can finally catch up on all that living you've been missing! Well, that's partly true. Puppies do demand a lot of time, but after they become fully housetrained and well behaved, that doesn't mean you can just return to your pre-Lab life. And why would you want to? Life with a Lab is a joy, especially when you take full advantage of all the ways your Lab can fit into your life at home, work and during your free time. All of these times offer opportunities for training, bonding and just being together.

A wonderful thing happens when you train your Lab both at home and away from home. Your Lab becomes better behaved and will be welcome in more places than you might imagine. Another wonderful thing happens when you train your Lab wherever you are. Your Lab obeys you wherever you are! "My Lab knows his commands. He'll obey them wherever we are!" you might protest. Trust us, dogs that are trained at home only tend to obey only at home. Follow our advice on training wherever you are and you won't be one of those frantic and apologetic dog owners who has to keep insisting, "He really does do it right at home! No, really!"

Don't assume that when you and your Lab are both home, you are spending time together. Bring him into your routine and he'll become a part of it. Pretty soon, you won't know how you ever brushed your teeth, watched television or worked at your computer without him!

Your Daily Routine

Humans thrive on routine and so do dogs. If you can incorporate your Lab into your daily routine, he'll know just what to expect and how to behave. You'll also find that you have more opportunities to spend time with your Lab than you thought you did. What a happy surprise!

The Long Down: Opportunities Abound

The long down is one of the most useful skills you can help your Lab develop (see Chapter 10 for instructions on how to teach your Lab the long down). You'll find the skill invaluable as you go about your daily routine, especially if your Lab likes to follow you around the house. When dealing with a younger Lab, make sure you do a few sit, stand, sit and down position changes before the long down so you burn up some of that Lab energy. That way, he'll welcome getting to lie at your feet.

➤ **At the computer.** These days, most people spend at least a little time on the computer each day. If you are like Joel and Eve, you may spend quite a bit of time sitting there hammering those keys. But you don't have to work alone! Computer time is a great time to train your Lab to do a long down. When practicing the long down, you should be stretching the time between request and reward. When you become engrossed in your work, you'll find this easy to do.

➤ **Phone calls.** If you tend to get involved in long phone calls, a long down with your Lab is a great way to get the most mileage out of that time. Remember, you don't have to praise your Lab verbally every time you give him a food reward or stroke his ears.

196

➤ **Meals.** Labs are very motivated by food, so aren't you just asking for trouble if you ask your Lab to hold a long down while you sit there eating all that delectable people food? If you never give your Lab treats from the table, he won't expect them. You can reward him with pieces of his own food, but as long as you refrain from tossing him a T-bone because he's being "So good!" you won't have a problem on your hands (or under your feet).

On the other hand, if you would like to enjoy your dinner Lab-free and you spend a lot of time with your Lab throughout the rest of the day, don't feel guilty about confining him to his doggy den or, if he can be trusted, letting him amuse himself in another room while you have your meals. You have every right to devote some time to the other humans in your life!

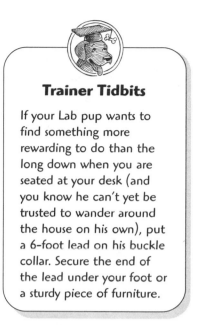

Trainer Tidbits

If your Lab pup wants to find something more rewarding to do than the long down when you are seated at your desk (and you know he can't yet be trusted to wander around the house on his own), put a 6-foot lead on his buckle collar. Secure the end of the lead under your foot or a sturdy piece of furniture.

➤ **In the bathroom.** Yes, we said in the bathroom. After all, you're just sitting there with nothing else to do, right? What a great time for your Lab to practice position changes, or if you want to read, a long down. Talk about using your time efficiently!

➤ **Grooming.** We mean you! When you are grooming yourself each morning (brushing your teeth, washing your face, combing your hair, taking a shower), bring your Lab into the bathroom and let him wait for you by your side. This is also a good time to groom your Lab. Don't forget to brush his teeth! (But remember, use doggy toothpaste for him, not your toothpaste.)

➤ **Watching television.** When you are watching television and your Lab is with you, do a few commands at every commercial break. You don't want to waste your time watching those commercials, anyway, and they are on so frequently that you'll get lots of opportunities for training breaks.

➤ **Shopping.** No, your dog can't go with you to the grocery store (there are health regulations), but many stores will be glad to let you and your Lab come in and browse. The nice thing about bringing your Lab shopping is that people who want to sell you something have an extra motivation to be nice to you and your dog. Just ask, and you'll be surprised how many retailers will welcome your Lab. Pet supply stores almost always welcome dogs.

Lab Lore

Many years ago, when Joel's Lab, Cocoa, started to have trouble jumping into his utility vehicle, Joel and Cocoa went vehicle shopping together. Guess what? Not one single car dealer said, "Get that dog out of here!" (That might mean a missed sale!) When Cocoa stepped into the back of a Dodge Caravan, lay down on the seat and looked at Joel as if to say, "Okay, buy this one," Joel did. Cocoa spent many happy years riding around in Cocoa's Caravan, and somewhere out there is a salesperson who probably remembers with great fondness that incredibly easy sale!

The Thirty-Minute (Plus) Labs-Only Daily Break

Daily mini training sessions aside, you should also reserve one training session for when you aren't doing anything else at the same time. During this special, you-and-your-Lab-only time, you devote all your attention to your beloved companion and the training activities you are working on together.

Young pups won't last for thirty minutes, but once your Lab is approaching his first birthday, you'll be able to work for half an hour. Just be sure to watch your Lab for signs of boredom. Training sessions should be fun for both of you. If your Lab tires of training before the end of his thirty minutes, spend some time together playing, retrieving and having less-structured fun.

The Training Walk

Because the health benefits of walking have become widely known, many people make a daily walk part of their regular routine. You can include your Lab in this health-bestowing daily activity by turning your walk into a training walk.

Training your Lab during a walk is a great way to teach your Lab to obey your requests wherever you are, not just in the house. A daily training walk will reinforce this behavior until it becomes second nature.

As you walk, stop occasionally and have your Lab do a few position changes: sit, stand, down, sit and so on. Then continue the walk. Do this about every 25 yards or so or whatever makes sense in your neighborhood. You could designate certain landmarks as training spots, such as street signs, trees or corners. The continuation of the walk will serve as a reward, and your dog will learn to follow commands at lots of different locations. What a fun way to teach good behavior!

The Practically Perfect Work Companion

If you run your own business or work for yourself, you can take your Lab to work with you! If you don't run your own business, however, you may still be able to convince your boss that your Lab can be a well-behaved member of the team. After your boss meets your well-trained Lab, you may be surprised by his or her response.

Certainly, some workplaces aren't dog-friendly, but many are. Follow our recommendations for training at the computer and on the phone, and your Lab will be the practically perfect office companion. In work situations where you or others move around a lot, consider bringing along your Lab's doggy den to keep him out of trouble (especially if he is still a pup). Although many office environments are potentially Lab-friendly, here are a few we have seen that work well:

➤ Many types of retail stores.

➤ Any pet-related profession, from veterinarian to dog groomer. Make sure your Lab is socialized well to other dogs.

➤ Informal offices (and even some formal ones).

➤ Landscaping, building and other outdoors work.

➤ Drivers of all kinds. Labs love to ride along, but see Chapter 15 for safety tips.

➤ Sales. If your clients are dog lovers, they'll take to you right away! If not, you can leave your Lab in the car (never on warm days!) or in his doggy den.

If you do bring your dog to work, you'll also find that the time spent driving to and from work is more fun with your Lab along for the ride. Just be sure to follow the Chapter 15 safety tips for riding in a car with your Lab.

Trainer Tidbits

If you think your Lab would do well at work but you aren't sure how he'll respond at first, take him there for one or two weekend practice sessions before you try him out on a workday. Show him around while he is on his lead, and then do some training so he gets used to obeying you in your work environment.

When You Can't Bring Your Lab to Work

If your work environment is unsuitable or unsafe for dogs, or if your boss just doesn't go for the idea of you bringing your Lab to work with you, don't feel guilty. Dogs usually sleep when they don't have anything to do and are generally happy to keep an eye on the house for you.

However, they would certainly love to see you over the lunch hour. When your Lab is a young pup, you will have to go home for lunch or have someone stop in to let your Lab out for a potty break. But after your Lab can hold it all day, it is still nice to come home so you can spend a little time together. What a lovely break in the middle of a grueling workday!

Labs Just Wanna Have Fun

When the workday is done or the weekend comes, you and your Lab can have fun, fun, fun! To your Lab, fun comes in all shapes and sizes, including training, working, retrieving and just hanging out with you.

But these activities can also be not-so-fun if they aren't handled the right way. Remember the management, relationship and education information we gave you earlier in this book? If you keep that information in the front part of your brain (or at your fingertips, if your memory isn't what it used to be), your Lab will have a wonderful life and will greatly improve your and your family's quality of life, too.

Labs are social animals, so to them, fun means doing things with you. Labs also like to do things that result in a reward (don't we all?). Labs feel rewarded by many of the same things as humans, including getting to see new places and getting to meet nice, new people. So when work is over and you are ready to play, or even to run your errands and take care of all the aspects of your life not related to work, bring your Lab along. Lab leisure time doesn't have to mean Frisbee in the park.

To help you track down more opportunities to spend time with your Lab on the weekends and after work, sit down and write out a typical schedule. What do you do in the evenings? What about weekends? Then analyze your schedule for Lab opportunities. Could your Lab join you as you drive through the bank and pick up dinner? Could he accompany you on visits to see friends or when you drive your kids to soccer practice?

Trainer Tidbits

If you can't make it home over the lunch hour and you worry about your Lab getting lonely or bored, consider hiring a dog walker or pet sitter to stop in and give your dog something to do over the noon hour. Or hire a trusted friend or family member to do the job. Your Lab will welcome the company, and you'll feel better, too.

If you can't find much time for your Lab, consider changing some of your activities. For example, if you spend time at a gym each weekend, consider taking up running or walking instead. Your Lab could join you, and it would be a whole lot less expensive, too. Do you like to browse the mall? Why not browse a local park, national forest or other outdoor landmark that allows dogs instead?

All in the Family

If you have both a Lab and kids, lucky kids! And lucky Lab! Labs and kids go great together, as long as the Lab is well socialized to kids and the kids are old enough to understand how to treat a dog with kindness and respect (although some Labs are great with toddlers, too, and very forgiving of an occasional tug on the ear or game of dress-up).

201

If you have kids, you are probably busy running them around to soccer practice, ballet class, choir practice, scouting or whatever other extracurricular activities your kids participate in. Chances are, you're also already in the frame of mind that involves finding fun things to do on the weekends and in the evenings. Kids just wanna have fun, too!

Trainer Tidbits

When you drive your kids around, consider taking your Lab in the car with you. Commuting with the kids gets your Lab out of the house, gives him a change of scenery, provides companionship for you on the trip home and as a further benefit, discourages car jackers, who are more likely to pass up a car with a dog in it.

Organizing leisure-time activities (if you can call weekends with kids leisurely) that involve both your kids and your Lab will be great for everyone involved. The more time your kids and your Lab spend together, the more they will learn how to act with each other and the better you will become at managing them all. Whenever you get the chance, introduce your Lab to other well-behaved children, as well. You want your Lab to be socialized to all kids, not just your own. What are some great family activities for you, your kids and your Lab? The list is endless, but we make a few suggestions in the following sections.

Hike It Up

If you live near a state or national park that allows dogs (they will probably require your dog to be on a leash), you and your whole family can go hiking together. Hiking is great exercise for people and dogs, and the fresh air and scenery are great for the soul, too. Your Lab will love to go on hikes, and if you come across a safe body of water, your Lab will be thrilled to go for a dip and retrieve a stick or two. Remember, always bring along water and a bowl for long hikes or any hikes on hot days or in warm climates. And don't forget the first aid kit!

In the Swim

Labs were bred to retrieve fish, fish nets and birds out of the water. No wonder they love water so much! However, just because Labs love

Labs are social animals, so make sure there's time in your family's day for just being together with and paying attention to your friend.

water doesn't mean you can toss your Lab puppy into the pond and expect him to love it. Would you toss your own child into the pond before he knew how to swim? Think about how you were taught to swim. Remember how scary it was at first?

Use gentle, loving care when teaching your Lab puppy to love the water. Find a natural body of water where you can wade in and wade out. Let your puppy follow you at his own pace. Don't get anxious if he doesn't jump right in. The bigger deal you make out of it, the more reluctant your pup may be to follow you. With a little patience, your pup will get his feet wet, so to speak. Joel likes to introduce his litters to the water (assuming the weather isn't too cold) when they are about 6 or 7 weeks old, and they all wind up swimming at that age. If your Lab is reluctant, return another day and let your pup see how much fun you are having in the water, or bring along another dog that is a veteran swimmer. Your pup will get the idea.

Trainer Tidbits

Because so many people love to hike with their dogs, manufacturers have come out with all sorts of products to make hiking easier on everyone. Look for the collapsible water bowls that fit into a back-pack or clip onto your belt. Doggy backpacks allow your Lab to carry his own supplies comfortably. You can even buy doggy shoes, sun visors, sunglasses and raincoats.

Labs are water-loving dogs! Take them to the beach, to a pond or to a river, or set them up with a baby pool. They'll love you for it.

Always bring along towels to dry off your pup after a water outing, before he goes back in the car. Don't let him overexert himself or become chilled. Remember, Labs are like children and cannot be trusted to use good judgment when it comes to doing fun activities. They can get carried away having a good time and trying to please you. It's up to you to say when enough is enough.

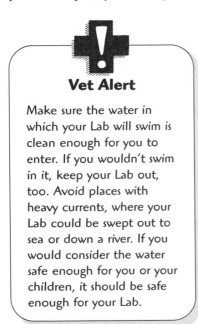

Vet Alert

Make sure the water in which your Lab will swim is clean enough for you to enter. If you wouldn't swim in it, keep your Lab out, too. Avoid places with heavy currents, where your Lab could be swept out to sea or down a river. If you would consider the water safe enough for you or your children, it should be safe enough for your Lab.

Also, always use common sense when your Lab is swimming in natural bodies of water. Labs are strong swimmers, but they can't battle strong currents. Joel learned this many years ago, when he was visiting his father-in-law's cabin on the Platte River in Nebraska.

It was early spring and he was with his first Lab, Bart, doing a little work and enjoying the day. All day long, Bart was bringing Joel a stick and encouraging him to throw it into the river. It was a relatively warm spring day, but there was ice in the river and a fairly swift current. Just before it was time for Joel and Bart to head home, Joel decided one retrieve in the river would be okay. Joel threw the stick, the stick very quickly began to drift down the river and Bart went swimming after it.

Bart was immediately swept down the river towards some ice, and as the river began to sweep him under the ice, Joel, wearing his boots and coat, prepared to jump into the river to save Bart. Just as he was about to jump, Bart managed to grab the edge of the ice with his front paws and claw his way to safety.

Bart almost drowned. Joel could very well have drowned if he had jumped in. When Joel returned to town and told his father-in-law, Gus, the story, Gus replied, "You have to be smarter than the dog." Wise words, which we hope you will take to heart.

Vet Alert

Always supervise your Lab when he is in a swimming pool, and be very sure he knows how to get back out. A bad swimming pool experience can traumatize a puppy and make him afraid of all water. If your puppy falls in the pool when you aren't watching and doesn't know how to get back out again, he could drown.

Sporty Labs

Labs love to play, and lots of sporting events that involve humans and dogs have evolved as people look for more fun things to do with their dogs (see Part 5). If you or your kids are playing in athletic events for humans only, however, your Lab can be a great spectator. Bring him along to Little League games, T-ball, soccer matches, flag football, beach volleyball or an informal game of basketball on an outdoor court.

Taking your Lab to outdoor events where lots of people are milling around, talking and cheering is good practice for your Lab's self-control and your management skills. Your Lab must know that he can't run onto the field just because his kid is up at bat. You have to know that you are responsible for your Lab's behavior. But if you and your Lab are ready for the challenge, go ahead and bring him along. The more practice he gets socializing, the better behaved he'll be, and any sporting event is more fun when the whole family is included.

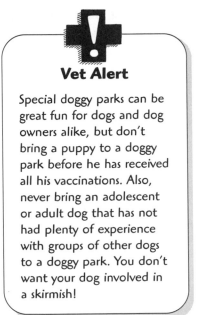

Park It!

If you regularly go to any parks, you already know whether dogs are allowed. If you aren't sure, read the signs or ask the park managers about the rules for dogs. Some parks require you to keep your dog on a leash. A flexi-lead that can extend up to 25 feet allows your dog to be under control and still run around. Even if the park allows for off-lead dogs (something becoming increasingly rare), make sure that you and your dog have mastered the come command before you find yourself screaming at your dog because he finds the park more interesting than you.

Cleanliness Is Next to Dogginess

Of course, no matter where you take your Lab, if you'll be there for a long period of time, he'll probably have to defecate. Yes, we know that bears defecate in the woods. We also know that a beer can will probably be around a lot longer than a pile of dog feces. We've heard all the arguments, but we still say that you should clean up after your dog.

When people clean up after their dogs, the people who run the parks, national monuments, hiking areas, playgrounds and sports fields have a good impression of dogs. When people don't clean up after their dogs, other people complain and that makes dogs look bad. Too many people have neglected to clean up after their dogs, and that is why dogs are banned from so many areas that would otherwise be wonderful places for you and your Lab to spend time together.

Lots of products exist to make poop scooping easier and more sanitary, but a few paper towels and a big plastic zippered bag also work fine. (Bring along some baby wipes or hand wipes to keep your own hands clean, too.) Set a good example, and if others do the same, perhaps more places will be opened up for you and your dog to spend your leisure time in the future.

The Least You Need to Know

➤ You can comfortably adjust your daily routine to include your Lab.

➤ You and your Lab will both be happier at home and at work when you can be together.

➤ Spend a little time exclusively with your Lab each day. He deserves it!

➤ Look for opportunities throughout your day to include your Lab and engage in mini training sessions.

➤ A well-behaved Lab can be a great companion for you and your family as you engage in your leisure activities.

➤ Always manage your Lab outdoors and in public, and always clean up after him.

Chapter 15

Around Town and on the Road

What could be more fun than driving all alone in a car? Plenty! Having your Lab along when you drive around town or go on a family vacation can make the ride much more enjoyable and can even make your trip safer (evil-doers don't want to tangle with people who have big dogs in their cars). Plus, you can rest easy knowing your dog is with you rather than home alone. Everyone will be happier.

Take Your Lab Along

If you are planning to take your Lab along, however, you'll need to be prepared. In this chapter, we'll give you some ideas about how to travel safely with your Lab and how to make the most of your car trips, whether they are around town or on the road. We'll also help you to find more ways to spend time with your Lab by taking her with you, even to places you might not have considered.

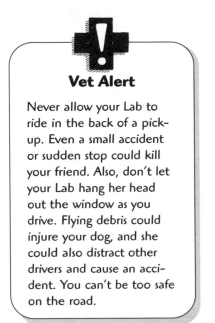

Vet Alert

Never allow your Lab to ride in the back of a pick-up. Even a small accident or sudden stop could kill your friend. Also, don't let your Lab hang her head out the window as you drive. Flying debris could injure your dog, and she could also distract other drivers and cause an accident. You can't be too safe on the road.

First, let's talk about local travel with your Lab. Take a few minutes to make a list of the trips you take on a regular basis in your local area. Where do you typically drive? The grocery store? The bank? The post office? To pick up your kids from school or from their extracurricular activities? Put a star by the trips you think would be made more fun with your Lab along. Don't worry about the details, all the "But how will I"?s that are popping into your head. We'll deal with those later. What? You have a star by every item on your list? So do we!

Your Lab can accompany you to more places than you think. Joel trains families to train their puppies and dogs all around the Washington, D.C., metro area and the suburbs. He does lots of driving and spends an hour or two at each of his client's homes on a weekly basis. For over a decade, he has brought at least one Lab with him, and now he usually has two Labs and a Rottweiler (that's another book). He does this year-round, and it works great with lots of planning. If you become a client of Joel in the summertime, he'll be asking you, "Where can I park my vehicle in the shade?" You, too, can take your Lab just about anywhere if you've planned it right, and one of the most important considerations is your vehicle.

Your Vehicle of Choice

Who would buy a vehicle just for their dog? Plenty of people! Although you can buzz your Lab around town in that little sports car, you won't want to leave her in there for very long. So what are your options for Lab-friendly vehicles?

Baby, You Can Drive My Car (Because It's Too Small for My Lab!)

Most cars have a relatively small airspace, and when your Lab is with you and will have to wait in the car, even for a short time, you'll have to think about ventilation and temperature. If you leave the windows open enough to ventilate a car and keep it cool, they'll probably be open enough for your Lab to escape after that squirrel in the parking lot. If you keep your Lab in her doggy den, you can crank the windows wide open, but then someone could steal your car and/or your Lab. You certainly don't want that to happen!

In the winter, you probably won't have to worry about heatstroke unless you live in a warm climate; plenty of dogs in Florida, for example, could get heatstroke on a warm day in January. Although Labs are more cold-tolerant than heat-tolerant, you won't want to freeze your buddy on a particularly frigid winter day.

Vans and Minivans

If you go to a dog show (a fun family activity, by the way), you'll see that the parking lot looks like a minivan dealership (you'll also see some full-sized vans and more than a few motorhomes). Minivans are great for every kind of dog because they offer lots of airspace, multiple windows that can be opened for ventilation and plenty of room to haul the kids, the dog and all the stuff that both need on any kind of trip.

Regular vans and sport utility vehicles offer lots of room and airspace for your Lab, too, but check to see how easy it is for your Lab to get in and out. If your Lab is aging and/or

Vet Alert

Always be alert to the dangers of heatstroke. When the temperature is just 85 degrees, the temperature in a parked car, even with the windows partially open, can easily reach 102 degrees in ten minutes, 120 degrees in thirty minutes. A dog can withstand a body temperature of 107 to 108 degrees for only a short time before irreparable brain damage or even death occurs.

Trainer Tidbits

Station wagons offer more air space than cars, but they aren't particularly well ventilated. Your Lab may have more room to move, but she can still get heatstroke easily in the back of a station wagon when the only air is coming through those little vents in the back windows. Even better than a station wagon or any kind of car is a minivan, van or motorhome.

suffering from arthritis, hip dysplasia or any other painful condition, a low-to-the-ground minivan may be just the ticket; it's easy to enter, easy to exit and very comfy. Remember Joel's Lab, Cocoa? A Dodge Caravan was her vehicle of choice, and Joel never regretted that dog-centered vehicle purchase.

Lab Lore

Even veteran travelers can face new challenges. Back in 1993, Joel and his Lab, Cocoa, drove from Maryland to California for a meeting of the Association of Pet Dog Trainers conducted by Dr. Ian Dunbar. Cocoa was an old pro at traveling, having accompanied Joel to many seminars. When Joel made the first potty stop in the desert, however, Cocoa looked around, puzzled, and then looked at Joel as if to say, "Well, where's the grass?" Joel laughed and said, "You're in trouble if you hold out for grass!" Cocoa decided to hold out for grass and convinced Joel, with her Labrador Retriever wiles, to stop at casinos along the way instead, where they had plenty of nice, lush grass. When Cocoa pottied, she gave Joel the look that meant, "Good job! Now clean it up, and let's get going."

Motorhomes

Motorhomes aren't cheap, and you may find the price to be more than you can justify for your life right now, no matter how much you love your Lab. But boy, do Labs love motorhomes! Motorhomes are the ideal vehicle for transporting your Lab. You may have trouble explaining why you drive a motorhome around town, but you and your Lab will be happy!

Of course, motorhomes make more sense for longer trips. If you are at a stage in your life where you would like to travel comfortably around the country with your Lab, a motorhome may be the ideal purchase. You'll have fun traveling from town to town, seeing the sights, meeting new people and relaxing in your home-on-wheels.

Joel's Vehicular Pick

Joel goes to lots of seminars, so when it came time for him to get a new, safe vehicle for his dogs when traveling both locally and far from home, he decided he'd better do some research. On the Internet, he found what looked like the perfect vehicle: the Volkswagen EuroVan Camper by Winnebago.

At first, it looked like this vehicle was only available in Europe, but after calling around, Joel found one in the Virginia suburbs of Washington, D.C., and bought it. The Volkswagen EuroVan Camper by Winnebago has lots of ventilation, including a vent in the roof and a couple of screened windows. For hot days, the top pops up and becomes a screened tent! The biggest drawback is the price. It isn't an inexpensive ride.

Your Vehicular Pick

Joel's pick may not be the right choice for your family and your Lab. A lot depends on your individual needs and the way you travel. But do consider your Lab when choosing your next vehicle. Here are some factors to consider when choosing a Lab-friendly vehicle:

➤ Does your Lab's doggy den fit inside?

➤ How well can it be ventilated?

➤ Does it stay cool in the shade (light-colored cars stay cooler)?

➤ Can your Lab easily get in and out?

➤ If everyone in your family is in the vehicle, is there still room for your Lab?

➤ Can your Lab be safely secured in the vehicle?

➤ Does it have room to pack all your Lab-related accessories, such as your canine first aid kit, water, dog bowl and items for retrieving?

If you have children, you may have noticed that suddenly that sports car didn't look quite like the ideal vehicle it once did, and if you bought back in your pre-parent days, you may now find it pretty inconvenient. Now that you are a dog owner, give your dog the same consideration, and your life will be easier when you take your Lab along. Spend some time looking around, trying out options and choosing a vehicle that will allow you and your Lab to spend time together on the road.

Vehicle Safety

Every time you drive in your car, you risk the possibility of having an accident. You put your seatbelt and shoulderbelt on to prevent injury (at least, we hope you do!). But what will prevent your Lab from getting injured if you are involved in a car accident?

As a dog owner, it is your responsibility to see that your Lab remains as safe as possible. Also, consider that your Lab could seriously injure you and the rest of your family in an accident if she becomes an unguided missile inside your car. Take all precautions and secure your Lab inside your car whenever she travels with you.

Confinement Options

You have two options when deciding how to confine your Lab inside your car. If your Lab has reached the point in her training where she only chews her chew toys, your best option is the doggy seatbelt. Available in pet stores and pet supply catalogs, these harnesses have a loop on the back through which you thread the seatbelt/shoulderbelt of your car. Your Lab can sit, lie down or stand up on the back seat and still be safe in a fender-bender. This is how Joel's Lab, Lady, travels, and she thinks it is just great!

If your Lab still chews, follow the training advice in Chapter 9 to teach your Lab what to chew and what not to chew. Seatbelts, of course, are in that not-to-chew category. Meanwhile, your pup should be secured in her doggy den while riding in your vehicle.

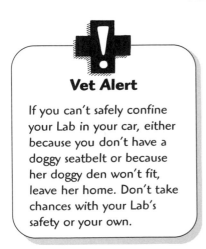

Vet Alert

If you can't safely confine your Lab in your car, either because you don't have a doggy seatbelt or because her doggy den won't fit, leave her home. Don't take chances with your Lab's safety or your own.

A well-secured doggy den, or crate, is another safe option for confining your Lab while on the road. Make sure the crate is secured to the vehicle with the seatbelt or by some other means so that it doesn't become a missile in your car in the case of an accident. The doggy den should be just the right size for your pup: big enough for her to stand up, turn around and lie down in, but not so big that she gets thrown around every time you turn a corner.

Family Vacations with Your Lab

When you brought home your Lab, you did so with the intention of making her a part of your family. You include her in your daily routine, so why wouldn't you want to bring her along on the family vacation? She is family, right? Although we understand that not every vacation is suitable for dogs, we hope that you will try to make your family vacations Lab-friendly whenever possible so you can bring your dog along. She wants to be with you, and the whole family will have a great time if your Lab is well trained and well behaved (as yours certainly is or soon will be).

Trainer Tidbits

The crate is the only acceptable option for a Lab that still chews. Don't give your Lab the opportunity to get in trouble by chewing up your car. That's proper management! Allow your Lab to ride along outside the crate in a doggy seatbelt only when you are absolutely sure she can behave and not destroy your car.

Labs add a special quality to a family vacation. Many people who wouldn't normally talk to a stranger on the road will warm up and strike up a conversation with you when they see your Lab. You'll get the chance to meet fellow Lab lovers and dog lovers wherever you go, and you just might forge some lasting friendships.

If you are a single person with a Lab, the enjoyment of traveling can be enhanced by having a buddy with which to share your vacation. People won't think twice if you discuss things with your Lab—at least not other dog lovers! ("Just look at that spectacular view, Skippy!") Again, having your Lab with you is a great way to meet new people, and your Lab will help keep you safe from people with less-than-good intentions, too. Nonetheless, use common sense and caution when traveling alone with your Lab.

In this next section, we'll give you some hints for making vacations with your Lab easier and more fun. Vacationing with your dog takes a little planning, but it is well worth the effort to make sure no family member gets left behind!

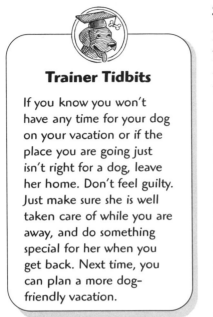

Trainer Tidbits

If you know you won't have any time for your dog on your vacation or if the place you are going just isn't right for a dog, leave her home. Don't feel guilty. Just make sure she is well taken care of while you are away, and do something special for her when you get back. Next time, you can plan a more dog-friendly vacation.

Success Is in the Planning

Labs are creatures of routine, and your Lab will have the same needs and will prefer the same schedule on the road that she has at home. Of course, your vacation schedule can't exactly mirror your schedule at home; otherwise, why take a vacation? But you can still plan to feed your dog and take her outside for potty breaks at the same times each day. If your dog normally sleeps in her doggy den, bring it along so she can feel secure at night. If she normally sleeps with you, don't suddenly banish her.

Also, you'll need to be prepared for emergencies. What if your dog gets sick? You'll have to be prepared to find a veterinarian in a strange area. And don't forget to take along your canine first aid kit.

Vet Alert

Water differs all over the country, and your dog's digestion may be sensitive to changes in the water (yours might be, too). Bring along a couple of gallons of the kind of water you give your dog at home and keep them in the trunk or the back of your van. To prevent a sudden bout of intestinal distress, give your dog "home water" only.

Part of the fun of a vacation is the planning. With a Lab, you may have a little more planning, but that just adds a little more fun! Enjoy the process.

Vacation Checklist

Whenever you travel with your dog, you absolutely must be prepared by taking the following precautions. The extra preparation time will be well worth it if emergency or misfortune should strike. Before you lock that front door and set out for destinations known or unknown, don't forget:

☐ A buckle collar complete with readable identification tags and a tag showing your dog has had a current rabies vaccine. Make sure your dog is wearing this at all times.

☐ An extra set of car keys. If you have to leave your dog in the car in very hot or very cold weather, you can leave the car running with the air conditioning or the heat on and still keep the car locked. Make sure you can see the car exhaust at all times so you know the engine has not quit. If the engine quits, the air conditioning wouldn't work and your Lab could die in just a few minutes.

☐ At least 2 gallons of water from home. Give only this water to your dog.

☐ A water bowl. The kinds that have a weighted bottom or that are heavy enough not to spill are good for in-the-car (or mini-van or motorhome) thirst quenching.

☐ The doggy den and, if your dog is able to keep from chewing up your car, a seatbelt harness.

☐ Enough dog food for the trip, plus some extra in case of spills or other mishaps.

☐ Your canine first aid kit.

☐ A chew toy or two.

☐ Something to retrieve. Hey, it's your dog's vacation, too—she should be able to have some good fun!

☐ An extra collar and an extra leash, just in case.

☐ A flexi-lead, for safe romping.

☐ Any medicine and/or vitamins your dog requires. Don't forget to keep your dog on her schedule of flea/tick control and heart-worm pills (those little critters don't take vacations).

☐ Grooming supplies. Keep your grooming routine the same, even when on vacation. Bring along the brush, nail clippers, flea comb, toothbrush and so on.

217

☐ Old towels, blankets and other clean-up items in case your Lab romps right into a muddy river, for example, and then is ready to bounce right back into your nice, new, clean minivan.

☐ Plastic bags and paper towels (or poop scoop) to clean up after your dog.

☐ This book! We'd love to join you on your vacation and will be glad to serve as a friendly reminder of how to manage your dog in any situation.

Trainer Tidbits

Keeping your dog's routine as normal as possible while on vacation will help her to feel secure and happy. Groom, train, feed and put her to bed at the same times you normally do. In between, have lots of vacation fun that includes your Lab: hiking, camping, swimming and retrieving.

Finding Dog-Friendly Lodging

Some people like to plan every aspect of their vacations before they ever set foot out the front door. If this is you, you'll be in a good position to arrange for dog-friendly, on-the-road lodging. If you like to see how far you can get each day and don't like to plan the journey too strictly (if you have small children, for example, you probably know that you can't plan too rigidly), you may find it a challenge to find dog-friendly lodging at the last minute.

It can be very frustrating looking for a motel, any motel, that takes dogs when it is late at night and you are tired and irritable. You can beg, you can plead, you can explain about the doggy den, you can even perform a training demonstration to the hotel management, but some of them won't budge (the old scrooges!).

We have to commend Holiday Inns for almost always taking dogs, and many hotels and motels will take dogs, but some of them will only take small dogs, and some insist that your dog remain in her doggy den. Be prepared to do a little driving around, and remember to start looking for lodging before it gets too late. Rather than trying to go just two more hours, get up two hours earlier in the morning, instead. You'll all be glad.

When you do find a great place that is happy to take well-behaved dogs, make a note of it and file it away in a place you'll be able to find later. If you compile your own list of dog-friendly lodging, you'll find it becomes a great resource both to your own family for future vacations and to your dog-owning friends who happen to mention, "Do you know where we could stay in Atlanta that would take our dog?"

Dog-Friendly Vacation Resources

Over the past few years, more and more books have been written to provide information that makes it easier for you to take your Lab on vacation with you. The Internet is another good source of information for dog-friendly vacations, and several publications exist that will keep you apprised of the latest information for successful family vacations with your dog.

If you are going to be spending some time in a particular location, contact the local chamber of commerce and ask for any information they have about dog-friendly resources in their area: lodging, parks and other tourist attractions that allow dogs, for example, as well as a list of local vets. They should be able to provide you with the information you need.

In addition, check out Appendix B for great resources for traveling with your dog.

Air Travel

Traveling by air? Leave your dog at home unless you can't avoid taking her along. Dogs that are too big to fit in a crate under the passenger seat (that means your Lab) have to ride in the cargo area of the plane. There's no heat and no air conditioning down there, and although we don't mean to scare you, some dogs die down there, usually due to overheating when flights are delayed.

If you absolutely must bring your dog, take the following precautions:

➤ Make a reservation (there will be a fee) and confirm it. Heck, confirm it twice.

➤ Don't put your Lab into her airline-approved crate until absolutely necessary, and be sure to take her for a potty break just before you put her in.

219

➤ Make sure your Lab's bedding, food bowl and water bowls are secured. Freeze one water bowl so the water doesn't spill and she'll have access to it during the flight.

➤ Stay with your Lab until the last minute, and then take her to the gate yourself and have her checked through there.

➤ Go immediately to the baggage area yourself after the flight to pick her up. Don't be afraid of annoying the airline staff just a little if they won't let you get your dog. Get her as soon as possible!

Chances are, your Lab will be fine, and when you have to fly with your Lab, well, you have to. But in general, we recommend that any vacation on which your Lab accompanies you be a driving vacation. If you have to fly, hire someone to stay in your house or drop in a few times a day instead and leave your Lab at home.

When Your Lab Absolutely Can't Join You

Yes, we understand. Sometimes your Lab absolutely can't come. Maybe it's a business trip, a ski trip or any type of vacation that will be primarily indoors in a place that doesn't allow dogs. Maybe you have to take a long plane trip and don't want to risk stowing your beloved Lab in the cargo hold. Maybe you are going overseas. Whatever the reason, if your Lab can't join you, that's okay. She'll probably miss you and wonder where you went, but you can make her stay at home as comfortable and normal as possible. And boy, will she be glad to see you when you get home! Nothing beats coming home from a vacation to a buddy that is overjoyed to see you. (Watch out for that tail because it'll be wagging like there's no tomorrow!)

If you do leave your Lab, you are responsible for making sure she has proper care in your absence. You can take care of her needs in several ways: by hiring a pet sitter, by boarding her in a kennel or by leaving her with a friend.

Pet Sitters

Hiring a pet sitter is a great solution for when you must leave your Lab at home. She can stay in her familiar environment, and although you'll be gone, everything else will be the same. Pet sitting is a booming business these days, so you probably won't have any problem finding a pet sitter. Although you can always hire a trusted friend or neighbor, a professional pet sitter has a reputation to maintain and a business to run, so he or she can probably be trusted to do a great job. Just in case, however, interview potential pet sitters before you hire them and ask the following questions (based on *Pet Sitter International's Recommended Quality Standards for Excellence in Pet Sitting*):

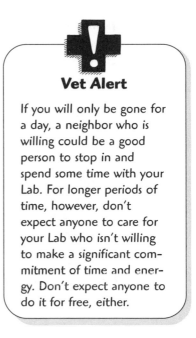

Vet Alert

If you will only be gone for a day, a neighbor who is willing could be a good person to stop in and spend some time with your Lab. For longer periods of time, however, don't expect anyone to care for your Lab who isn't willing to make a significant commitment of time and energy. Don't expect anyone to do it for free, either.

➤ **How much experience do you have?** Many pet sitters are also or were previously animal professionals, such as veterinary technicians or trainers. Also ask how long the pet sitter has been pet sitting. Knowledge and skill come with experience.

➤ **Can you provide references?** Don't just accept the references—check them. You'll be glad you did. Personal referrals from friends who have already used a pet sitter and had a good experience are the best way to find a good pet sitter.

➤ **Are you bonded and insured?** Pet sitters should be bonded to protect you against theft and insured for liability protection. Insurance is one of the benefits of membership in a professional pet-sitting organization such as Pet Sitters International or the National Association of Professional Pet Sitters. Although membership in a professional organization and being bonded and insured don't guarantee quality of service, they do show that your pet sitter is serious about his or her profession.

➤ **Do you provide written literature describing your services and fees? What about a service contract?** Having everything in writing protects both you and the pet sitter from misunderstandings about both fees and duties. Make sure your contract describes everything you expect from the pet sitter.

221

➤ **What do you need to know about my Lab?** You should already know the answer to this question. The pet sitter must have contact information if he or she needs to reach you and phone numbers for your vet, an emergency pet care facility and a poison control center. The pet sitter also needs to know any medical condition your dog has, how to access the canine first aid kit, your dog's name, age, routine, what she eats and when, where she sleeps, her favorite toys and activities, the location of her leash and any other personal things about her that would improve her care. Ask this question to reassure yourself that your pet sitter is ready to find the answers to these questions; your pet sitter may even come up with things you wouldn't have considered.

➤ **Do you keep regular office hours? Are you easy to find?** Because many pet sitters work at their business full time, they are often out and about, walking dogs and petting cats. Most pet sitters carry a pager or have an answering machine and should return your calls promptly, at least by the end of the day. How easy was it to get a hold of your pet sitter to schedule this interview? You might want to try calling him or her once after the interview to confirm the day you'll be leaving. This will give you one more chance to be reassured that your pet sitter is responsible enough to call you back in a timely manner.

➤ **What crime-deterrent precautions do you take?** Part of the benefit of having someone watch your pet is having someone watch your home. Pet sitters are trained to make your house looked lived-in so would-be thieves won't pick your house as the one that is obviously empty. Careless actions (leaving doors unlocked or windows open) or disclosures (chatting with the neighbors about your fantastic vacation in the Bahamas) by an irresponsible pet sitter could also signal that your house is vulnerable. Most pet sitters will also take in mail and newspapers and will turn lights on at dusk and off in the morning.

➤ **Are you aware of federal, state and local laws pertaining to animal care?** Laws differ depending on where you live. For his or her own protection and yours, your pet sitter should know the relevant laws. (It wouldn't hurt for you to brush up on them, too.)

➤ **Do you have a veterinarian on call for emergencies?** Of course you will want to provide your pet sitter with contact information for your own veterinarian, but in the event your veterinarian can't be reached in an emergency, a good pet sitter should have a reliable backup plan.

➤ **What's your policy if you get sick or the weather prohibits you from getting to my house?** A good pet sitter will have a contingency plan in the event he or she can't make it to your house for any reason. Many sitters have other good pet sitter contacts they can depend on to step in. If you have neighbors or friends you trust, you could also give the sitter those phone numbers. A friendly neighbor will probably be glad to trudge across the yard in a blizzard to feed your Lab if the pet sitter is snowbound. Some pet sitters will live in your house while you are away, so getting to your home won't be a problem.

➤ **Will you call to confirm I've arrived home?** You may have every intention of getting home on time, but sometimes the unavoidable occurs. You may end up stranded in an airport where a pet sitter can't return your call to his or her pager. Your pet sitter should confirm that you are home, and if you aren't, should make sure your pets are taken care of until your return.

➤ **Do you provide a service rating form?** Good pet sitters are always trying to improve their service. A service rating form allows them to recognize areas in which they might do better next time. It also helps them to see what aspects of their service are particularly appreciated. (When filling out a service rating form, don't forget to mention the good things as well as the things you think could be improved.)

This process may seem like a lot of work, but would you do any less in hiring someone to watch your children when you leave town? Don't take chances with your Lab. Make sure she has the best of care so you can truly enjoy your vacation.

Boarding Kennels

Another option is to take your Lab to a boarding kennel. You'll find quite a range in quality in boarding kennels, so always check out the kennel and ask for a tour well before your date of departure. If your Lab has to be away from her home, at least make sure she gets a nice little vacation of her own. Some kennels offer extra play time, activities and walks for your Lab. Some have play areas and offer luxurious grooming services. Some are even called doggy spas and doggy resorts.

Although your dog certainly doesn't need to be in the lap of luxury while you are away, you'll at least want to be confident that the kennel is clean, well-maintained and that your Lab will be fed well and exercised at least twice each day. Ask your vet for recommendations about good boarding kennels, talk to the staff of the kennel and don't skimp. This isn't the time to worry about saving a few bucks, and although more expensive doesn't always mean better, in many cases you get what you pay for.

A Friend Indeed

No matter how experienced the pet sitter, some people aren't comfortable leaving their pets with someone they don't know. If you have a friend or neighbor you can trust, you might consider having him or her stay in your house while you are away. If he or she can't stay at your house, he or she could stop in several times a day to spend time with your Lab. Just be sure your friend is responsible and will take the time to keep your Lab company. If you choose someone your Lab already knows and who has a good relationship with your Lab, that's certainly ideal. If they can live in the house, even better. Your Lab will probably do very well while you are away. Make sure you pay your friend for the service. Your Lab and your friend are both worth it!

Preparing Your Pet

You can prepare your pet for her time away from you by making sure she will be well cared for, comfortably confined and able to stick as closely as possible to her regular routine. Do lots of positive training and give her an adequate amount of exercise just before you leave, and then let her spend some time in her doggy den resting before you go out the door. This is a good time to get suitcases into the car; this is something that makes many dogs nervous—they know something's up.

224

If you feel guilty about leaving and shower your Lab with excessive attention, it will be an even bigger shock to her when you leave. If you want to spend lots of time with her, do it when you get back. Before you leave, keep things as normal as possible. Don't make a big deal about leaving, or she'll think there must be something to worry about. Act normally, don't disrupt your dog's routine on the day you leave and tell her good-bye matter-of-factly, as if you are going off to work, and leave without incident. If you trust the person who will care for your dog and know that you have taken all possible precautions, relax and enjoy your vacation. Your Lab will be fine.

Trainer Tidbits

Do not have your pet sitter or boarding kennel staff train your Lab while you are away unless you do a very thorough job of making sure the person training your dog understands and uses positive training methods. Your Lab doesn't need choke collars, reprimands or rough handling. You can pick up training when you return. Your Lab won't forget what she has learned.

The Least You Need to Know

➤ Minivans and motorhomes make great vehicles for transporting Labs.

➤ Keep your Lab safely confined in any vehicle by securing her in her doggy den or in a doggy seatbelt.

➤ Never leave your Lab in a car on a warm day. She could die from heatstroke. It happens all too often!

➤ Don't take your dog along if you are traveling by air, unless absolutely necessary.

➤ Planning will assure successful travel with your dog.

➤ If your dog can't join you, take every precaution to assure that your Lab will be well cared for in your absence.

Chapter 16

The Times, They Are a' Changing

In This Chapter

➤ Moving with your Lab

➤ Introducing a new baby into the family

➤ Should you get another dog to keep your Lab company?

➤ How Labs handle family tragedies such as major illness, divorce and death

➤ What if you die? What happens to your Lab?

We've said it before: Labs are creatures of habit. Your Lab loves his routine, loves his home, his yard, his doggy den and his family. When any of these aspects of his regular life becomes upset, your Lab will feel the stress of the change.

Major life changes are pretty stressful on humans, too, but we have the benefit of being able to understand, at least some of the time, why the change is taking place. Your poor Lab is at the mercy of whatever changes you inflict upon him. However, you can also manage your Lab in ways that will make major life changes easier to handle. If you help your Lab through life transitions, he'll turn right around and help you through them, too.

When You Move

Moving is a highly stressful event for humans (just ask Eve, she moved across the country right in the middle of writing this book). But don't let the stress of moving be an excuse to ignore your Lab. Imagine how your Lab must feel being suddenly uprooted from the home he knows and loves and transported to a whole new territory! He needs you right now, and even though you have boxes to pack and arrangements to make, you also have a responsibility to help your Lab maintain a regular routine and to spend your normal amount of time together. Don't leave him wandering around in the chaos, without any attention from you, wondering what is happening.

Vet Alert

Even if your Lab seems healthy, take him to your vet for a checkup a week or two before you move, and make sure he is up-to-date on all his vaccinations, tests and heartworm pills. While you're there, ask your vet about anything that should concern you about moving with a dog. He or she might have some additional great suggestions that would apply to your individual Lab and situation and might even be able to recommend a good vet in the area where you are moving.

Preparing Your Lab (and Yourself)

One of the best ways to prepare your dog to move is to keep everything as normal as possible. Take a break from moving preparations to engage in your normal grooming, training and play sessions. Busy as you are, continue to feed your Lab at the normal times, keep his water bowl full and take him on his walk. Keep bedtime about the same if you can.

Also important: Practice stress management yourself! If you are getting too stressed out, your Lab will think something is wrong. He'll worry. Really! Labs are very perceptive, and if you are suffering, your Lab will suffer right along with you. Enjoy stress-reducing walks in the fresh air with your Lab. Take time out to just sit on the couch for ten minutes and pet your Lab. Remember, the more organized you are and the more you plan ahead, the less everyone in your family, your Lab included, will feel the strain.

The third and most important thing to remember is to continue to take your Lab to different places. If you have followed the advice in this book about training, socialization and traveling with your Lab (both locally and on longer trips), well done! The move will be much easier on him. If you haven't been taking him to various locations and introducing him to new people periodically, it's time to start.

Ideally, you will begin training him in various locations and getting him used to riding in the car at least several months before the move. Make it as important a part of your moving plans as changing your phone service or booking the moving van. A Lab that is a veteran traveler will take a move to a new location in stride, especially if his routine remains relatively intact and you remain relatively calm about the whole affair. If your Lab is feeling good about the move, he'll be a source of comfort to you when you get to your new destination, too. Exciting as moving can be, it sure is nice to have a familiar and well-loved friend along!

No Dogs Allowed?

If you have children and have to move, you would never say, "Well, it looks like we'll have to give up the kids. It isn't easy to find places that allow them, and it's such an inconvenience to move across country with kids in the car!" Don't get a dog if you aren't willing to make the effort to include him in your life changes. Finding places to live that allow dogs is tougher if you are renting, but it certainly isn't impossible.

Although some landlords will only accept small dogs, don't necessarily assume that a landlord won't accept your well-trained Lab on his or her rental property. Take your Lab with you when you look at possible rentals

Trainer Tidbits

When you're giving away stuff you don't use so you don't have to move it, make sure you don't toss any of your Lab's things into the giveaway pile. Your Lab's doggy den, dog dishes, chew toys, retrieval objects and even bedding—no matter how old and ratty it's getting—will be sources of comfort and reassurance for your Lab in your new location.

and let the landlord see how well behaved and well managed he is. You may just be able to seal the deal! Of course, in some situations, dogs are absolutely not allowed. Find this out on the phone beforehand and don't even waste your time looking.

Don't give up! If finding a place is taking longer than you anticipated, see whether a trusted friend or family member can temporarily house your Lab while you are looking for a more permanent situation. All your positive training will pay off when you find the perfect place to live, where your Lab is welcome because of his good manners and friendly ways.

And Baby Makes . . . Four?

Your family is blessed with a baby, and you already have a well-trained Lab. This is a formula for success! Of course, bringing any new family member into the mix necessitates management. You can't just expect everyone to adjust without a little direction. Many couples have a dog before they have a baby, and until baby comes along, their dog is their baby. But guess what? After your new little human comes home to stay, your Lab is still just as in need of your love and attention as he was before. As far as he is concerned, he was the first child, and the addition of a new pack member shouldn't downgrade his status any.

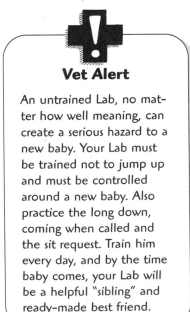

Vet Alert

An untrained Lab, no matter how well meaning, can create a serious hazard to a new baby. Your Lab must be trained not to jump up and must be controlled around a new baby. Also practice the long down, coming when called and the sit request. Train him every day, and by the time baby comes, your Lab will be a helpful "sibling" and ready-made best friend.

First-time parents may find it difficult to make time for their old friend. Even die-hard dog lovers may feel, in those first hectic, sleepless, stressful weeks with a newborn, that their Lab has somehow transformed into "just a dog." The feeling that your Lab will have to do without your attention because you are spread so thin and feeling so stressed is natural, but also unfair to your dog. New moms, especially, are experiencing major hormonal fluctuations and may feel a little blue and extra emotional after baby comes home. It's easy to block out everything but the new baby and even to feel irritated and annoyed with your Lab, though he doesn't deserve it.

All your Lab wants is to welcome you home. He is so glad to see you after your absence and so curious about the new little one! This is where Dad can help if Mom isn't quite feeling up to consistent management. New fathers, you are under a lot of pressure now, too, but managing your Lab can be an important part of your job. Give him lots of love and attention, keep his routine consistent and continue to train him. Plus, introduce him to the new baby in steps.

Introductions

The very first introduction between your Lab and your new baby should be scent-only. Your Lab knows something's up. Mom hasn't been home for a few days, and everyone is acting differently! He may not be worried, exactly, but he is probably extra alert for any clues about what's going on. You can help him by keeping his routine regular, but also by introducing him to the baby before the baby ever comes home.

How? Take a receiving blanket you can spare or even a clean T-shirt or other soft cloth item to the hospital or birthing center and wrap the baby

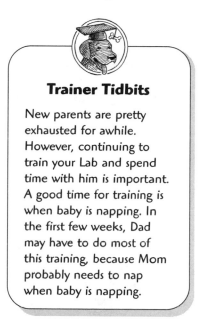

Trainer Tidbits

New parents are pretty exhausted for awhile. However, continuing to train your Lab and spend time with him is important. A good time for training is when baby is napping. In the first few weeks, Dad may have to do most of this training, because Mom probably needs to nap when baby is napping.

in it for a few hours. If the baby spits up on it, great, but it's not necessary. His scent will soon be all over the blanket. Then, Dad or another family member can bring the blanket home and offer it to your Lab. Let him sniff it, play with it, even sleep with it. Let it be his blanket. When he meets the baby for the first time, he'll already be familiar.

When you first bring the baby home, take the next step. While one parent holds the baby, the other parent holds onto the dog. You've seen the way dogs greet each other, right? Let your Lab sniff the new baby's well-diapered rear. Your Lab doesn't need to lick the new baby, and of course, you don't want him to lick the baby's face, although he may try (he's just being friendly, no need to get upset about it). But let him sniff, and encourage him with lots of positive words and gentle strokes, especially when he acts calm. Tell him the baby's name and explain that this is a new family member for him to love. He'll understand what you're saying, in his way.

After you've introduced him to the baby, let him take a nap in his familiar doggy den while you attend to the baby and show the baby around his new home. Don't feel guilty about confining your Lab when only one parent is home and is caring for the new baby. When baby takes a nap, you can do a lot of positive training with your Lab so he knows he is still an important member of the family.

Child-Proofing Your Lab

A well-behaved and well-trained Lab still needs child-proofing. He will probably understand that the baby is like a puppy and will take a friendly interest in this new member of the pack. You may find he takes to sleeping outside the nursery door or staying nearby as a sentinel wherever the baby is playing or napping.

You should take a few child-proofing precautions. Train your Lab to be conscious of the baby. If baby plays on the floor on a blanket, teach your Lab that he can't step on the blanket. If baby swings in a baby swing, you can teach your Lab to make a wide birth around the swinging seat so baby and Lab don't collide. You may need to remind him that some toys are for babies to chew and others are for Labs to chew, and that toys aren't mutually interchangeable. Use the off request to teach your Lab what not to touch, the kennel request to teach him where to go when you need him to be out of the way and the long down or long sit to keep him in one position while you move around.

An important part of training your Lab when you have children around, and even when you don't, is to teach him not to guard his food. It is natural, and a survival mechanism, for dogs to be protective of their food. Dogs had to make sure they got enough to eat; otherwise, they wouldn't be able to pass their genes on. By using the lure-and-reward method of training, you have given your Lab the idea that food comes from you and that you don't steal it, you give it. You will want to teach him the same thing about your children.

It is best to feed your Lab in his doggy den away from toddlers and children until you teach him that your child is very rewarding to have around during meals. While you are still at the point of managing meals without training, remember that if your Lab gets used to eating alone, he may very well warn you or your child if you approach.

If you follow Joel's advice of using food as a lure and reward, you'll be using so much of your Lab's daily allotment of food for training that your Lab will not be eating much food out of a dish. When he's used to getting most of his food from your hand, you can train him to love the fact that your hand is near his food dish.

Make sure your dog is well versed in the "take it" and "off" commands (see Chapter 10). Then, put a piece of food in your Lab's food dish and say, "Take it." What a great reward, getting to eat food out of a dish that you put in there with your own hands! Your Lab will never have the chance to think it is bad to have you around his food dish!

When he is used to eating some of his food out of his dish, occasionally and regularly take a tasty morsel (some kind of special treat your dog loves) and, while he is eating, reach your hand into his dish, add the treat to his regular food and then say, "Take it." He will love you approaching his food dish!

Because all relationships are unique, you will have to carefully train other family members to do the same training. Small children will have to be carefully supervised during this type of training. If your Lab shows any signs of guarding his food, consult a qualified canine behavior consultant at once.

Trainer Tidbits

When teaching your children that dogs should be handled with gentleness and respect, also teach them never to approach a strange dog without first asking the owner's permission. Not all dogs are as well mannered or well socialized as your Lab, and many aren't used to children. Don't teach your child to assume every dog is friendly or let your child become a dog bite statistic.

Lab-Proofing Your Child

When your baby develops an interest in your Lab and begins to reach out for him, do lots of positive training with baby and Lab together, teaching your baby how to handle your Lab gently and not to touch his eyes, pinch or hit. Some babies are naturally gentle and would never hit. Others

By training your Lab and your child to accept each other, you will encourage a great friendship.

are more boisterous and tend to experiment with their environment in a more raucous manner.

If your Lab is already well trained, your baby will probably need more training than your Lab! Always supervise your Lab and baby when together, as much for what your child might do to your Lab as anything! Continue to train and manage both kids and dogs to ensure a lasting, successful relationship. Following are a few more management tips:

➤ Teach your child to leave your Lab alone when he is eating (except when training), drinking and outside relieving himself. Even a friendly Lab has to have privacy once in awhile.

➤ Doggy dens are for Labs only. Teach your children that your Lab is off limits when in his doggy den. Keep your Lab's special, private place sacred, so he can escape the family fray and the prodding and poking of small children if he needs to.

➤ Keep dry dog food out of reach of small children. Kibble is a choking hazard.

➤ Babies love to play and splash the water in dog bowls, yet your Lab needs plenty of fresh, clean water available at all times. Always know where your baby is, and keep him away from the water bowl.

➤ If your Lab ever shows any sign of aggression towards your child, immediately separate dog and child and contact a canine behavior consultant. Depending on the cause, aggression can almost always be managed and doesn't mean you have to get rid of your dog. (By aggression, we mean a snarl, a warning nip that doesn't break the skin or a low growl.)

➤ Make sure your child (or anyone, for that matter) never comes into contact with dog feces. The accidental ingestion of roundworm eggs can pose a serious danger to humans. Have your Lab wormed regularly and talk to your vet about ways to minimize this risk.

➤ A child who can talk can learn positive dog training. Joel has seen children who learned their dog's name and the sit request right after they learned to say Mommy and Daddy.

Pet Number Two (or Three, or Four)

Many folks think it would be a good idea to get another dog, a friend for their Lab. The common thinking is, "We are gone all day. How nice if our Lab had company!" Well, maybe this is true, but maybe it isn't. If your Lab could talk and you asked him, he might very well say something to the effect of, "Another dog? Nah. You're all the company I need. When you can't pay attention to me, I'd just as soon take a nap." He might even say, "What? You don't spend enough time with me as it is, and now you want me to share you?"

If your Lab isn't yet very well trained and you are still working out certain commands or the management of certain behaviors, getting another dog will only complicate the matter. It's harder, not easier, to manage two dogs than it is to manage one. The first dog won't train and manage the second dog for you. You'll have to do it all over again.

> **Lab Lore**
>
> If you have two dogs, you may wonder how they know which of them you are speaking to. Dogs understand that if you are looking at them, you are talking to them. If you have any doubt, go ahead and use your dog's name. Joel likes to have a way of requesting all the dogs to do something. Instead of saying, "Red, Memphis, Mr. Bojangles, sit," he will simply say, "Dogs, sit." It works!

235

Remember all the work it took to get your puppy or dog housetrained and to get him to be a good member of the family? Remember those sleepless nights standing out in the middle of the front lawn in the wee hours of the morning while your puppy relieved himself? Remember all the work to manage your Lab's naturally exuberant behavior? Remember how nice it was when your Lab finally began to respond, behave and understand what you wanted?

You'll have to do it all over again. You'll have to do the same great job with the new dog, put in all the same effort and continue to manage your first Lab at the same time. Plus, you'll have twice the vet bills, twice the cost of pest control, twice the cost of heartworm pills, twice the cost of food, double the doggy dens, two collars, two leashes, two sets of tags, more grooming supplies and at least four chew toys. Is having two or more Labs impossible? No. Is it difficult? Time-consuming? Expensive? Chaotic? You betcha. Are you sure you're ready for that kind of commitment?

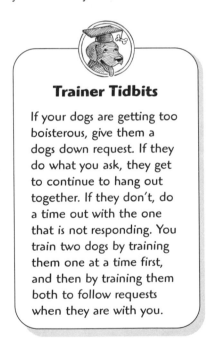

Trainer Tidbits

If your dogs are getting too boisterous, give them a dogs down request. If they do what you ask, they get to continue to hang out together. If they don't, do a time out with the one that is not responding. You train two dogs by training them one at a time first, and then by training them both to follow requests when they are with you.

Another consideration when getting a second dog is the time you'll need to spend managing the relationship between your current dog and the new dog. You'll need to introduce the new puppy or dog properly, being careful to show more, not less, attention to your first dog whenever the new dog is present. Train your new pup when your first dog is sleeping securely in his doggy den so he doesn't feel displaced and you can work with your new puppy or dog one on one. They both need their individual time with you, as well as time learning to get along together (those of you with two or more kids know exactly what we mean).

Managed well, the relationship will probably work out just fine, but may well present continual challenges to work through: squabbles over chew toys, battles for your attention and the room-destroying menace of two frisky Lab pups playing an exuberant game of Labrador tag.

You'll also need to consider what gender to choose for your second Lab. Although the gender of your first Lab isn't as important as finding a Lab with the right personality, gender becomes more important when a second Lab enters the picture. The highest probability of success is having one male and one female. With proper introductions and training, this pair is likely to get along.

Two males can result in problems when the youngest reaches social and sexual maturity at about 18 months, although castrating one of your males may minimize this problem, because the more different the two dogs are, the fewer problems they'll have. Two females are more likely to get along than two males, but if they do dislike each other, the fighting can be much more intense. If you do have problems between your two dogs, the sooner you seek the services of a qualified canine behavior consultant, the better!

If after a lot of soul-searching and planning, you decide you are ready to manage a multidog household, wel-come to an interesting and challenging way of life! You will learn a lot about doggy/doggy behavior. Sometimes, you may think that you do little else with your time at home than train, feed, groom, pet and talk to Labrador Retrievers. But then again, some people think that's an awfully nice way to live!

Trainer Tidbits

Can you walk two dogs at once? Yes! Simply teach each dog to walk on a loose lead. Then connect a Y (available at pet stores) to the end of your lead so you can hook both dogs up to one lead. You can then walk two dogs at once. You can even walk four dogs at once, like Joel does, by having two leads with Ys.

Illness, Divorce, Death

These subjects aren't pleasant, but they are all too often a part of life. If you help your Lab to cope when illness, divorce or death strikes your family, he'll help you to cope, too. You need each other!

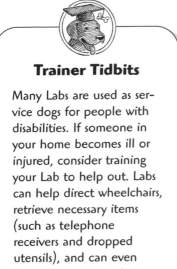

Trainer Tidbits

Many Labs are used as service dogs for people with disabilities. If someone in your home becomes ill or injured, consider training your Lab to help out. Labs can help direct wheelchairs, retrieve necessary items (such as telephone receivers and dropped utensils), and can even learn to open certain types of doors and fetch help. On top of all that, they are a great comfort and make superb confidantes.

When Someone Gets Sick

When a new baby enters the family, it is a stressful yet joyful event consuming everyone's time. When someone becomes seriously ill, you have all the stress and none of the joy. Your Lab can offer you and your family love, companionship and a positive focus for any family member who is ill. Labs make excellent therapy dogs, and if a Lab can cheer up a sick person he doesn't even know, imagine what he can do for those people he loves!

Of course, when someone becomes ill, adjustments will probably have to be made in your Lab's routine, especially if the person who is ill is the Lab's primary caretaker. But Labs are resilient, and although they love their routine, they love you even more. With good, positive training and quality attention, your Lab will be fine and will do his best to help you in whatever way he can.

The Big D

One of the big reasons dogs are left in animal shelters or with rescue groups is divorce. Divorce happens a lot. But if you and your partner split up, please try to decide which of you would provide the best home for your Lab. Many folks work out joint custody arrangements. Getting rid of your Lab because you can't agree on who should have him is the worst possible outcome. Don't punish your Lab for your personal problems. Do what is best for him.

If your family is going through a divorce, your Lab probably knows something is wrong. Labs are very sensitive to their owners, and when people in the family are upset, angry or distraught, the dog will feel the same way. It may sound silly, but try to protect your dog from outbursts and arguments the same way you would protect your children. Labs are easily upset by family dissension because they are so sensitive to what their owners need and want. For the sake of your dog, as well as your children, keep it as friendly as possible.

Plan Ahead for Your Lab's Future

When tragedy strikes and someone in your family dies, your Lab will grieve with you. He knows when someone is gone, and he knows when his family is sad. Your Lab can help you to deal with your grief because he shares it.

But if you are your Lab's only caretaker and you die, what will happen to your Lab? Please amend your will to specify who will take your Lab (make sure that person agrees). If you can't find anyone willing and qualified, consider leaving a donation to the local Labrador Retriever rescue organization along with instructions for your Lab to be placed with that organization. The organization will find him a good home.

We certainly hope none of these scenarios befalls your family, but if they do, please be aware of the effect of family tragedy on your Lab. Be ready and willing to do what it takes to help your Lab adjust, whether that means making a great effort to keep his routine intact or making provisions for him in your will. He is a family member, after all, and what happens to your family happens to him.

The Least You Need to Know

➤ For an easy transition, prepare your Lab for a move to a different home with lots of practice travel.

➤ When you bring home a new baby, make sure your Lab is already well trained.

➤ Lab-proof your kids!

➤ Think carefully about the extra time, effort and money involved before buying another Lab.

➤ When tragedy strikes your family, it strikes your Lab, too. Be prepared to help him adjust.

➤ Please make provisions for your Lab in your will.

Part 5

Fun with Your Lab

Time for some real fun! In this section, we'll tell you all about the great organizations and events out there providing arenas for dog fun. From organized obedience competition to hunt tests to flyball, freestyle and Frisbee, this section has everything you need to know to get started.

And if your Lab is simply gorgeous? We'll introduce you to the world of the dog show. Who knows, yours might just be the next champion! Of course, official champion or not, we know your Lab will always be a champion to you, and the more time you spend together, the better life with your Lab will become.

Chapter 17

Obedience
Is Bliss

In This Chapter

➤ Your dog is ready to try something more challenging than basic commands. What can you do?

➤ Is your Lab Canine Good Citizen material?

➤ The ins and outs of obedience competition

What could be nicer than a happy, well-trained, well-behaved dog? If that describes your pal, and if you are running out of things to do in your training sessions because your Lab has mastered all the basic commands, why not consider a little friendly competition?

Obedience competition can be great fun for you and your Lab and can also get quite competitive, depending on the types of trials you choose. The best way to start is through obedience classes (although be absolutely sure they only employ positive training methods before signing up with your Lab). Obedience classes range from puppy classes and Canine Good Citizen classes to advanced obedience classes that train you to train your dog for the CD, CDX and UT titles.

Your Good Citizen

If you and your Lab would like to pursue some obedience work and have already aced the basic classes, a fun and useful endeavor is to let your Lab try for a Canine Good Citizen award, a sort of feather in your Lab's cap. Any dog can take the Canine Good Citizen (CGC) certification test, but only dogs well trained in basic obedience will pass. This is one award even a mixed-breed dog can win, so if you have a Lab mix, go for it!

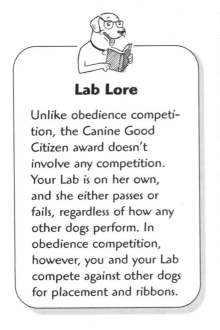

Lab Lore

Unlike obedience competition, the Canine Good Citizen award doesn't involve any competition. Your Lab is on her own, and she either passes or fails, regardless of how any other dogs perform. In obedience competition, however, you and your Lab compete against other dogs for placement and ribbons.

Many dog organizations, including AKC clubs, and other organizations such as 4-H offer the CGC test, so call your local All-Breed Obedience club, Labrador Retriever Club or the AKC office to find the nearest opportunity for testing (see Appendix B). The test is a non-competitive, one-time, pass or fail set of ten tests designed to recognize those dogs (and owners) that have such excellent control of their behavior that they make excellent citizens. The ten tests are as follows (so start practicing):

1. **Accepting a friendly stranger.** In this test, your Lab must remain quiet and well behaved when a friendly person your Lab doesn't know approaches you and speaks to you. You will shake hands with the stranger and talk pleasantly. Your Lab must not show any sign of guarding you, of shyness or of moving toward the stranger. She must stay in position next to you.

2. **Sitting politely for petting.** In this test, your dog sits at your side, and a friendly stranger approaches and pets your Lab on the head and body and walks behind and around you and your Lab. Your Lab must not show shyness or any resentment.

3. **Appearance and grooming.** The purpose of this test is to show that your dog can be safely and easily examined and handled by a stranger, such as a vet, groomer or friend. The evaluator will comb or brush your Lab and lightly examine her ears and each front foot. Your Lab, of course, must allow it and not act shy or aggressive.

4. **Out for a walk on a loose leash.** In this test, you demonstrate that you are in control of your Lab. Your Lab must walk
on either side of you on a loose leash. Together, you must make
a left turn, a right turn and an about turn, stopping once during
the middle of the test and again at the end. Your Lab must stay
in a good heel and can either sit or stand during the stops.

5. **Walking through a crowd.** In this test, your Lab must show
that she can remain under control in a public place. You and
your Lab must walk around and by at least three people. Your
Lab may show interest in the people, but she shouldn't get
excited, shy or resentful. You may talk to your dog, encouraging
her, praising her and giving her direction during this test, but
your Lab must not strain at her leash and should remain next to
you and under control.

6. **Sit and down on command, staying in place.** In this test,
your Lab demonstrates her knowledge of basic commands. You
request a sit and a down. You are allowed to make the request
more than once and to use more than one word to make the
request (such as, "Come on, Shivers. Would you please sit?").
Then, when instructed, you ask your dog to stay and walk down
a 20-foot line away from your Lab. She must stay in place,
although she can change position.

7. **Coming when called.** In this test, your Lab shows that she
understands the come request. First, you must walk 10 feet away
from your dog. You can ask her to stay, or you can simply walk
away if the evaluator is petting her or distracting her. Then you
turn, face her and call her to you. She must, of course, come.

8. **Reaction to another dog.** In this test, your Lab shows how
well behaved she can be around other dogs. You and your Lab
must approach another handler and dog from about 10 yards
away. You and the other handler will stop, shake hands, talk
pleasantly and then continue on for another 5 yards. Both dogs
should show casual interest in each other, but they shouldn't
break position or act shy or aggressive.

9. **Reaction to distractions.** In this test, your Lab proves she is
confident and well behaved in distracting situations. The evaluator will set up some common distractions, such as a loud noise,

245

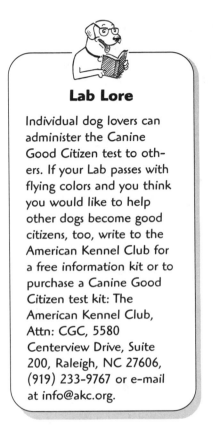

Lab Lore

Individual dog lovers can administer the Canine Good Citizen test to others. If your Lab passes with flying colors and you think you would like to help other dogs become good citizens, too, write to the American Kennel Club for a free information kit or to purchase a Canine Good Citizen test kit: The American Kennel Club, Attn: CGC, 5580 Centerview Drive, Suite 200, Raleigh, NC 27606, (919) 233-9767 or e-mail at info@akc.org.

like a large book being dropped to the floor, or a jogger running by in front of the dog. Your Lab must show some natural interest and curiosity and may appear a little startled, but she shouldn't act panicky, fearful or aggresive. Your Lab must also not try to run away or bark.

10. **Supervised separation.** In this final test, your Lab shows that she can behave herself when left alone and will contin ue to demonstrate good man ners and training. The evaluator will say something to the effect of, "Would you like me to watch your dog?" and you will agree. Hand the leash to the evaluator and walk out of sight. The dog will be held for three minutes, and although she doesn't have to maintain a position (such as a sit), she should not spend the whole three minutes barking, whining, howling, pacing or acting very nervous. She can, however, act slightly agitated. After all, you are such a wonderful companion and have trained her so well that she misses you!

Lab Lingo

The **UKC,** or **United Kennel Club, Inc.,** is the second oldest and second largest all-breed dog registry in the United States. The UKC registers purebred dogs and hosts conformation shows, obedience trials, agility trials, field trials, water races, night hunts, bench shows and hunting tests for retrievers, among other events.

If you passed, congratulations! If you didn't, you can try again another time. Keep working with your Lab. When she does earn her CGC certification, you can both be very proud.

Obedience Is Fun!

If you are looking for titles for your Lab, you'll need to attend trials and tests sanctioned by the American Kennel Club, in which your Lab can earn points towards obedience titles such as Companion Dog Excellent (CDX) and Utility Dog (UD). If you're just looking for some fun, attend fun matches and matches sanctioned by the AKC and *UKC (United Kennel Club, Inc.)* that don't count for points towards titles.

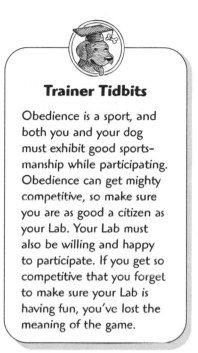

Trainer Tidbits

Obedience is a sport, and both you and your dog must exhibit good sportsmanship while participating. Obedience can get mighty competitive, so make sure you are as good a citizen as your Lab. Your Lab must also be willing and happy to participate. If you get so competitive that you forget to make sure your Lab is having fun, you've lost the meaning of the game.

The purpose of obedience trials is more than just proof that your Lab obeys. Obedience is meant to show how useful purebred dogs are as companions to humans. In obedience trials, dogs are expected to show they can behave themselves in all venues, including in the presence of other people and other dogs. Advanced obedience work includes tracking, which demonstrates your Lab's natural ability to follow a scent. Tracking is a rigorous sport requiring lots of energy on the part of both your Lab and you, so if you would like to try it, be sure you are both in good shape!

Titles

In obedience, your Lab may earn certain titles, each of which requires the performance of certain exercises. Titles are earned in different classes, including Novice, Utility and Open. Exercises for titles become progressively more difficult, of course.

Obedience titles are Companion Dog (CD), Companion Dog Excellent (CDX), Utility Dog (UD), Utility Dog Excellent (UDX) and Obedience Trial Champion (OTCh). Your dog can also earn titles in tracking, a competition that tests his ability to follow a scent. Titles include Tracking Dog (TD), Tracking Dog Excellent (TDX), Variable Surface Tracking (VST) and Champion Tracker (CT).

The Least You Need to Know

➤ Obedience trials and matches can be a fun way to spend time with your Lab.

➤ Train your Lab to earn her Canine Good Citizen certificate, and you'll both be proud of how well behaved she is.

➤ Obedience matches and trials consist of exercises by which you and your Lab can show how well you work together and communicate.

➤ Obedience trials give your Lab an opportunity to earn points towards titles, including Companion Dog (CD), Companion Dog Excellent (CDX), Utility Dog (UD), Utility Dog Excellent (UDX) and Obedience Trial Champion (OTCh.).

➤ Tracking tests give your Lab the opportunity to achieve the following titles: Tracking Dog (TD), Tracking Dog Excellent (TDX), Variable Surface Tracker (VST) and Champion Tracker (CT).

Chapter 18

It's in the Blood: Hunting Tests and Field Trials

> **In This Chapter**
>
> ➤ Hunting test rules and format
>
> ➤ The difference between hunting tests and field trials
>
> ➤ Field trial rules and format

Labs were bred for the hunt. The earliest Labrador Retrievers, way up north in Newfoundland, helped man survive by aiding him in the hunt and retrieving fish and game. Even today, many hunters bring along Labs as their companions and helpers, and Labs are still bred to excel at hunting and retrieving game.

If you aren't interested in hunting or field trial competition, you can skip this chapter. If you are a hunter or are interested in the sport of hunting or in pitting your Lab against other Labs to see who demonstrates the most precise and impressive retrieving skills in the field, this is the chapter for you.

Hunting Tests

The purpose of hunting tests is to test how well your Labrador Retriever can work with you on the hunt. Hunting tests test and evaluate the suitability of retrievers as hunting companions in the field, so hunting tests, although structured, simulate as closely as possible actual hunting conditions.

Lab Lore

Not all breeds are eligible to participate in hunting tests. Eligible breeds are Labrador Retrievers, Chesapeake Bay Retrievers, Curly-Coated Retrievers, Flat-Coated Retrievers, Golden Retrievers, Irish Water Spaniels and Standard Poodles. Most hunting tests are open to all of these breeds, although specialty clubs for a particular breed may conduct hunting tests for that breed only.

The ability of your Lab to retrieve game birds will be tested under many possible conditions, including on land and in the water, and all tests and conditions are organized and orchestrated by the judges. These judges usually have a lot of experience hunting waterfowl and upland game (like pheasants) and must attend AKC Retriever Hunting Test seminars.

Like obedience, hunting is a sport, and both dogs and handlers are expected to behave with proper sportsmanship. That means no handlers abusing dogs (or judges) and no dogs attacking other dogs.

The Program

Although each hunt test is unique because every environment and every judge is different, the basic setup works something like this: When it is your Lab's turn, the judge will call his number. You and your Lab approach the line. Once your Lab is at the spot where the test begins, he is considered as being tested until the test is over and he moves back out of view of the test area.

Everyone, judges included, is dressed in customary hunting garb. When a bird is shot, your Lab must be able to see it fall. Then, when you instruct your Lab, he should run to where the bird fell, find it and bring it back to you, gently, without dropping it. Your Lab will be tested on both land and water, having to retrieve birds under all sorts of conditions. Dogs are scored on *marking*, their style in retrieving, the perseverance, courage and hunting ability used to find and retrieve a fallen bird and their trainability, which involves their steadiness, control, response and delivery.

➤ **Marking.** A dog that doesn't find a bird that the judges believe he should have found will receive a low score in marking.

Lab Lingo

Marking is a dog's ability to observe and remember where a bird fell so he can find the bird and retrieve it.

Marking, or memory of where the bird fell, is considered one of the most important qualities in a retriever and a natural ability. Even if your Lab doesn't see exactly where a bird fell, he has good marking if he looks towards the fall, is paying attention to where it went and goes straight towards the area. Marking scores are lower for dogs that unnecessarily disturb the area while looking for or getting to the bird (the fall).

➤ **Style.** Your Lab's retrieving style is the way he acts, how alert he is, how eager he is and how quickly he retrieves. Style also includes the manner in which your Lab enters water, picks up birds and returns them. Dogs that are a pleasure to watch have great style. Marking and style are considered the two most important natural abilities of retrievers. According the *Regulations & Guidelines for AKC Hunting Tests for Retrievers*, style includes "an alert and obedient attitude, a fast, determined departure both on land and into the water, an aggressive search for the fall, a prompt pick-up and a reasonably fast return."

➤ **Perseverance/courage/hunting.** This category is evidenced by your Lab's determination.

Lab Lore

If your dog is too rough on the bird so that it is unfit for human consumption, he cannot receive a qualifying score. However, the judges should closely inspect the bird because the dog may not have been resposnsible for the condition of the bird. *Hardmouth* is a term applied to a dog that is so rough on birds that he crushes their bones or otherwise severely damages them. This term carries a stigma and marks a retriever as undesirable.

If your Lab's a natural bird dog, you may want to test his skills in an organized hunt test or field trial. (photo by Marianne and Jessica Cook)

How aggressively does he go for the bird? Does he hesitate, or is he systematic in his approach? When the going gets rough, does he enter cold water or mud with disdain? Does he come back without the bird or look for it without much interest? Does he keep looking back to you for directions or does he find the bird but then fail to pick it up? Hesitancy, lack of confidence and lack of drive are all considered faults in the perseverance/courage/hunting area.

➤ **Trainability.** Although considered less important than natural ability, trainability is nonetheless an important consideration in judging a Lab's hunting skill. In other words, you have to do some of the work, too! If you've taught your Lab to be steady on the line without moving around too much, to be under control at all times with good manners, to be responsive to your requests and direction and to deliver the bird to your hand willingly and easily without dropping it, you've done a good job with your dog, and he's done a good job, too. Trainability is judged according to your Lab's steadiness, control, response and delivery.

Rules and Titles

Qualifying scores in hunting tests go toward the titles of Junior Hunter (JH), Senior Hunter (SH) and Master Hunter (MH).

Field Trials

According to the AKC, field trials "are practical demonstrations of the dog's ability to perform, in the field, the functions for which they were bred." That means that field trials are completely different for different breeds. Retrievers have their own field trials and so do pointing breeds, spaniels, Beagles, Basset Hounds and Dachshunds. Of course, we'll limit our discussion to retriever field trials.

Although hunting tests are a little like Canine Good Citizen tests, field trials are more like obedience trials. Also called *non-slip retriever* trials, they test a retriever's ability to retrieve game birds under all conditions. Like hunting tests, field trials are meant to simulate an ordinary shoot. However, field trials are more formal and a lot more competitive than hunting tests.

Other than that, however, they are fairly similar. Conditions vary in different areas, and judges are responsible for arranging the trials to best simulate a natural shooting scenario.

Lab Lore

The North American Hunting Retriever Association (NAHRA) is a not-for-profit organization created in 1983 to preserve the hunting instincts of retrievers. The NAHRA believes retrievers often don't fulfill their hunting potential and attempts to provide a structure for the evaluation of hunting and retrieving work, including tests and competitions in which dogs don't place, but instead compete against an ideal standard. To learn more about the NAHRA, check out their Web site at http://www.starsouth.com/nahra/.

The Least You Need to Know

➤ You and your Lab can participate in hunting tests to earn the titles of Junior Hunter, Master Hunter and Senior Hunter.

➤ In hunting tests, your Lab will be judged on marking, style, perseverance/courage/hunting and trainability.

➤ Field trials are more formal, expensive and competitive forums for evaluating the ability of retrievers to retrieve fallen game.

➤ Whatever sport you and your Lab engage in together, remember to keep it fun for both of you and to practice good sportsmanship.

Your Agile Lab: Agility Trials

Maybe you and your Lab have tackled obedience and think it's fun but are looking for something more. Does your Lab excel at tricks, jumping and running? Do you think she would be great at maneuvering an obstacle course? If you are looking for some serious fun, consider training your Lab to compete in the sport of Agility.

Agility

Agility is one of the latest rages in dog events. Why? Because it's a whole lot of fun! Your Lab gets to perform on a playground of equipment, competing against other dogs to see who can maneuver the courses with the most accuracy, speed, attention to their handlers (that's you!) and grace.

Agility is a great way to keep your Lab in shape, have fun, reinforce and add to basic training and demonstrate to an appreciative crowd how well behaved, talented, responsive and agile your Lab is. Agility trials often draw large crowds because they are almost as fun to watch as they are to do.

The Course

The fun part of the agility trial is the obstacle course itself. If you are competing in the Novice class, you may walk your dog through the *contact obstacles*, before the competition begins. Your Lab may do a few warm-up jumps, but these must be done off the course.

Lab Lingo

Contact obstacles are the obstacles in an agility obstacle course with painted areas with which the dog must make contact while tackling the obstacle. Any part of a dog's foot may touch the contact zone, but the dog will be faulted and lose points if she misses the contact point. Contact zones are often painted bright yellow and are on the A-Frame, Dog Walk and Seesaw obstacles.

The following obstacles are part of an agility trial obstacle course:

➤ **The A-Frame.** Dogs must go up one panel of the A-frame and go down the other panel in whatever direction the judge orders. Contact zones are painted on the A-frame, often bright yellow. Your dog must touch the contact zone points with part of her foot on the way down only. The A-frame is about 5 to 5½ feet tall, and the top surface is painted with a non-slip surface.

➤ **The Dog Walk.** This structure has a center section with two ramp sections, all about 1 foot wide and either 8 or 12 feet long and about 3 to 4 feet off the ground and painted with a non-slip surface. This structure is also painted with contact zones. Your dog must go up one ramp, cross the center section and go down the other ramp in whatever order the judge specifies, touching each contact zone with part of her foot.

➤ **The Seesaw.** This structure is a plank or panel on a center fulcrum. The plank is about one foot wide and 12 feet long, and the base extends 2 inches past the sides of the plank so your dog can see where the center point is. The plank is painted with a non-slip surface, and contact zones that are 42 inches long are painted on each end. Your dog must ascend the plank, cause it to seesaw the other way and then descend. Your dog must wait for the opposite side of the plank to touch the ground before getting off the seesaw, and she must touch each contact zone with part of her foot.

➤ **The Pause Table.** This table has about a 36-inch square top painted with a non-slip surface or carpeted. The height of the table depends on your dog's height division. For Labs, it would be either 16 inches or 24 inches tall. Your Lab must jump onto the table, pause for five seconds in a sit or down position (according to what the judge decrees) and then dismount.

➤ **The Open Tunnel.** This flexible tube can be formed into different shapes, and the openings are either round or rectangular and are no higher than 26 inches. The tube is 10 to 20 feet long, although the AKC recommends a 15-foot length. It must be positioned so that your dog cannot see the end of the tunnel when she enters the tunnel and must also be secured so it doesn't move or roll around when your dog is in it. (Securing the tunnel isn't your responsibility.) Your dog must go in one end of the tunnel (the one the judge indicates), go through the tunnel and come out the other side.

➤ **The Closed Tunnel.** This tunnel has a rigid entrance connected to a chute. The opening section is 24 to 36 inches long and about 2 feet in diameter. The bottom inside surface is non-slip. The rest of the tunnel is made of a lightweight, sturdy material such as rip-stop nylon. This chute isn't rigid so the tunnel looks closed to the dog. It is open, however, flaring to a 96-inch opening at the end. Your dog must enter the tunnel and exit through the chute.

➤ **The Weave Poles.** This part of the obstacle course consists of six to twelve poles mounted on a base or stuck in the ground. Each pole is about an inch in diameter and at least 3 feet tall, uniformly spaced at about 2-foot intervals. The poles must be

257

Trainer Tidbits

If your dog makes a mistake when moving through the Weave Poles by missing an interval or going the wrong way, she must go back to the beginning of the Weave Poles or back to the place where the error occurred and start again.

flexible so that they can bend to make way for very large dogs. Your dog must enter the section of Weave Poles by going between the first two poles from right to left, then moving from left to right between the second and third poles, right to left between the third and fourth poles, and so on, going through the entire section with this weaving movement.

➤ **The Single Bar Jump.** This portion of the course has bars on supports positioned so the base can be adjusted for different height divisions. Usually, two or more bars are on the supports for the jump. Your dog must jump over the top bar without knocking it off, in the direction the judge specifies.

➤ **The Panel Jump.** In this jump, six boards are arranged on upright supports to look like a solid wall. Dogs must jump over the top board without knocking it off, in the direction the judge specifies.

➤ **Other Single Jumps.** Courses can also include other types of single jumps for your dog to jump over, without knocking off the top crosspieces, of course.

➤ **The Double Bar Jump.** This jump has two parallel bars positioned at the correct height for your dog's height division; it resembles two single bar jumps placed together. The distance between the two crossbars is one-half the jump height division. For example, if your Lab is in the 20-inch division (22 inches and under at the withers), the distance between the two bars in the Double Bar Jump would be 10 inches. For the 24-inch division, the distance would be 12 inches. Your dog must jump over both top bars without knocking off either one in whatever direction the judge specifies.

➤ **The Triple Bar Jump.** In this jump, the dog must clear three bars of gradually increasing heights. For a dog in the 20-inch height division, the horizontal distance between each bar is 10 inches, but the three bars are 10, 15 and 20 inches in height, respectively. For a dog in the 24-inch division, the bars are 12 inches apart horizontally, and 12, 18 and 24 inches in height. Your Lab must jump over all three bars without knocking off any in whatever direction the judge specifies.

➤ **The Tire Jump (or Circle Jump).** This jump consists of a tire or other, similar object suspended from a frame. The inner diameter of the tire must be about 2 feet, and the frame must allow the tire to be suspended at different heights appropriate for different height divisions. Your Lab must jump through the tire opening in the direction the judge specifies.

➤ **The Window Jump.** This jump looks like a wall with a window in it. The window must be about a 2-foot square or a circle with a 2-foot diameter. The wall must extend for at least 1 foot around the window, and the frame must allow for the window to be adjusted to different jump heights. Your Lab must jump through the window opening in the direction the judge specifies.

➤ **The Broad Jump.** This jump consists of four 8-inch sections or five 6-inch sections, each about 4 to 5 feet long and of different heights, either arranged in ascending height or in a hogback arrangement (ascending then descending). The length of the entire jump is twice the height of the division. For example, if your Lab is in the 20-inch division, the broad jump length would be 40 inches. If your Lab is in the 24-inch division, the broad jump length would be 48 inches. Your Lab must jump over all the sections without touching them, entering between marker poles placed near the front and exiting between marker poles placed near the back.

That's it! That's the course. Of course, depending on how advanced your Lab is and what titles she's acquired, the number of obstacles will vary. All courses must clearly show where the beginning and ending are, and each obstacle or jump must be clearly numbered so

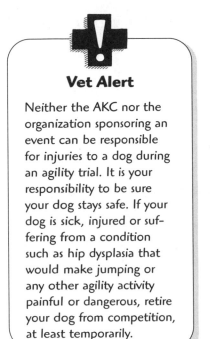

Vet Alert

Neither the AKC nor the organization sponsoring an event can be responsible for injuries to a dog during an agility trial. It is your responsibility to be sure your dog stays safe. If your dog is sick, injured or suffering from a condition such as hip dysplasia that would make jumping or any other agility activity painful or dangerous, retire your dog from competition, at least temporarily.

you know the order. You'll have at least a half an hour before the start of your competition to see the order and survey the obstacle course layout.

Jumpers With Weaves

Jumpers With Weaves is a whole separate agility class further demonstrating how well you and your dog work together. This course is faster because it doesn't include contact zones or a Pause Table. You and your Lab can just go, go, go! The course is mostly jumps, and your dog will be judged primarily on her speed and jumping ability.

The Least You Need to Know

➤ Agility is a fun, competitive sport in which you and your Lab can participate together.

➤ Agility trials consist of obstacle courses through which your dog can run, jump, crawl, balance, climb and weave.

➤ The agility titles your dog can earn are Novice Agility (NA), Open Agility (OA), Agility Excellent (AX), Master Agility Excellent (MX), Master Agility Champion (MACH), Novice Jumper With Weaves (NAJ), Open Jumper With Weaves (OAJ), Excellent Jumper With Weaves (AXJ) and Master Excellent Jumper With Weaves (MXJ).

Chapter 20

The Three F's: Flyball, Freestyle and Frisbee

In This Chapter

➤ The fast and furious sport of Flyball

➤ Canine Freestyle, when you and your Lab have rhythm

➤ The art and sport of Canine Frisbee

If you and your Lab are born athletes or are looking for some creativity in your activities together, or if you just want to get into a really good game, look into Flyball, Freestyle and Frisbee. These sports are catching on fast, and if they aren't available in an organized form in your area, they probably will be soon. Fun to participate in, fun to watch, less stringently regulated and less formal than many AKC events and a great way to spend time with your dog, these activities may be just what you are looking for.

Flyball

Flyball is a team sport, but the teams are made up of dogs, not people. Invented in California in the late 1970s, Flyball soon became immensely popular, and in the 1980s, the North American Flyball Association (NAFA) was formed.

Lab Lore

A dog named Rocket Relay broke the world record time for running a Flyball course (which was 16.70 seconds) by running the course in 16.35 seconds at a June 1998 Flyball tournament in Cookstown, Ontario. The North American Flyball Association (NAFA) has officially declared this a world record. A different dog scored a time of 16.20 seconds in November 1998 at the Flyball Triple Crown in Brampton, Ontario, but these results are still awaiting ratification by the NAFA at the time of this writing.

Trainer Tidbits

You can start training your Lab to learn Flyball when he is just a puppy. Whenever practicing retrieving, always run away from the puppy after you throw an object to be retrieved. This will encourage him to chase after you, increasing his speed and his instinct for the relay race.

How It Works

Flyball is a relay race. Each team consists of four dogs that run a course with four hurdles, spaced 10 feet apart, and a spring-loaded box 15 feet from the last hurdle. When stepped on, the box shoots out a tennis ball.

The total length of the course is 51 feet (including a 6-foot distance between starting line and the first hurdle). Hurdle heights depend on the height of the dogs and must be 4 inches lower than the height at the withers of the shortest dog on the team. The minimum possible height is 8 inches, and the maximum possible height is 16 inches.

The dogs line up at the starting line and must then jump all four hurdles, jump onto the box so the tennis ball shoots out and then run to catch the tennis ball, returning over the four hurdles. When the first dog crosses back over the starting line, the next dog takes off. The first team to have all four dogs run the course without making a mistake wins that heat.

If you like the idea of Flyball, attend a few tournaments and watch the action. You'll see all kinds of breeds participating and lots of mixed-breed dogs, too. If it looks like fun, start training your Lab to jump over hurdles and to bring tennis balls back to you.

If you want more help in training your Lab for Flyball, contact NAFA (see Appendix B) and look at its Web site. Also check out the Flyball Home Page at http://muskie.fishnet.com/ ~flyball for training information and Flyball contacts, people who can tell you what has worked for them. And remember, use positive training methods only!

Lab Lore

The Flyball Newsletter, *Finish Line*, lists all tournament events and results and is available for $20 for a one-year subscription (which includes four issues). Write to Melanie McAvoy, 1002 E. Samuel Avenue, Peoria Heights, IL 61614, 309-682-7617, e-mail: melmcavoy@ worldnet.att.net.

Freestyle: Gotta Dance!

Maybe you are more creatively inclined or want to be out there playing with your dog, not just watching him run relays. Then perhaps Canine Freestyle is for you! Canine Freestyle, sometimes called Canine Musical Freestyle, is an extension of obedience training that is set to music and choreographed using basic and advanced obedience moves. First popular in Canada, it is now becoming increasingly popular in the United States. When your Lab has earned his CD (Companion Dog obedience title) or knows enough that he could earn it if you chose to participate in competition, you and he are probably ready to begin learning Canine Freestyle.

The Canine Freestyle Federation, Inc., or CFF, was founded in 1995 and incorporated in 1996. They are an international organization that has provided structure, rules, competitions and demonstrations to organize and promote the sport of Canine Freestyle. Musical Canine Sports International (MCSI) was also created to regulate Canine Freestyle, providing competitions, regulations, guidelines and titles. In 1994, the Illini Obedience Association adopted the MCSI Freestyle rules and guidelines,

Lab Lore

Where did they get the idea to set obedience training to music? From horses! Equine dressage is a sport in which horses perform to music, and if horses can do it, so can dogs.

and MCSI now sanctions competitions in the United States (the sport was first popular in Canada).

Canine Freestyle is great fun to watch, so attend a demonstration or competition if you can. Important to a successful performance is creativity and originality, so you'll see some interesting stuff.

Lab Lingo

Turns can be to the right, left or an about-face. Turns are performed while in a heel position. **Pivots** are in-place turns with your dog in a heel position. Either the handler or the dog remains in place.

Trainer Tidbits

Although many types of Frisbees will work for competition and training, many Canine Frisbee pros recommend the Fast Back 2000 Freestyle Frisbee by Mattel, weighing 119 grams. This disc is reportedly lightweight and easy to throw.

Frisbee: The Ultimate Retrieve

If you and your Lab like to play Frisbee, and especially if your Lab seems to have a particular skill and love for the game, you may enjoy getting involved in Canine Frisbee events. Labs make excellent Frisbee dogs because they have the retrieve instinct. Some dogs have to be taught to retrieve, but chances are, your Lab will bring that Frisbee back to you without more than a hint of suggestion on your part.

But do you and your Lab have what it takes to compete in serious Canine Frisbee competition? The sport is growing quickly, and Canine Frisbee competitions are held all over the country. Canine Frisbee clubs abound, and other dog clubs and even city recreation centers are holding Canine Frisbee events.

Attend a Canine Frisbee event to see if you think you and your Lab would enjoy competing. One of the main organizations regulating Canine Frisbee is the International Disc Dog Handlers Association (IDDHA). IDDHA sanctions the worldwide Canine Disc trials and competitions and holds tests, gives titles, keeps records and ranks competitors.

Getting Started

If you like the idea of trying Canine Frisbee, the first step is to get a Frisbee and try it out with your Lab. Although your Lab might catch the Frisbee on the first throw, don't be disappointed if he doesn't get it. You have to show him what to do. You can start by rolling the Frisbee like a ball. Reward your dog with praise and a piece of food whenever he chases the Frisbee and brings it back to you.

If your Lab knows the take it request (see Chapter 10), you can use it to teach him to take the Frisbee. First, let him take it from your hand as you stand still. Then let him take it from your hand as you run. Next let him take it from the air as you toss it, just

> **Trainer Tidbits**
>
> Never let your Lab use the Frisbee as a chew toy. Plastic can develop sharp areas around chew marks that could injure your dog's mouth, not to mention decrease the life of the Frisbee. If your Lab mouths and chews on the Frisbee after catching it, reward him for quick, focused returns. Then, if he's in the mood to chew, give him a chew toy.

a short distance at first. Pretty soon, if you keep it fun, your Lab will be chasing that Frisbee with glee and leaping to catch it.

Of course, you'll need to practice your throwing skills, too. Practice makes perfect! Practice snapping your wrist to produce greater spin. Start with short throws and work up to longer throws, maintaining good control.

The Internet is a great source for Canine Frisbee information. See Appendix B for Web sites and other Canine Frisbee resources. Then start working with your Lab. Keep it fun, and get ready to show those Border Collies and Australian Shepherds how it's done!

The Least You Need to Know

➤ Flyball is a fast, fun, competitive relay race for dogs involving jumping over hurdles and retrieving a tennis ball.

➤ Flyball titles include Flyball Dog (FD), Flyball Dog Excellent (FDX), Flyball Dog Champion (FDCh), Flyball Master (FM), Flyball Master Excellent (FMX), Flyball Master Champion (FMCh), ONYX and Flyball Grand Champion (FGDCh).

➤ Canine Freestyle, also called Canine Musical Freestyle, is obedience work set to music. It often involves costumes and is meant to show both technical skill and artistry.

➤ Although not all Canine Freestyle competitions award titles, possible titles include Musical Freestyle Dog (MFD), Musical Freestyle Excellent (MFX) and Musical Freestyle Master (MFM).

➤ Canine Frisbee is another popular sport involving both single-disc tosses judged for speed and distance, and freestyle work involving multiple discs.

➤ Canine Frisbee titles include Basic Disc Dog (BDD), Disc Dog Expert (DDX), Advanced Disc Dog (ADD) and Master Disc Dog (MDD).

Chapter 21

Your Showstopper: A Guide to Dog Shows

In This Chapter

➤ Does your Lab have what it takes to be a show dog?

➤ What is a dog show and how does it work?

➤ The ideal Lab versus the practically perfect Lab

Sure, you like to have just as much fun as the next guy. But maybe, just maybe, when you look at your Lab you see a true beauty, a rare specimen, the closest thing to Lab perfection you can imagine. Maybe you've known from the start that you wanted a show dog, or maybe you hadn't considered it until your Lab grew into a dog with star quality. In either case, if you are considering showing your Lab, you'll want to know what's involved, how dog shows work and, most importantly, whether dog shows are something in which both you and your Lab will enjoy participating together.

A Star Is Born

How do you know if the dog show circuit is for you? Most people show their dogs in dog shows for at least one of two reasons:

➤ To earn the Champion of Record title, which will make a dog a more valuable breeder

➤ For fun

267

No matter what your reason is, to do well in competition, you have to have the right kind of dog. What is the right kind? This is a loaded question. The right kind of dog for you may very well not have anything to do with the right kind of dog for a dog show competition.

For dog shows, experts in that breed judge dogs for how closely they match the standard for that breed. Breed standards are developed and periodically updated by national breed clubs. AKC-member clubs must then have their standards approved by the AKC. Once approved, that standard becomes the ideal for that breed. Over the years, priorities for various breeds change, so to see how a breed has changed, you can look at old breed standards. The breed standard for Labs approved in 1957, for example, is far less detailed, has a lower weight limit and doesn't even mention the Labrador Retriever temperament. The current breed standard is what the judges will use to evaluate Labs in the show ring today.

Lab Lore

Other breed clubs, such as the United Kennel Club (UKC) and kennel clubs in other countries, have differing standards for each breed and recognize different breeds than the AKC. The AKC is the largest breed club in the United States and has the most widely accepted standard, but many people choose to join and breed their dogs by the standards of other clubs.

For example, the standard for the Labrador Retriever says: "Eye color should be brown in black and yellow Labradors and brown or hazel in chocolates. Black or yellow eyes give a harsh expression and are undesirable." It also says: "The tail should also be covered in thick, short fur all the way around (called an "otter tail") rather than long, feathery fur as on a Golden Retriever," and that Labs should be between 55 and 80 pounds.

Does that mean your 47-pound, yellow-eyed Lab with a long, thin, feathery tail won't be the best pet you ever had? Certainly not. But she might not do very well in a dog show. If, on the other hand, your dog does closely match the standard, loves to perform, thrives on the attention of a crowd and is proud to strut her stuff, you may have the makings of a champion.

Lab Lingo

Majors are wins of three, four or five points in a dog show. Points are based upon how many dogs are in a competition. The more dogs competing, the more points possible because your dog has won over more competitors (it's a lot tougher to be the best of 500 dogs than the best of 50 dogs).

The Ideal Lab Versus the Practically Perfect Lab

Although having a champion is great and is something to be proud of, we'd just like to emphasize one more time that your practically perfect Lab needn't ever see the inside of a dog show ring. Many good breeders, while breeding for the ideal, put the health and temperament of their puppies ahead of physical characteristics. Joel breeds first and foremost for excellent family pets, and we both believe that is an excellent priority for a breeder. Using the term "pet quality" to denote "inferior" specimens misses the point of breeding dogs. Dogs are what they are today because humans wanted companions, helpers and partners. A dog that looks beautiful but isn't friendly isn't worth much, even if she does have a *Ch.* before her name.

Lab Lingo

People who aren't breeders tend to giggle when a female dog is called a **bitch**, but to breeders and dog show veterans, bitch is the only accurate word for a female dog. **Dog** usually refers to the male, although it is sometimes used to refer to both sexes.

That being said, part of the most-recent Labrador Retriever breed standard (approved in 1994, see Chapter 2) adds a section on temperament not present in earlier standards. This section is worth repeating because although we love a good-looking Lab, we think the

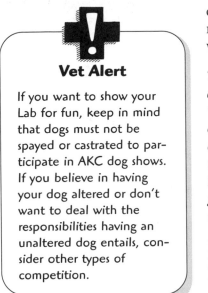

Vet Alert

If you want to show your Lab for fun, keep in mind that dogs must not be spayed or castrated to participate in AKC dog shows. If you believe in having your dog altered or don't want to deal with the responsibilities having an unaltered dog entails, consider other types of competition.

description of the ideal Lab temperament is the best way to measure the worth of a Labrador Retriever:

True Labrador Retriever temperament is as much a hallmark of the breed as the "otter" tail. The ideal disposition is one of a kindly, outgoing, tractable nature; eager to please and non-aggressive towards man or animal. The Labrador has much that appeals to people; his gentle ways, intelligence and adaptability make him an ideal dog.

If this description fits your Lab, you have a champion on your hands, title or no title. If it doesn't describe your Lab, don't give up on her. Follow the advice in this book, work with your Lab every day, faithfully adhere to positive training methods and give your Lab good care and boundless love.

Puppy or senior dog, perfectly shaped or a little bit crooked, healthy or health-challenged, a Lab that is well trained and well loved will repay her owners with loyalty, affection and the kind of unconditional love you rarely find. Love like that is worth every ounce of effort. It means being the object of a Labrador Retriever's devotion—and we can't think of many things we'd rather be.

The Least You Need to Know

➤ Dog shows are arenas for determining which dog most closely matches the ideal, as written in the breed standard.

➤ Dogs that are very close to the ideal, are well trained and enjoy performing for a crowd make good show dogs.

➤ Accumulating sufficient points earns a dog the title of Champion of Record. You can then put a *Ch.* before her name.

➤ Your dog doesn't have to match the breed standard to be ideal for you!

The Lab Lingo Glossary

AKC Canine Good Citizen Test   This test is offered by dog clubs around the country. Dogs are tested and either pass or fail at ten different activities. Tests include allowing a stranger to approach, walking on a loose lead, walking through a crowd, sitting for examination, reacting to another dog and reacting to distractions such as loud noises or unexpected people. Any dog can qualify to be a Canine Good Citizen, not just purebred or AKC-registered dogs.

AKC limited registration   A dog is registered with the AKC as a purebred dog, but no litters produced by that dog will be eligible for registration. Dogs with limited registrations are ineligible to compete in conformation, but they are eligible to compete in obedience and other types of competition, such as tracking and hunting tests.

allopathic medicine   A method of health care that seeks to relieve symptoms and focuses treatment on the problem itself.

American Kennel Club (AKC)   A non-profit organization, established in 1884, devoted to the advancement of purebred dogs. The AKC maintains a record of all registered dogs; publishes ideal standards for each recognized breed; sponsors a variety of dog events including dog shows, obedience and field trials, agility and the Canine Good Citizen program; and publishes educational information.

backing   In Freestyle, when your dog moves backwards.

bitch   A female dog.

breed standard   A description of the ideal specimen of a particular breed. No dog is expected to completely match the standard, but breeders use these standards to help define and improve a breed, and dog show judges judge show dogs based on the breed standard.

brindle   A type of coat pattern in which black is layered in areas of light color (often tan), producing a tiger-striped look.

brisket   The chest area, or the front half of the torso (the thorax).

Canine Eye Registration Foundation (CERF)   An organization that works in conjunction with the American College of Veterinary Ophthalmologists (ACVO) to maintain a registry of purebred dogs that have been examined and found to be unaffected by any major inheritable eye disease such as PRA.

clicker   A simple device that makes a click when you press it. The thin metal tab inside this plastic box makes the clicking sound.

cloddy   A description of a dog that looks low, thickset and heavy.

complementary medicine   Combining holistic and allopathic care for a complete health care program.

contact obstacles   Obstacles in an agility obstacle course with painted areas with which the dog must make contact while tackling the obstacle. Any part of a dog's foot may touch the contact zone, but the dog will be faulted and lose points if he misses the contact point. Contact zones are often painted bright yellow.

cow-hocks   Turned-in ankles and turned-out toes.

croup   The pelvic girdle.

dam   The mother of a litter of puppies.

dewclaws   "Toes" on the inside of a dog's leg, separated from the other "toes" and comparable to a thumb, except that they aren't used. They are commonly removed because they serve no function.

distance work   In Freestyle, any movement in which you and your dog are more than 6 feet apart.

distemper   A highly contagious virus. Symptoms may include discharge from the eyes and nose, a dry cough, vomiting, diarrhea and loss of appetite. Neurological problems may develop in the advanced stage (at which time the chance of recovery is slight), including head shaking, drooling, seizures, twitching and uncontrollable chewing motions. It is the main cause of death in dogs that are not vaccinated.

docking   The procedure of shortening a dog's tail by cutting it. In th e United States, many breeds have their tails docked.

dog   A male dog or used generally to refer to all dogs.

ewe neck   A neck in which the topline has a concave, or sunken, curve rather than a convex, or protruding, curve.

field trials   Competitions that test a dog's ability to perform his designated function in the field. For retrievers, of course, that function is hunting and retrieving.

foreface   A dog's muzzle area.

forequarters   The front of the dog, from shoulder blades to paws.

front work   In Freestyle, when your Lab is sitting, standing, lying down or moving while facing you with his body centered in front of your feet.

gastrocolic reflex   A physiological process in young mammals that results in defecation shortly after a meal. In dogs, feeding at regular times usually results in regular defecation, aiding housetraining.

heeling   In Freestyle, when your Lab is sitting, standing, lying down or moving at your left or right side, in line with you and facing the same direction.

hindquarters   The back part of the dog, from hips to paws.

hock   The hind-leg joint corresponding to the human ankle joint.

holistic health care   A method of health care that treats the body as a whole.

homeopathy   A type of health care based on the principle that "like cures like." It treats system imbalances with minute doses of substances that would produce those same symptoms when given in large doses. Although based in ancient healing techniques, homeopathy per se was developed by a German doctor named Samuel Hahnemann (1755–1843).

Kong   The king of chew toys, an indestructible, hard rubber, roughly cone-shaped, hollow toy that is perfect for the exuberant chewing nature of Labrador Retrievers, both young and old.

273

Labrador Retriever Club, Inc. (LRC)   An AKC-sanctioned national breed club. The LRC's current breed standard (a description of the ideal Labrador Retriever) was approved by the AKC in 1994. The LRC issues working certificates for Labrador Retrievers, sponsors Labrador Retriever events and educates the public about Labrador Retrievers, including maintaining a directory of breeders.

lateral work   In Freestyle, any movement in which your dog moves sideways.

level bite   A bite in which the upper and lower incisors meet exactly, rather than overlapping one way or the other.

lure-and-reward training   A method of training that has been used for many years by progressive trainers to teach puppies and dogs the meaning of simple commands by luring them into position and offering a reward.

majors   Wins of three, four or five points in a dog show. Points are based upon how many dogs are in a competition.

management   Part of the MRE system involving guiding your dog toward good behavior by removing the opportunities for unwanted behaviors.

marking   In hunt tests, a dog's ability to observe and remember where a bird fell so he can find the bird and retrieve it.

MRE system   A system developed by Joel Walton designed to demonstrate the three most important aspects of handling dog behavior: proper management, a good dog-owner relationship and continual training or education.

non-slip retriever   A dog who walks at heel, looks for and remembers where a bird fell and retrieves game on command. Non-slip retrievers aren't expected to find birds they didn't see fall, nor are they expected to flush out game.

obedience trials   Competitions that test dog and owner in performing certain exercises.

Parvovirus   Commonly known as Parvo, this deadly virus targets bone marrow, the gastrointestinal lining, lymph nodes or the heart. Symptoms of the enteric form include loss of appetite, vomiting, diarrhea, fever and depressed behavior. The myocardial form usually occurs in young puppies, may cause sudden death and may also result in chronic congestive heart failure. Parvovirus is transmitted through contaminated feces, is extremely contagious and is one of the biggest killers of puppies.

pasterns   The forelegs between the "ankle" and the joint where the toes begin.

patella   The knee cap.

pedigree   A dog's family tree. This written record of a dog's ancestry must go back at least three generations.

perseverance/courage/hunting   In hunt tests, a dog's determination to perform a task and to face difficult conditions to complete the task.

pivots   In Freestyle, in-place turns with your dog in a heel position. Either the handler or the dog remains in place.

professional handler   Someone hired to handle your dog in the show ring. Handlers are trained to know how to bring out the best in a dog in the ring and can sometimes make the difference between winning and not even placing.

Progressive Retinal Atrophy (PRA)   An untreatable, degenerative genetic eye disorder that causes eventual blindness. The disease can be detected by a veterinary ophthalmologist when a Lab is anywhere from 18 months to 4 years old. Labs affected by this problem usually go totally blind at between 6 and 8 years old.

scissors bite   A bite in which the outside of the lower six front teeth (incisors) touches the inner side of the top six front teeth (also incisors).

short-coupled   A dog relatively short in length from the shoulder blades to the hips, as opposed to longer-bodied dogs.

show champion pedigree   The family tree of a dog that is descended from dogs that have earned champion titles in dog shows.

sickle hocks   Hocks that can't be straightened.

sire   The father of a litter of puppies.

socialization   A method of getting your puppy used to lots of different kinds of people by introducing him to many types of people under controlled conditions when he is still young. Socialized dogs tend to be friendlier and more trusting.

spay-neuter agreement   A contract you sign that states you agree to have your dog spayed or castrated, and that you will not breed that dog. Many breeders require these agreements for dogs they don't think should be bred.

spread hocks   Hocks that point outward.

stifle   The "knee" joint.

style   In hunt tests, a dog's manner, alertness, eagerness and speed on retrieves, as well as his entry into water and style of picking up and returning birds.

throatiness   Excessive loose skin under a dog's throat.

topline   The outline of a dog's back (in profile) from just behind the top of the shoulder blade to the base of the tail.

tracking   Competitions that test a dog's ability to follow a trail by scent.

trainability   In hunt tests, a dog's ability to acquire steadiness (no excessive movement on the line), control (response to directions and manners on the line, including noise), response (how the dog takes direction) and delivery (how he returns the bird) through training.

turns   In Freestyle, turns can be to the right, left or an about-face. Turns are performed while in a heel position.

underline   The outline of the dog's underside (in profile) from the front of the chest to the base of the abdomen.

United Kennel Club, Inc. (UKC)   The second-oldest and second-largest all-breed dog registry in the United States. The UKC registers purebred dogs and hosts conformation shows, obedience trials, agility trials, field trials, water races, night hunts, bench shows and hunting tests for retrievers, among other events.

weedy   A description of a dog that looks light-boned or that has an insufficient amount of bone for his size.

withers   The top of the shoulder blades, used to measure a dog's height.

Retriever Resources

Labrador Retriever Clubs

Labrador Retriever Club, Inc.
Corresponding Secretary: Mr. Christopher G. Wincek
Breeder Contact: Ms. Judy Meyer
P.O. Box 454
Chesterland, OH 44026
Phone: (216) 729-2064
www.thelabradorclub.com/

Alaska

Alaska Labrador Retriever Club
Vicky Olson
4256 Birch Run Dr.
Anchorage, AK 99507
Molson@arctic.net

Arizona

Papago Labrador Retriever Club
Deborah Sheppard
301 S. Hayden Rd.
Tempe, AZ 85281
http://users.aol.com/labradane/terri/plrc.html

California

Golden Gate Labrador Retriever Club
Georgia Burg
16306 Redwood Lodge Rd.
Los Gatos, CA 95030
www.k9web.com/clubs/gglrc/

High Desert Labrador Retriever Club
Doris Engbertson
15331 Wyandotte St.
Van Nuys, CA 91406
Labrador@relaypoint.net

Labrador Retriever Club of Southern California
Nancy Talbott
9365 W. Avenue I
Lancaster, CA 93536
www.io.com/~tittle/LRCSC/

San Joaquin Valley Labrador Retriever Club
Judy Heim
15002 Cambridge Dr.
Lathrop, CA 95330
Hyspire2@aol.com

Sierra Vista Labrador Retriever Club
Trudy Rose
12031 Cresthill Drive
Elk Grove, CA 95624
Talimar@aol.com

Colorado

Labrador Retriever Club of Greater Denver
Denise Aamel
6259 S. Monaco Way
Englwood, CO 80111
Pndrgnlabs@aol.com

Connecticut

Labrador Retriever Club of Central Connecticut
Julie Pease
95 Thankful Stow Rd.
Guilford, CT 06437

Labrador Retriever Club of the Pioneer Valley
Oddny Bolduc
123 Burbank Rd.
Ellington, CT 06029

Labrador Retriever Club of Southern Connecticut
Ellen Plasil
5 Smoke Rise Ridge
Newtown, CT 06470

Pawcatuck River Labrador Retriever Club
Catherine Mason
5 Hardwick Rd.
Quaker Hill, CT 06375
www.uconect.net/-chmason/prlrc/prlrc.html

Florida

Southern Florida Labrador Club
Debbie Bates
2913 Riverland Rd.
Fort Lauderdale, FL 33312

Georgia

Greater Atlanta Labrador Retriever Club
Carol Quaif
2263 Ashton Place NE
Marietta, GA 30068
www.kellyn.com/galrc

Hawaii

Labrador Retriever Club of Hawaii
Marie Tanner
95–138 Kuahelani Ave., 120
Mililani, HI 96789

Indiana

Hoosier Labrador Retriever Club
Lynn Traynor Pannicke
1805 N. Alabama St.
Indianapolis, IN 46202
http://members.aol.com/HLRCInc/index.htm

Winnebago Labrador Retriever Club
Barbara J. Holl
1291 Joliet St.
Dyer, IN 46311
Djhamel@facstaff.wisc.edu

Kansas

Shawnee Mission Labrador Retriever Club
Michelle Lewis
P.O. Box 652
Desoto, KS 66018
Dmlewis462@aol.com

Kentucky

Miami Valley Labrador Retriever Club
Connie Stutler
13394 Green Rd.
Walton, KY 41094
www.geocities.com/Heartland/Plains/7946

Massachusetts

Labrador Retriever Club of Greater Boston
Wendy McNaughton
156 Barker Hill Rd.
Townsend, MA 01469
Wendy McNaughton@digital.com

Michigan

Huron River Labrador Retriever Club
Annie Cogo
1408 N. Kellogg Rd.
Howell, MI 48843
thornwyck@aol.com

Minnesota

Labrador Retriever Club of the Twin Cities
Linda L. Weikert
51767 Highway 57 Blvd.
Wanamingo, MN 55983
www.tc.umn.edu/nlhome/m260/halst001/labrador.htm

Missouri

Spirit of St. Louis Labrador Retriever Club
Patty Wilcox
10208 Blackberry Lane
Catawissa, MO 63015
RCKWOODLAB@aol.com

New Jersey

Jersey Skylands Labrador Retriever Club
Laura Dedering
121 Thackery Dr.
Basking Ridge, NJ 07920

Mid Jersey Labrador Retriever Club
Tony Ciprian
386 Stokes Rd.
Shamong, NJ 08088

New Mexico

Labrador Retriever Club of Albuquerque
Juxi Burr
4401 Yale Blvd. NE
Albuquerque, NM 87107
www.geocities.com/Heartland/Meadows/5942

New York

Iroquois Labrador Retriever Club
Jim Forsyth
965 Farmington Rd.
Macedonia, NY 14502
LBFool@aol.com

Long Island Labrador Retriever Club
Valarie Severn
65 Beverly Rd.
Massapequa, NY 11758

North Carolina

Labrador Retriever Club of the Piedmont
Colleen Kincaid
141 Lauren Ct.
Gastonia, NC 28056

Raleigh-Durham Labrador Retriever Club
Evie Glodic
5308 Sandy Trail Dr.
Knightdale, NC 27545
www.virtualrealeigh.com/labrador

Ohio

Central Ohio Labrador Retriever Club
Jan Eichensehr
5414 Vinewood Ct.
Columbus, OH 43229

Lake Erie Labrador Retriever Club
Cathy Chisholm
3721 Strandhill Rd.
Cleveland, OH 44122
www.lightstream.net/~chisholm

Miami Valley Labrador Retriever Club
Martha Couch
4010 Idlewild Rd.
Burlington, KY 41005
www.geocities.com/ad_container/pop.html

Northern Ohio Labrador Retriever Club
Geraldine Gauger
3522 East State St.
Barberton, OH 44203

Oregon

Rose City Labrador Retriever Club
Greg Huntzinger
30940 SW RiverLa Rd.
West Linn, OR 97068

Pennsylvania

Greater Pittsburgh Labrador Retriever Club
Gina Gross
714 Fordham Ave.
Pittsburgh, PA 15226
Ginagross@mindspring.com

South Carolina

Labrador Retriever Club of the Piedmont
Rita M. Powell
320 Beechwood Dr.
Greer, SC 29651

Texas

Dallas-Ft. Worth Labrador Retriever Club
Marion Harris
1780 Chapman Ct.
Aledo, TX 76008

Heart of Texas Labrador Retriever Club
Kerri Schooler
24912 Singleton Bend E. Rd.
Travis Peak, TX 78654
Kerins@flash.net

Virginia

Labrador Retriever Club of the Potomac
Sandy Schroeder
590 Treslow Glen Dr.
Severna Park, MD 21146
http://lrcp.com/

Washington

Puget Sound Labrador Retriever Association
Shelah Frey
14701 SE Allen Rd.
Bellevue, WA 98006

Other Dog Organizations

The American Kennel Club
Public Education Department
5580 Centerview Dr.

Raleigh, NC 27606-3390
Fax: (919) 854-0168
www.akc.org/

Continental Kennel Club
P.O. Box 908
Walker, LA 70785
Phone: (800) 952-3376

The Kennel Club of Great Britain (KC) or (KCGB)
1–5 Clarges St.
Piccadilly
London W1Y 8AB
Phone: (171) 493-6651
www.the-kennel-club.org.uk/

United Kennel Club, Inc.
100 East Kilgore Rd.
Kalamazoo, MI 49002-5584
Phone: (616) 343-9020
www.ukcdogs.com/

Guide Dog/Assistance Dog Organizations

Canine Companions for Independence
National Headquarters
P.O. Box 446
Santa Rosa, CA 95402-0446
Phone: (800) 572-2275 (voice & TDD)
www.caninecompanions.org
(provides mobility-assist and hearing dogs—always looking for volunteer puppy raisers)

Delta Society
289 Perimeter Rd. East
Renton, WA 98055-1329
Phone: (800) 869-6898
Fax: (206) 808-7601
www.petsforum.com/delta

Guide Dogs for the Blind, Inc.
P.O. Box 151200
San Rafael, CA 94915-1200
Phone: (800) 295-4050
Fax: (415) 499-4000

www.guidedogs.com
(provides guide dogs, uses volunteer puppy raisers)

Therpay Dog Organizations

Delta Society (see above)

Therapy Dogs International
88 Bartley Rd.
Flanders, NJ 07836
Phone: (973) 252-9800
Fax: (973) 252-7171
Tdi@gti.net
(certifies Therapy Dogs)

Flyball Contacts

British Flyball Association
(BFA)
Nigel Bouckley
49 Tremear Green St
Columb Rd.
St Columb
Cornwall TR9 6RB
United Kingdom
Nigel@nigelb.demon.co.uk

Flyball in Australia:
Reg Dwyer
PO Box 144
Calwell ACT 2905
Australia
Phone: (61-6) 2922919
r-dwyer@pop.cc.adfa.oz.au

Flyball in Belguim:
Mark Dewilde
Antwersesteenweg 107
2660 Hoboken
Belgium
Phone: Int. Code + 32.3
828 86 71
Jumasoft@glo.be

Flyball in Poland:
Tomasz Pecold
ul. Trzyniecka 14/11
41–506 Chorzow
Poland
Phone: +48 032 2464425
leszko@silesia.top.pl

North American Flyball
Association, Inc. (NAFA)
1400 W. Devon Ave., #512
Chicago, IL 60660
www.flyball.org/

Canine Freestyle Federation Contacts

England
Sandra Russell
33 Sycamore Rd.
Eccle, Manchester
M30 8LN
1617894819

USA Mid-Atlantic
Joan Tennille
4207 Minton Dr.
Fairfax, VA 22032
Phone: (703) 323-7216
ctennille@aol.com

USA Midwest
Rae Tanner
25060 Cedarwood Lane
Ingleside, IL 60041
Phone: (847) 740-1782

USA New England
Alison Jaskiewicz
576 Jackson Rd.
Mason, NII 03048
Phone: (603) 878-2590

USA Southeast
Dee Dee Rose
506 Crosskeys
Clinton, MS 39056
Phone: (601) 924-3244

USA West
Susan Colledge
Apt. C-19, 3860 Midland Dr.
Roy, Utah 84067
Phone: (801) 731-6027

Canine Frisbee Contacts

ALPO Canine Frisbee Disc Championships
(free training manual available)
4060-D Peachtree Rd., Suite 326
Atlanta, GA 30319
Phone: (800) 786-9240
Bloeme@aol.com

International Disc Dog Handlers' Association (IDDHA)
1690 Julius Bridge Rd.
Ball Ground, GA 30107
www.iddha.com/
IDDHA@aol.com

For regional clubs and competitions, check out the IDDHA Web site at www.iddha.com/clubs.htm.

Additional Web Pages

Labrador Retriever Clubs

American Pointing Labrador Association:
www.pointinglabs.com/apla/

287

High Desert Labrador Retriever Club:
www.geocities.com/Heartland/Plains/5498/

Labrador Retriever Club of GD: www.kellyn.com/lrcgd/

Midwest Labrador Retriever Club: www.para-shift.com/ssllrc/

National Labrador Retriever Club, Inc.: http://kellyn.com/nlrc/

The New GALRC (Greater Atlanta Labrador Retriever Club) Home
Pages: www.kellyn.com/galrc/

Papago Labrador Retriever Club:
http://users.aol.com/papagolrc/plrc.html

Shawnee Mission Labrador Retriever Club:
www.geocities.com/Heartland/9618/

Swedish Labrador Retriever Club: www.norrblom.se/labradork-
lubben/rasinfoe.html

Labrador Retriever Rescue Sites

Labrador Retriever Rescue Contacts:
http://mmg2.im.med.umich.edu/~kleung/rescue.html

Training

American Dog Trainers Network: www.inch.com/~dogs/

Association of Pet Dog Trainers: www.apdt.com/

Clicker Trainers:
www.wazoo.com/~marge/Clicker_Trainers/Clicker_Trainers.html

A Dog and Cat Behavior and Training Center by Perfect Paws:
www.perfectpaws.com

Green Acres Training: www.greenacreskennel.com/training.html

Jean Donaldson's Dogs Behaving Badly! Homepage:
www.lasardogs.com

Karen Pryor's Clicker Training Homepage:
http://dontshootthedog.com/

Narnia Pet Behavior, Training, and Consulting:
http://users.aol.com/jemyers/narnia.htm

Walton Family Dog Training LLC:
http://pages.prodigy.com/MD/wfdt/wfdt.html

Activities

AKC Agility Information: www.akc.org/agregs.htm

AKC Canine Good Citizen Information: www.akc.org/cgc.htm

AKC Dog Show Information: www.akc.org/Begnshws.htm

AKC Field Trial Information: www.akc.org/ret1.htm

AKC Hunt Test Information: www.akc.org/rehunt.htm

AKC Obedience Information: www.akc.org/obedreg.htm

AKC Training Information: www.akc.org/train.htm

Canine Freestyle Federation: www.canine-freestyle.org/

Canine Frisbee WebRing, containing many great sites about the sport. Start at http://members.tripod.com/~frisbee_dog/webring/.

Canine Musical Freestyle Information:
www.woofs.org/freestyle/whatis.html

Flyball FAQ: http://muskie/fishnet.com/~flyball/FAQ/html

The North American Hunting Retriever Association (NAHRA): www.starsouth.com/nahra/

United Kennel Club Information: www.ukcdogs.com/about.htm

On Travel

DogGone Newsletter Online: www.doggonefun.com/

TravelDog—For People Who Travel With Their Dogs: www.traveldog.com/

Travel Guide for Dog Owners: www.inch.com/~dogs/travel.html

Travel With Your Dog—Internet Resources:
http://dogs.miningco.com/msub6.htm

Working Dogs Page travel info:
http://workingdogs.com/doc0020.htm

E-mail Lists

A Complete List of Dog-Related E-Mail Lists: www.k9web.com/
dog-faqs/lists/email-list.html#lab

Labrador Retriever Lists

LABRADOR-L is the original mailing list started in 1994 for and about
Labradors. Cindy Tittle Moore and Liza Lee Miller administrate the
list. To subscribe to this list, send an e-mail message as directed:

> To: listserv@iupui.edu
> Subject: leave blank
> Body: subscribe LABRADOR-L your-name

LABRADOR-H is a Hoflin list moderated by Jake Scott. To subscribe to
this list, send an e-mail message as directed:

> To: requests@h19.hoflin.com
> Subject: leave blank
> Body: subscribe LABRADOR-H

LABSR4U is a list moderated by Bud Cravener and Lori Dodd. To subscribe to this list, send an e-mail message as directed:

> To: listserv@shrsys.hslc.org
> Subject: leave blank
> Body: subscribe LABSR4U your-name

Training Lists

The Aggressive Behavior List (AB-L) is hosted by Joel Walton and is
for pet dog trainers and pet dog owners to talk to one another about
aggressive behavior in dogs. The list is limited to unwanted aggressive

behavior directed toward humans or dogs by canines. To subscribe to this list, send an e-mail message as directed:

> To: majordomo@esosoft.com
> Subject: leave blank
> Body: subscribe AB

The Start Puppy Training list is hosted by Joel Walton and is for breeders, puppy trainers, veterinarians and puppy owners to talk to one another about puppy training. Topics include: early puppy training by breeders, early puppy training by owners, puppy classes, normal puppy behavior including housetraining, puppy/play-biting, chewing, jumping up and not listening.

The Pre-Puppy Primer List is the list to join before you get a puppy or a dog. The Pre-Puppy Primer list is hosted by Joel Walton and is for breeders, puppy trainers, veterinarians and potential puppy owners to discuss the training required before you acquire a puppy or dog. Topics include: choosing a compatible type or breed, recognizing whether the puppy has been socialized, early puppy training by breeders, puppy parties, early puppy training by owners, puppy classes and normal puppy behavior including housetraining, puppy/play-biting, chewing, jumping up and not listening. The Pre-Puppy Primer list is part of the SPT list. To subscribe to either of these lists, send an e-mail message as directed:

> To: majordomo@esosoft.com
> Subject: leave blank
> Body: subscribe SPT

The Pettable-L list is hosted by Joel Walton and is for pet dog trainers and pet dog owners to talk to one another about dog training, behavior and temperament problems. Topics include: housetraining, puppy/play-biting, chewing, jumping up, not listening, biting, fearfulness and attacking other dogs. When you subscribe, you will receive a reply explaining how you can participate on the Pettable list as a pet dog owner or a pet dog trainer. To subscribe to this list, send an e-mail message as directed:

> To: majordomo@esosoft.com
> Subject: leave blank
> Body: subscribe PETTABLE

Clicker Training is an open mailing list devoted to the use of the clicker and targeting in training. The list is owned by Kathleen Weaver. To subscribe to this list, send an e-mail message as directed:

> To: majordomo@listservice.net
> Subject: leave blank
> Body: subscribe CLICK-L

Isabel M. Gordon owns clicktrain for those more experienced with the techniques of training with a clicker. To subscribe to this list, send an e-mail message as directed:

> To: majordomo@gcstation.net
> Subject: leave blank
> Body: subscribe CLICKTRAIN

Flyball Lists

To subscribe to the Flyball Mailing List, send an e-mail message as directed:

> To: listproc@ces.com.
> Subject: leave blank
> Body: subscribe flyball your_name

Videos

Dunbar, Ian. *Sirius Puppy Training.* New York: Bluford & Toth, 1987.

CD-ROMS

Donaldson, Jean. *Jean Donaldson's Dogs Behaving Badly.* Montreal: Lasar, 1998.

Books

On Labs

Churchill, Janet I. *The New Labrador Retriever.* New York: Howell Book House, 1995.

Coode, Carole. *Labrador Retrievers Today.* New York: Howell Book House, 1993.

Coykendall, Jr., Ralf W. *You and Your Retriever.* New York: Doubleday & Co., 1963.

Farrington, Selwyn Kip. *Labrador Retriever, Friend and Worker.* New York: Hastings House, 1976.

Hill, Warner F. *Labradors.* New York: Arco, 1966.

Martin, Nancy A. *The Versatile Labrador Retriever.* Wilsonville, OR: Doral, 1994.

Roslin-Willaims, Mary. *Advanced Labrador Breeding.* London: H.F.&G. Witherby LTD: 1988.

Roslin-Williams, Mary. *All About the Labrador.* London: Pelham, 1985.

Warwick, Hellen. *The New Complete Labrador Retriever.* New York: Howell Book House, 1986.

Weiss-Agresta, Lisa. *The Labrador Retriever: An Owner's Guide to a Happy Healthy Pet.* New York: Howell Book House, 1995.

Wiles-Fone, Heather and Julia Barnes. *The Ultimate Labrador Retriever.* New York: Howell Book House, 1997.

Wolters, Richard A. *The Labrador Retriever: The History—The People, Revisited.* New York: Dutton, 1992.

On Training and Behavior

Arden, Andrea. *Train Your Dog The Lazy Way.* New York: Alpha Books, 1998.

Donaldson, Jean. *The Culture Clash.* Oakland, CA: James & Kenneth, 1995.

Donaldson, Jean. *Dog Are From Neptune.* Montreal: Lasar, 1998.

Dunbar, Ian. *Dog Behavior: An Owner's Guide to a Happy Healthy Pet.* New York: Howell Book House, 1998.

Dunbar, Ian. *How to Teach a New Dog Old Tricks.* Oakland, CA: James & Kenneth, 1996.

Hodgson, Sarah. *Dog Perfect.* New York: Howell Book House, 1995.

Holmes, John and Mary. *Reading the Dog's Mind: Learning How to Train from the Dog's Point of View.* New York: Howell Book House, 1998.

Pryor, Karen. *Don't Shoot The Dog.* North Bend, OR: Sunshine Books, 1985.

Pryor, Karen. *On Behavior: Essays and Research.* North Bend, OR: Sunshine Books, 1995.

Reid, Pamela. *Excel-Erated Learning!* Oakland, CA: James & Kenneth, 1996.

On Health

Giffin, James M., MD, and Delbert G. Carlson, DVM. *Dog Owner's Home Veterinary Handbook.* New York: Howell Book House, 1992.

Siegal, Mordecai (editor). *UC Davis Book of Dogs: The Complete Medical Reference Guide For Dogs and Puppies by the Faculty and Staff, School of Veterinary Medicine, University of California at Davis.* New York: Harper Collins, 1995.

On Traveling

Barish, Eileen. *Vacationing With Your Pet!* Scottsdale, AZ: Pet-Friendly Pub., 1994.

General

American Kennel Club. *The Complete Dog Book*, 19th edition, revised. New York: Howell Book House, 1998.

Hodgson, Sarah. *The Complete Idiot's Guide To Choosing, Training, and Raising a Dog.* New York: Alpha, 1996.

Index